For George
With best wishes for the
new year
January, 1992,

Chris

UNIVERSITY OF NEBRASKA PRESS • LINCOLN & LONDON

THE PROUSTIAN FABRIC

ASSOCIATIONS OF Memory

CHRISTIE McDONALD

Acknowledgments for the use of
previously published material appear
on pages x–xi.

The paper in this book meets
the minimum requirements
of American National Standard
for Information Sciences –
Permanence of Paper for Printed Library Materials,
ANSI Z39.48–1984.

Library of Congress
Cataloging in Publication Data
McDonald, Christie, 1942–
The Proustian fabric : associa-
tions of memory /
Christie McDonald.   p. cm.
Includes bibliographical
references (p.) and index.
ISBN 0–8032–3150–4 (cloth)
1. Proust. Marcel. 1871–1922.
A la recherche du
temps perdu. 2. Memory in lit-
erature. I. Title.
PQ2631.R63A834 1992
90–21940 843'.912—dc20 CIP

Book cover: detail of a dress
fabric by Mariano Fortuny.
Silk. Italian, ca. 1914.
Reproduced, courtesy of the
Metropolitan Museum of
Art, gift of Miss Mercedes
Acosta, 1952. (52.37.1a),
Photographed by John Hill.

TO MICHAEL

A general is like a writer who
sets out to write a certain
play, a certain book, and then
the book itself, with the
unexpected potentialities which
it reveals here, the impass-
able obstacles which it presents
there, makes him deviate
to an enormous degree from
his preconceived plan.—
Marcel Proust, *Time Regained*

CONTENTS

ACKNOWLEDGMENTS

M any people contributed to the project of this book. Stephen Mitchell first drew me into Proust's world when we were students in Paris, a world in which I dwelled for two years. Then, in the early 1980's, I reread Proust and taught an interdisciplinary seminar on *Remembrance of Things Past* with Jean-Jacques Nattiez, and began to gather material for the book. In that context, David Mendelson shared his insights on and passion for Proust's text, and Jean-Jacques Nattiez engaged me in many lively discussions which, through our differences, helped me to see where I was going. Antoine Compagnon gave his guidance in the ways of Proustian microfilms at the Bibliothèque Nationale in Paris prior to the appearance of the new Pléiade edition of *A la recherche du temps perdu,* and Jean Milly made several suggestions, helpful to me at a crucial time, in tracking down material.

Ginette Michaud lent her keen critical eye to the manuscript at an important moment, and Nicole Deschamps generously gave it a meticulous reading. Michel Pierssens and Jean Le Tourneux both read portions and made helpful suggestions. Material from the project was presented to audiences, who offered valuable comments and criticism, at Columbia University, The Graduate Center of the City University of New York, Critical Futures, The Johns Hopkins University, The Learned Societies of Canada, two meetings of the Modern Language Association, The Hebrew University in Jerusalem, The University of Haifa, The University of Minnesota, the Université de Montréal, The State University of New York at Binghamton, and the University of Tel Aviv.

A sabbatical leave from the Université de Montréal during the year 1988 allowed me to complete much of the work on the book, with a grant provided by the internal granting committee of the Université de Montréal (CAFIR) in 1987–1988 to consult the Proust manuscripts on microfilm at the Bibliothèque Nationale in Paris.

My thanks to John Hill for his photographic art and Jeffrey Lawrence for help in producing the cover; and to Jean Drusedow, Curator in charge of the Department of the Costume Institute, Deirdre Donahue, and Kim Fink for their help in locating the dress created by Mariano Fortuny in the collection of the Metropolitan Museum of Art and permission to reproduce it. For technical assistance with the manuscript, I thank Jean-Vincent Blanchard, Véronique Cnockaert, Benoît, Dugas, and Yannick Portebois.

Conversations with Mary Ann Caws, John McDonald, Dick Miller, Joan McD. Miller, Nancy Miller, Adam Vance and Jacob Vance have contributed in ways that do not always appear in footnotes. I am, of course, solely responsible for the outcome.

Portions of this book have been published in earlier versions. Chapter 6 appeared as "Proust's Mosaic" in *Poetics Today* 10:2 (Summer 1989). I thank Hurtubise HMH for the permission to publish as Chapter 5 a new and revised English language version of "Re-parutions" from *Dispositions* (Montreal:Hurtubise HMH, 1986). An English translation of the original chapter appeared as "Republications," translated by Gloria M. Smolenski,

in *Reading Proust Now,* edited by Mary Ann Caws and Eugene
Nicole (New York: Peter Lang, 1990). An early version of Chapter 1 appeared as "Literature and Philosophy at the Crossroads:
Proustian Subjects," in *Writing the Politics of Difference,* edited
by Hugh Silverman (Stony Brook: SUNY Press, 1990.)

ABBREVIATIONS

ASB	*Against Sainte-Beuve and Other Essays,* trans. John Sturrock
Corr.	*Correspondance,* ed. Philip Kolb
Corresp. gén.	*Correspondance générale,* ed. Robert Proust and Paul Brach
CSB 1954	*Contre Saint-Beuve,* ed. Bernard de Fallois
CSB 1971	*Contre Sainte-Beuve,* ed. Pierre Clarac with Yves Sandre
JS	*Jean Santeuil,* ed. Pierre Clarac and Yves Sandre
JS Hopkins	*Jean Santeuil,* trans. Gerard Hopkins
RTP	*Remembrance of Things Past,* trans. by C. K. Scott-Moncrieff and Terence Kilmartin
RTP Gall.	*A la recherche du temps perdu,* Pléiade ed., 1987-1989

Note on translations:
Quotations in the text from most
Proust writings are in English;
the original French may be found
in the endnotes. Small differences
occur between the French and
the English in some passages from
Remembrance of Things Past
because the Scott-Moncrieff and
Kilmartin translation draws upon
the 1954 Gallimard edition of
A la recherche du temps perdu,
whereas the French quoted in the
notes is taken from the 1987–89
Gallimard (Pléiade) edition.

I n *Remembrance of Things Past,* Proust shows that the life of writing, like the life of thought, involves an essential wandering through particulars. Sense comes through the association of memories. He had found an analogue to this wandering while looking at Monet's painting *Water Lilies*: "We are there . . . trying to chase away all thought, to understand the meaning of each color, each one calling up in our memory past impressions; these impressions are associated in an architecture as airy and multicolored as the colors on the painting, and they build a landscape in our imagination."[1]

Proust develops a principle of individuation as the basis of memory and art, as that which both demands and resists generalization.[2] Truth resides in the reconstruction of events without precedent, where nothing ever repeats itself exactly. By probing the way in which associations seem to guide thought, by translating the simultaneity of associations into the necessarily successive, temporal sequences of writing, Proust attempts to generalize the ungeneralizable. Out of individual experience, he wishes to tease some general quality resembling a scientific law and still maintain what is unique. This effort makes of association the unanalyzed domain of thought and the premise upon which Proust's sense of literature is to be constructed. He develops "literarily" theories of knowledge on the margins of rationalism, overtly opposed to positivism, which then become implanted and affect thought thereafter.

Around the turn of this last century, while Freud was developing the clinical method of psychoanalysis with the basic rule in "free association," Ferdinand de Saussure founding semiology (as a system of signs) on the association between signifier and signified[3], and James Joyce writing *Ulysses*, Proust was incorporating association into the literary text as an operation fundamental to language and thought. Within the same generation all four of these thinkers were grappling, and without apparent influence upon each other, with the way in which disparate associations integrate irrationality within a system of thought. What interested me was the quasi-simultaneous emergence of association as the basis of thought; the way in which deterministic structures emerge through the indetermination of association; the way in which a paradigmatic organization of thought, previously unanalyzed, provokes change in the order of knowledge.

Association has long been considered a nonessentialist philosophy developed in order to explain the functioning of memory and the way in which memory sequences are stored in the imagination or thought. The fundamental problem has been to account for the relationship of the principles or laws that regulate these sequences to the instance of sensation and reception. Aristotle located a definition of association in relations of similarity, contrast, or contiguity. And although Proust's immediate associationist predecessors were from the second half of the nineteenth century,[4] he was able to integrate philosophical questions that resurfaced from the eighteenth century by questioning the organization of thought: how does one thing evoke others? Can thought pass from the discontinuity of contiguous memories and perceptions to some continuity, unity, and even truth of the self?

I have limited myself in the following chapters, to a discussion of Proust,[5] taking as a premise that literature "says" something special or particular; that it is, moreover, this particular force, as the force of the particular, that Freud diverted from literature to speak about creation.[6] In making public the private process of association through the narrational use of the first person, Proust's novel reflects the swirl between centuries that transforms thought. *Remembrance of Things Past* straddles the dominant thinking patterns of two centuries: the nineteenth century, in which the association of fragmentary thought was to be subsumed into the notion of a totality; and the twentieth century, in which the notion of associative thinking was to move toward an infinite process of referral and interpretation.[7]

Proust's notion of association initially, like Freud's, was "firmly anchored to a mechanistic concept of determinism."[8] Freud developed the technique of free association for psychoanalysis between 1892 and 1898. It still remains the most widely accepted part of psychoanalytic technique. The basic rule, as Freud called it, required evenly poised attention on the part of the analyst and a form of uncensored thought characterized as free fall (the literal meaning of the German expression *einfall*) on the part of the analysand: the patient says anything and everything that occurs to him or her, allowing a kind of thought outside the norms of daily, habitual, and rational discourse to emerge. What is striking is that the (seeming) accidents of association become intelligible only through a rigorously determined structure of the psyche. One analyst describes it this way: "The analyst looks behind the chain of free associations . . . for the affective attitude which governs this sequence and is as it were the law of its intelligibility."[9] That Freud related this search for intelligibility through association with the "false connection" or "mésalliance" in the transference of the patient to the analyst shows the extent to which association operates by a displacement of feeling, calling for interpretation.[10] The lack of an abstract formulation or theory of association, even in Freud's own writings on the question, is striking, however. It is as though association operates out of the control of theory, subject mainly to the construction of series, interlocking analogies, and clusters of examples.[11]

Very early, Proust begins to gather his forces for his project while translating Ruskin, taking notes on the way in which thought skips about. He goes on to invent arbitrarily but definitively the terms of a program to be worked out during the rest of his life, until his death in 1922. In Chapter 1, I look at Proust's search for and defense of the compositional structure of his novel. From *Contre Sainte-Beuve* on, he sets up a balancing act between the affective side of narrative and the analytic or intellectual function of thought, located between literature and philosophy. For this, a complex notion of the unconscious has become necessary, one which, though based on the affect, does not fall into a "crude association of ideas" located in collective psychology.[12] Though at times the narrator lapses into a kind of mechanical associationism, [13] the goal is to situate different levels of association in order to understand the workings of creative thought.

Eighteenth-century inquiries into association focused on the relation between the accidents of experience coming through the senses and conceptual understanding of those experiences as guided by the faculty of reason. John Locke, the first to use the term "association of ideas," placed association at the source of error;[14] David Hume made of it the basis of all thought. Thus, the very same principles accounted for both what was true and what was erroneous in the relation of experience to sensations, perceptions, memories, imaginations, and rational thought. These thinkers, like those who followed, attempted to comprehend the organization of thought through an associative process: Hobbes called it "mental discourse," Tucker "translation," Thomas Brown "suggestion."[15]

Proust distances the narrative from the history of associationism, ironically commenting, for example, how one of his characters (Mme Chemisy, an early incarnation of Mme Cambremer, whose thought patterns are mechanical) spends her mornings reading works by Herbert Spencer. But he assumes responsibility for the issues raised by that history: both Hume's question, why do associative connections seem to be *necessary* connections? and Kant's, how can causal relations that emerge from a subjective origin take on universal validity?

In order to account for change, Proust takes up the questions of necessary and contingent connections as he seeks a form of association, located in memory, that moves from a subjective origin in the individual to a universalizing principle. He seeks to describe the heterogeneous experience of the world through perception and time in its relation to language. By reconciling what is most unique with general laws of thought, he strives to activate its creative forces. Schopenhauer warned of the dangers of such thinking: "One idea rapidly calls forth another, until all that occupied us yesterday is present once more. On the fact that this takes place properly depends the health of the mind in contrast to madness, which . . . consists in the occurrence of great gaps in the continuity of the recollection of the past. But how completely sleep breaks the thread of memory, so that it must be resumed again each morning, is seen in particular instances of the incompleteness of this operation."[16] In his reformulation of this problem in *Remembrance,* Proust gives it a Cartesian twist. Doubting the fundamental spatiotemporal coordinates of thought, he queries whether, by mixing perceptions together, associations may not result in misconceptions and deceive. "The associations of ideas", he writes in a sketch, "have the force of beliefs, error."[17] And yet he senses that a process of mental wandering—which is neither madness nor simple error—underlies the emergence of all new thought; that only by upsetting habit and conceptual certainty can change occur. Such a destablizing activity puts everything into question: rationality, causality, the order of discourse and analogical thinking. Proust has a strategy, however, to ward off any untoward consequences of this questioning: the fidelity of his writing to an initial project which, while always different, will always be the same.

As set out in the fragments of a preface to *Contre Sainte-Beuve,* the project is totalizing, and totality corresponds to a principle of intelligibility. This identification of thought with the totality means that the total work emerges only as it produces and contains its own genesis, recounting throughout the novel the discovery of the narrator's vocation as a writer. It is a project in which the end as the beginning must lead to the completion of understanding and meaning in writing; that is, Proust proposes a hermeneutic project. That deviation from the project inheres within it, however, as Proust's remark placed as an epigraph to this book suggests, makes a unitary working-out of the text problematic.

Association is a mode of thinking that functions by deviation and digression, perhaps the only one to allow for a "mnemonic hermeneutics:"[18] a process of learning to comprehend the self and the world based upon the repetition of events inscribed through memory and association from the very first pages of the book. Proust writes: "A writer reasons, that is to say he goes astray, only when he has not the strength to force himself to make an impression pass through all the successive states which culminate in its fixation, its expression" (RTP 3:916). [19] And this is because "the impression is for the writer what the experiment is for the scientist, with the difference that in the scientist the work of the intelligence precedes the experiment and in the writer it comes after the impression" (RTP 3:914).[20] For the writer, "certain obscure impressions . . . had solicited [his] attention in a fashion somewhat similar to these reminiscences, except that they concealed within them not a sensation dating from an earlier time, but *a new truth*" (RTP 3:912; emphasis added).[21]

What Schopenhauer designated as madness and Locke called error, in both cases referring to association, is an interminable process of thought in which no truth can ever be certain or fixed. It is this aspect of association that both fascinates Proust and makes him wary. As an always unfinished process, association can be reduced to neither of two polarized functions: either a theoretical systematization based on the intelligibility of the affect, or the abandonment of all meaning in the anarchy of empirical discovery. In Proust's texts, association allows the reader to locate the resistance to rational thought, and rational philosophy, that he first articulates in *Contre Sainte-Beuve* in relation to the conception of the work of art.

Proust is able to walk the line between development of an individualist psychology, which allows for freedom of choice, and the need to displace rational thinking into a theory and practice of affect. Chapter 3 deals with the disjunction between thought and its enactment in the world. Proust dramatizes the relationship of determinism to freedom, of atavism to opinion, in writing about reaction to the Dreyfus case. Short sequences and remarks on this subject, peppered throughout the novel, introduce the ethical and political dimensions of association and establish their narrative function.

In *Remembrance of Things Past* Proust creates his literary landscape in relation to music and painting, though the immediate models are not those cited above; he creates it from impressions linked by association in which memories and feelings combine and recombine disjunctively in thought. Proust seeks to establish the truth of being through the way in which associations signify within the heterogeneity of time and space. He translates the experience of the arts—in the models of music and painting—in order to recreate and analyze the itinerary leading to a "discovery": his vocation as a writer. As quintessential artist, he is to write the book of the self, both general and particular, that will bring together private obsession with art and the laws of thought. Proust conferred the figural status of book upon the life, even though the life was not to explain the book, and this leads to a textual repetition of problems formulated in spiritual terms.[22] In Chapter 2 I discuss the passage from ontology to aesthetics in the relationship of involuntary memory to metaphor and music, as the idealized models for creation. The entry into writing as art can ultimately be entertained because of the exemplary status granted to the subject through the singular epiphanic association of involuntary memory. Translation, however, as the operative mode of the writer, requires the superimposition of life on text. And the possibility of passing from this ideal to the pluralized performance of meanings within the text raises serious questions about the establishment of a sense of the absolute.

Swann's Way appeared in 1913, an extraordinary year. It was the year that Arnold Schoñberg listened to the premiere of his *Gurrelieder,* a massive nineteenth-century work, with the the late quartets perking in his head, the quartets that launched music into atonality and the twentieth century; it was also the year that Gustav Klimt painted *The Maiden. Swann's Way* was announced in three parts. Then, during and after the war years, a proliferation of writing brought about the addition of interim volumes, — *The Guermantes Way 1 and 2, Cities of the Plain 1 and 2, The Captive, The Fugitive (Albertine disparue)*—in which the original structure (Proust called it a "severe construction") no longer seemed to dominate.[23] It was as though an autonomous grafting operation was to take place from "within, " much of it concerning the narrator, Marcel, whose love for and jealousy of Albertine comes to occupy the center of the later volumes of the novel. With the focus on jealousy a shift in tone occurs, marking the narrator's desperate attempt and failure to enclose meaning within the frame of the original project. This panoramic view suggests that both the genesis of the writing and the order of the text posit the conditions for the work of art to emerge, only then to exceed them in a compelling way. Changing the project from within, a new "style" emerges in the search for the self in time, displacing the notion of an absolute truth through sequences leading to associations and repetitions without end.

THE EDITIONS

Maurice Blanchot referred to Proust's first novel, *Jean Santeuil,* as a book that was "never made . . . [but] was harvested."[24] *Remembrance of Things Past* is a book that has also been harvested, editorially, the results appearing in the late 1980s and becoming tangible to the reader through the presentation of massive amounts of material previously unavailable. On October 5, 1987, the Proust papers came into the public domain, although they had been accessible since 1984, the year when the Bibliothèque Nationale acquired the near-totality of the manuscripts.[25] The year 1987 marked the end of an era for readers of Proust, an era of readings largely determined by the edition established in 1954 under the editorship of Pierre Clarac and André Ferré, who based their edition on the uncorrected typescripts and did not take account of Proust's indications for changes. And 1987 began a new era for readers of Proust with the appearance of *A la recherche du temps perdu* from three publishers: Gallimard, Garnier-Flammarion, and Bouquins-Laffont, each with a separate approach to the text. Gallimard, which possesses the rights to the previously unpublished material, presented a large critical edition complete with many sketches, variants, and notes; Garnier-Flammarion included critical notices, chronologies, and biographies but no sketches; Bouquins-Laffont offered the text without critical apparatus other than a guide to the life and work for the general public.

All three editions revised the text, basing changes on Proust's own corrections, the most important of which were from the portions published posthumously: *The Captive, The Fugitive,* and *Time Regained.* In the Pléiade edition published by Gallimard, from which I take my quotations in French, the editorial principle is the following: to base the first part of *Remembrance* on the original edition from Proust's first publisher, Grasset, but to produce the text that Proust might have dreamed of had he not had been obliged to cut and rework it; to base *The Captive* and *The Fugitive* on the typescripts and *Time Regained* on the manuscript. The editors privileged the last drafts, presenting earlier drafts as variants. The idea was to demonstrate how the textual wanderings lead up to some final moment of the text, to show the richness of a process of thought in which Proust constantly reevaluated what he was writing. As director of the Gallimard edition, Jean-Yves Tadié saw no major change in the meaning of the text but suggested that the revised edition would add a new kind of pleasure to it, allowing the reader to follow the growth and superimposition of thought from one variant to another. Jean Milly, director of the Garnier-Flammarion edition, invited readers to read like a psychoanalyst with poised attention so as to taste the open-ended quality of the text, lik-

ened to musical variations. Bernard Raffalli, head of the Bouquins-Laffont edition, stakes his edition on the greatness of a
text that sums up all previous literature and announces what is
to come.[26]

What none of these editiors apparently foresaw was the publication by Proust's first publisher, Grasset, of a separate little
volume, heavily cut and edited by Proust himself in 1922, which
a relative found in a trunk purely by chance (the ultimate dream
of the archivist) not long before the other editions were sched-
uled to appear; it is entitled *Albertine disparue*[27]. One wonders if
by some quirk of history this is to be Grasset's editorial revenge,
in the form of a commercial coup, for losing Proust to Gallimard. Whatever one's fantasy, there is a question about what
status to grant this text. How does its publication affect, for
example, the "last draft" theory for establishing a definitive version of a text? None of the three editions can take account of the
changes in this text, because Proust would probably have relo-
cated the 250 pages he cut from it and prepared the material to
follow in sequence. In Chapter 6 I look at the kind of problem
that the preparation for and final suppression of a scene in Venice poses.

Along with the sketches and variants contained within the
other editions, this little volume grants us a rare privilege: the
ability to see not only what a writer added or retained while he
was writing but what he discarded.[28] All demonstrate more than
a dilemma limited to archivists and manuscript scholars, and
perhaps more even than a battle of publishers; all demonstrate
the movement of association in thinking as a process of both
textual revision and self-revision in which the two become synonymous. New texts offer the reader an editorial performance of
the very same concerns that the narrator expresses about the establishment of meaning: how to fix and control meaning in a
seemingly endless and arbitrary network of associations. Access
to the genesis of the text helps to pose the question of totality in
both a concrete and an abstract way because, at some level, new
documents demand a reevaluation of past assumptions. One
may envisage totality either as the always incomplete repertory

of empirical discoveries, in which new information may indeed upset prior hypotheses, or as the nontotalizable substitution of an infinite process in which, since there is no center to ground substitution, no such thing as a "new" fact can emerge. In the latter view, empirical facts would be integrated into a predetermined system whose parameters regulate their meaning.[29]

What interests me is the way in which the two sides of Proust's thought—one tending toward a notion of totality and ultimate meaning, the other toward the unraveling of meaning in the infinite movement of piecing together fragmentary knowledge—are reproduced in the recent editions. Albert Feuillerat sensed this kind of a riptide as early as 1934.[30] More recently, Alain Buisine, evoking the two sides of Proust in order to break them down, remarks that there is a Proustian hagiography which dictates that criticism follow avowed Proustian doctrine.[31] The comment implies that critics often indulge in the kind of idolatry for which Ruskin criticized others and was criticized by Proust. I rather think that if this is so, it is because criticism also passes through what one might call the idolatry of systems in different generational periods. There have been several such periods since Proust entered the canon, and we are surely not through.

CRITICAL PERSPECTIVES

O ver three decades the criticism of *Remembrance of Things Past* has changed considerably. Three general approaches have dominated: phenomenological criticism in the period prior to the mid-1960s tended to concentrate on the phenomenology of mind inscribed in the project; during the period of structuralism within literary studies in the 1960s and 1970s, critics tended to concentrate on the semiological aspects of the text; in the 1980s "genetic" criticism developed with the access to variants and previously unavailable material. The phenomenological studies dealt with the concept of the object and analyzed consciousness and time in relation to it.[32] The semiological studies explored the levels of linguistic patterning within the text; through the explicit movement away from rhetoric as traditionally conceived, they sought to establish a form of systematization that ensured, at a linguistic level, the coherence of the work of art.[33] The genetic approach began largely with work on the manuscripts and the preparation of new editions.[34] In the exploration of a work in progress, it has brought to light problems of uncertainty, similar to those teased out of the finished text in deconstructive criticism.[35]

No one approach alone proved adequate to the model of Proust's project: phenomenological studies risked leaving aside the problem of language and the unconscious, as central preoccupations, whereas semiological studies left the problem of the subject and the truth of the structure to a large extent unquestioned. Deleuze wrote: "What is essential in the Search is not memory and time, but the sign and truth. What is essential is not to remember, but to learn. For memory is valid only as a faculty capable of interpreting certain signs, time is valid only as the substance of type of this or that truth."[36] As remarkable as Deleuze's book is as a semiological study of Proust's text, this statement remains partial. To exclude memory was also to exclude access to and the belief in truth, the certainty of which was assured through a feeling of joy. Paul Ricoeur argues that Deleuze's interpretation does not exclude the question of time; rather, the apprenticeship of signs imposes a long and circuitous route that substitutes for the shortcut of involuntary memory. For Ricoeur, the totality of the work is to be found in neither of these ways alone: if one can allow that the work is a fable about the question of time, this is so because it poses the problem of relating involuntary memory to the apprenticeship of signs. Ricoeur sees in the discovery of an extratemporal dimension the final revelation toward which the entire work tends: its hermeneutic key.[37] As for genetic criticism, until the publication of the recent editions, much of the work dealt with the external history. Antoine Compagnon takes a theoretical position beyond the external historical reconstruction of manuscripts by suggesting that the reinsertion of a literary event in its historical context allows the reader to measure the plurality of meanings within a text.[38]

Vincent Descombes distinguishes between the historical, the aesthetic, and the philosophical readings of Proust by critics in the past. If the argument is based on facts, he says, then the reading is historical. If it relies on interpretation, the reading is aesthetic (or critical in the sense of literary criticism). If the argument turns on arguments grounded in philosophical reasons, the reading is philosophical. Philosophical reasoning comes out of the logic of concepts. The purpose of the philosophical reading would be to see whether the meaning that one gives to the text is philosophically clear. Descombes's own reading depends on the distinction between the thought of the novelist and the thought of the theoretician. He seeks to show that Proust-the-novelist is superior to Proust-the-theoretician: specifically, the theoretician in him balks at a sociological comprehension of human life, while the novelist, who must create characters and dramatic scenes, shows a remarkable flair for sociology. Ultimately, he pits the philosophy of the novel against the philosophy of the essay, and the novel wins.[39]

I argue that the quest for the general laws of love and emotion frame, in rational terms, the desire to write. The project of writing forms a coherent whole as a philosophical endeavor to discover the nature of the creative and creating subject in its "essence." However, although Proust searches for the invariant, the generalities of art and life, at another level this is not the grounding for his project. Attempting as a writer to make sense out of impressions, he addresses the relationship of the singular idiom to the universal in what may seem to be an ongoing quarrel between poetry and philosophy: the separation of individual literary self-creation in the recognition of contingency from the traditional philosophic endeavor of achieving universality through its transcendence.[40]

The passage from phenomenology to rhetorical analyses and then to genetic criticism within Proustian studies opens the way for analysis of *the ways in which the mechanisms of association, as the mechanisms of thought (be they philosophical or artistic), deal with the sub-theoretical level present in all theorizing.* For Proust, the rational notion of totality and the concept of an all-encompassing theory are at some level synonymous. By putting in place a practice for which there is no adequate speculative theory, Proust's texts raise a key epistemological question of how association in literature leads to a redefinition of thought which is neither rational nor irrational.

The analyses that follow in this book diverge from the phenomenological, structuralist, and genetic models yet draw in some measure from each. From the phenomenological studies I retain the notion of a subject (the narrator) seeking to found an existence in thought and feeling. That this subject operates from within language—in association—as the determining force emerges from the impetus of semiological studies. To understand the way in which associations combine in memory, and lead to art, requires an understanding of Proust's project; I look at some aspects of its historical development as it is manifest in the letters and sketches. The English translation of *Remembrance of Things Past* cited here tacitly subscribes to certain phenomenological concepts, particularly evident in the use of the word "mind"; I have tried to use the word "thought" to indicate a distance on the the term, and to point out problems in that translation as they arise.

I analyze how Proust steers a course between literature and philosophy in order to challenge and ultimately transform the tradition of rationalism. My hypothesis is that Proust tacks away from an initial structure by displacement: the project is designed to mediate rational thought in the search for a total work and a theory of the artistic subject; the text is the operator of affective movements which, without being classifiable as simply irrational, escape the logic of rationality.

ORGANIZATION

The book is divided into two parts. Part I deals with "the Project" of the novel, largely those sections sketched out in 1908-9; Part II deals with what I call "the Text, " those sections that exceed the project and ultimately question its unity. That is, what interests me here is to examine the constitution of the writing subject as that which both furthers and questions the tradition that puts reason at the center. I propose to locate a working concept for the subject that is neither modern, postmodern, nor poststructuralist; one that returns to the particular, the idiom, but for which there is no pivotal faculty, no self centered in reason. My approach is to open theoretical questions through close textual readings. Quotation and paraphrase form integral parts of the arguments, for theoretical reasons. My strategy is to reconstruct the sequence of a number of microstories within the novel, as Proust's theory of association demands, in order to understand the relationship between singular events and their formulation in general terms. Proust wrote literature, as Heidegger and Wittgenstein were to write philosophy, in order to display the universality and necessity of the individual and the contingent. He was a master at making the contingent into a given, at linking the singular and the universal. I define his subject as an agent for whom hierarchical thought ceases to be pertinent. The absence of hierarchy creates an anxiety: the "anxiety of indeterminacy," which the letters, sketches, and rewritten passages display in varying degrees.

I take as a premise in this book that all documents, whether private or public, sketch or "final" draft, have gained the status of text because, like the sketches and drawings hung in a museum, they present a retrospective on the artist; we can now "x-ray" Proust's text, as it were, as machines might perhaps a Rembrandt. The infinitely patient work demanded of the editors has passed out of the hands of specialists into the public domain of readers. The chapters of this book move from issue to issue by displacing the resolution of serious questions concerning the possibility of a literary and personal identity: Chapter 1, the structure of thought and art; Chapter 2, the foundation of aesthetics in the translation of memory; Chapter 3, the ethical dilemma of relativism revealed in political change (the Dreyfus affair), and the literary wisdom of uncertainty; Chapter 4, the possibility for newness in the irruption of desire for women; Chapter 5, the epistemological gain that accompanies the devastation of jealousy in love; Chapter 6, association—the foundation of art and disruption of life, from the image of the cathedral to the dress. Each chapter deals with specific events in the novel; I reread some of the best-known or canonically accepted passages in Part I to prepare for others in Part II that are equally important for the questions asked here.

In the association of memories, Proust emphasizes the topic of *ethos* (the root meaning of which goes back to the self) in such a way that a Platonistic model of the self lying behind or beyond the empirical world of events is posited as an ideal. Then Proust's brand of association leads the way to new thinking, by revising schemata inherited from the past through what Freud called *Nachträglichkeit*: "aftering" or "delayed signification." Along with the temporal gaps which allow for interpretation through memory, the spatial movement "to the side of objects" also concerns me.[41] Associations give meaning (often, it seems, in the semblance of causal relations) to change. And the beauty of what they convey, as Proust says of Giotto, is not so much the ideas but a *feeling of form*.[42] When it is taken away, the scaffolding totters.

ART ONE: THE PROJECT

1

In a notebook, Proust wrote that his "philosophy, like all true philosophy, comes down to justifying, to reconstructing what is."[1] The difficulty was to understand *what it is that is* and to reclaim this *whatness* through writing. "Should it be a novel? a philosophical study? am I a novelist?" he queried in a notebook from 1908.[2] Proust chose the novel. He did not choose it in order to make literature the successor to philosophy or to have literary anecdotes serve as the illustration of abstract principles. He chose it to transform the philosophical question "How to think?" and the more existential one "How to become what one is?" into the literary challenge of "How to become a writer?"

As Proust asked who is the subject which "is," which "functions" socially and politically in the world, and which "writes," he was able to break from the opposition between perception and reflection and to understand that the dualism of binary thinking would be altered through what he called "the rectification of an oblique interior discourse" (RTP 3:926).[3] Thought would not be *either* philosophical *or* literary, perceptive *or* reflective, conscious *or* unconscious. In *Remembrance of Things Past* the paths of literature and philosophy, as ways of making the world intelligible and giving meaning to it, would so intertwine as to become almost inseparable.

Since Proust states that the movement of thought "deviates gradually more and more widely from the first and central impression" (RTP 3:926), [4] the question was, why does literature resist philosophy while asking the profoundest of philosophical questions? And as it renders the affect intelligible, how does it mark the reassessment of limits in the shifting domain of art and philosophy?

In a letter dated October 12, 1912, Proust wrote: "You know, perhaps, that ever since I have been ill, I have been working on a long book, which I call a novel . . . I don't know how to describe the *genre*."[5] His hesitation about the genre grew out of the need both to write something akin to memoirs and yet oppose contingency to necessity in the search for an as yet invisible overall structure. Proust chose the first person singular for his "autofiction"[6]—"There is a Monsieur who narrates and who says 'I' "[7]—to show a delicate balance between contingency and freedom within the novelistic framework. The narrator then questions the philosophic grounding of being, as the search for self-creation in art becomes the only consistent, hence necessary, point of reference in a text where everything else is questioned.

While the novelistic qualities of the narration and freedom of tone suggest a form akin to memoirs, Proust maintains that in reality a "very severe composition" differentiates them. Whatever part is played by contingency merely expresses the contingent part of life, a logic according to which there can no longer be anything contingent in the book.[8] The idea for the "severe composition" (he referred to it later as "a construction and a dogmatic work")[9] may have occurred to Proust when he was finishing his translations of Ruskin's work in 1905—the same year, traumatic for him, in which his mother died. Proust encountered the basic idea in *Sesame and Lilies* while correcting proof for his translation; he writes in a note that Ruskin "goes from one idea to another without apparent order. But in reality the fancy that leads him follows his profound affinities which in spite of himself impose on him a superior logic. So that in the end he happens to have obeyed a kind of *secret plan which, unveiled at the end, imposes retrospectively on the whole a sort of order and makes it appear magnificently arranged up to this final apotheosis.*"[10]

This superior logic, the secret plan leading to a final apotheosis, grants a cadence to what appears to be disordered thought. With the idea of a retrospective ordering, Proust lays the groundwork not only for the overall structure of the novel but for the method of its working out in association as well. His definition of memory comes close to Ruskin's sense of association: "The accidental connection of ideas and memories with material things, owing to which those material things are regarded as agreeable otherwise, according to the nature of the feelings or recollections they summon: the association being commonly involuntary and often times so vague that no distinct image is suggested by the object, but we feel a painfulness in it or pleasure from it, without knowing wherefore."[11]

But beyond the instant of association, what Proust saw in Ruskin's work was a unitary and totalizing thrust, a movement pulsing toward an end, that he would later espouse as his own: "From the beginning Ruskin thus reveals . . . themes and at the end . . . he will inextricably combine them in the last sentence where *the tonality of the beginning . . . will be recalled in the final chord.*"[12]

"I have tried to transmit my whole philosophy, to make all my 'music' resonate," Proust wrote of *Swann's Way*.[13] The totality of his philosophy, figured in this musical image, could not be the result of chance alone: "One might sit at the piano for fifty years, trying out all possible combinations of notes, and still never come up with a phrase as 'divine' as that of a great musician." No, the artist is chosen, and truth presumed to be an invariant: "I believe that (literary) truth is discovered each time, like a law of physics. One finds it or one doesn't."[14]

Like Ruskin, Proust senses that the artist does not choose the subjects of art: "The subject of the novelist, the vision of the poet, the truth of the philosopher are imposed on them in a manner almost inevitable, exterior, so to speak, to their thought." Like Ruskin too, Proust feels a higher order stirring in art: "It is by subjecting his mind to the expression of this vision and to the approach of this truth that *the artist becomes truly himself.*"[15] Proust thus scrutinizes the way in which Ruskin pulls a work together: "If th[is] disorder is the same in all his [Ruskin's] books, the same gesture of bringing in the reins together at the end and of feigning to have constrained and guided his steeds, does not occur in all of them. Here . . . we should see more than a game."[16] Vision and craft join together at the beginning and the end of the work to establish the parameters within which everything signifies. The beginning and end confer unity on the disparate elements, providing them with the needed structure.

But if the invariant in his novel was the structuring principle, this was not apparent to the reader when the first volume appeared in 1913. Proust argued vehemently that despite its complexity, the overall compositional structure was tight; he manifested impatience with those who did not understand that a structure of deferral binds together the mass of details and episodes. "This book . . . is a very structured whole, although the composition is so complex that I fear no one perceives it and that it seems like a series of digressions. It is the very opposite."[17] And "there are many characters; they are prepared from the first volume. . . . The complexity of the composition only appears much later, when all the themes have begun to combine."[18] In structuring the unity of the project thus, this book would be unlike the works from the nineteenth century whose unity, Proust suggested, comes after the fact.[19] This would be a work whose unity was to be inscribed from the inception of the project and whose vitality would be propelled through the expression and torment of feeling.

But the problems of structure and chronology could not be resolved with such quick dispatch. Proust may have at one point confused the problem of endings with the problem of finishing; he may, that is, have confused structure with genesis. In 1909, a year after he began the notes for *Contre Sainte-Beuve,* he wrote jubilantly to Madame Straus what may well be the understatement of the century: "I have just begun—and finished—a very long book"—though he did caution that if "everything is written, many things remain to be revised."[20] And of course we know that the book Proust first sketched in 1908 would not be finished even at his death in 1922, and to this day remains problematic because of textual and other difficulties. Indeed, the 1987–89 Pléiade edition contains at least as many pages of variants as there are pages of text, and it reactivates questions about how to relate closure to incompleteness, structure to writing, project to text. The editors took their general comprehension of the text and based editorial decisions on the assumption that *Contre Sainte-Beuve* was a first version of the *Recherche.* Proust had indicated that *Contre Sainte-Beuve* "was composed of events, the reflection of events upon each other at a distance of many years."[21] None of the notebooks in which he wrote these fragments, however, suggests that he had in mind at that time a unified work, unless by "unified" one again means a complex composition.[22] Nor does any single literary form dominate: fragments of essay alternate with fragments of narrative, correcting, completing, and revising one another.

Even the editorial history of this text remains divided and fragmentary; no "definitive" version of the *Contre Sainte-Beuve* exists. There are two quite dissimilar editions: one published by Bernard de Fallois in 1954, and another by Pierre Clarac in 1971.[23] Fallois makes the case for "continuous creation" in which the birth of the novel, *Remembrance of Things Past,* emerges from the failure of an essay about criticism. He takes the genesis of a work of art to be a linear operation. According to this argument Proust produced only one great book, the teleology of which was etched in the early fragments. There, one could already see the dissociation between creative and critical thought, between abstract and concrete thinking, which tended toward an anti-intellectualist stance. Yet even if one takes the opposite view, as Maurice Bardèche does when he suggests that personal memories lead to a theoretical meditation on literature, a cleavage between the critical and narrative sections of the text remain in which one part precedes and gives birth to the other. Pierre Clarac refused Fallois's theory, suggesting that no relation existed between the essay and the novel and minimizing the importance of the narrative sequence. The projects are separate and separable, he maintained: one was a theoretical essay and the other a conversation with Proust's mother. For the reader, the problem is that neither edition bears out the theory proposed in its respective presentation of texts. Fallois's reconstruction is artificial and arbitrary, and while Clarac plays down the importance of the narrative on principle, he nevertheless still includes narrative passages in his edition.[24]

The apparent happenstance anthologizing from the manuscripts in both editions points up a general problem in the thinking about Proust's manuscripts. Bernard Brun suggests "an impossibility of thinking about the Proust project beyond the limits of a rigid framework, whether it be the order of the 'narrative' [récit] or the order of 'discourse,' in any other ways but through the categories of criticism which obliterates the work of the writer."[25] He goes on to show that the manuscripts corroborate the notion of a discontinuous, episodic kind of writing within which fragments display dogmatism. They corroborate the simultaneity of Proust's conception of the project as an essay both on and of criticism *and* a narrative in dialogue form in which his mother would figure as interlocutor.

At the origin, then, there was a project composed of many styles: criticism, parody, theory, and narrative; at the origin there was also Proust's mother. He writes in a letter dated mid-December 1908: "I am going to write something on Sainte-Beuve. In my thought, I have *built two* articles. . . . One is an article in classical form. . . . The other would begin with the story of a morning, Maman would come close to my bed, and I would recount the article that I want to do on Sainte-Beuve. And I would develop it for her."[26]

The "plot" of *Contre Sainte-Beuve* consists of how the narrator, "I," sleeplessly waits for morning and his mother. He remembers two different places, the country and the ocean where he lived his bedtime drama, and the walks that he takes along two separate paths. In the morning, his mother brings him a newspaper in which an article he had written appears. Sounds from the street stir up memories of a trip to Venice with his mother. He speaks to her about the discovery of characters and the world. The book was to end with "A conversation with *Maman*" which, Proust wrote in a letter dated 1909, one would see as the working out of aesthetic principles, a kind of *preface* placed at the end of the text.[27]

Proust evokes his mother indirectly in the final pages of *Time Regained* in a passage written in 1909, about the same time as the preface to *Contre Sainte-Beuve*.[28] The narrator hears the sound of the garden bell, the very same bell that signals the departure of Monsieur Swann and the arrival of his mother to kiss him goodnight: "When the bell of the garden gate had pealed, I already existed and from that moment onwards, for me still to be able to hear that peal, there must have been no break in continuity . . . since that moment from long ago still adhered to me and I could still find it again, could retrace my steps to it merely by descending to a greater depth within myself" (RTP 3:1105–6).[29] This continuity is between self and self, the one present and the other past, in relation to the unprecedented night when his mother stayed and read to him in his room, the scene of the goodnight kiss which Proust placed early in "Combray."

In this celebrated scene the narrator suffers because his mother does not come to kiss him goodnight in his room when Swann comes to dinner. One evening in particular, the narrator's father and grandfather both break what the young boy considers to be their contract with him by sending him to bed early. In his room a sense of revolt comes over him, and he reacts by writing a letter to his mother imploring her to come to his room for an important, secret matter. In the novel this is the narrator's first act of writing. Receiving no response, he waits tormentedly until his parents retire. Buried in his bed, the boy anticipates a punishment, which will come neither from his father nor from the knowledge that all must die. For death here portends resurrections through memory: the first will be "Mamma regained."[30] When both the mother and the father do finally come up the stairs, a most remarkable reversal occurs: the father, seeing the boy's distress, sends his wife to spend the night in the room with him. The arbitrariness of his father's acts seem incomprehensible, coming from "chance expediencies" rather than any "formal plan": "When I had just committed a sin so deadly that I expected to be banished from the household, my parents gave me a far greater concession than I could ever have won as the reward of a good deed" (RTP 1:40).[31]

The drama of separation from and return to his mother when the father "gives in" in *Swann's Way* inscribes a structure of intermittency within the project of the *Contre Sainte-Beuve*. It resurrects a world now absent: "The house where this happened no longer exists. And the image of it in my memory is perhaps the only 'proof' that remains of it, and it will soon be destroyed. The possibility of such hours has been obliterated forever. For some years now, my father and my mother have been able to do no more than continue to influence me from beyond the grave."[32]

It is during the same night that his mother reads to him from *François le Champi*, a novel by George Sand that the boy's grandmother had given to him. The dialogue between mother and son takes place in the form of a reading in which the plot is obscured, first because "when I read, I used often to daydream about something quite different for page after page," and then because "the gaps which this habit left in my knowledge of the story were widened by the fact that when it was Mamma who was reading to me aloud she left all the love-scenes out" (RTP 1:45).[33] Unconsciously screening the book through the gaps and blanks of reading, the young boy reinforces his mother's deliberate censorship. As "unfaithful" readers, the two are complicitous: both rewrite the book. As unconscious on the part of the boy as it is conscious on the part of the mother, this process explains the necessity of interpreting the story after the fact: the "key" to the strange relations between Madeleine, the miller's wife in the Sand novel, and the boy François is not, as he then believed, the "strange and mellifluous name of *Champi,* which invested the boy who bore it" (RTP 1:45);[34] the key may be found in the suppression of the love scenes in the novel. Those scenes prepare the change in François: the young hero of the novel is transformed from son into lover and then husband of his adoptive mother. The narrator conveys his understanding of suppression and a heuristics of denial in the process of reading, but at no time does he make the connection or ponder the way in which this reading informs the novel as a primal scene of reading. Yet that is what it is.

What this extraordinary moment shows is the force of reading in the gaps, the sense that "true" meaning emerges from a collage: the connections and misconnections of thought in reading. What this scene also shows is the necessary incompleteness that allows meaning to emerge through time and subsequent interpretations. Thus this important scene, along with the projected dialogue with his mother in *Contre Sainte-Beuve,* provides a key to aspects of both the genesis and reception of the novel. As a sequence of fragments in which both mother and son suppress and displace material, this inaugural reading demands a delicate balance, an attention poised between intellect and feeling. The gaps in the mother's reading foretell, albeit fortuitously, parts of the text that have been (or will be editorially) suppressed, a subject to which I return in Chapters 6 and 7.

Identification with his mother is what allows Proust to articulate the unitary ideal of the work. "I am so tired," he writes to her in 1904, "that I don't know if you can feel through these incoherent lines the joy of feeling you closer to me and thinking about how soon we will no longer be but one person, as we are only one heart."[35] And in *Time Regained,* when the narrator happens on a copy of *François le Champi* in the Guermantes' library, the force of feeling brings on tears, not as he once thought because *Champi* stands for the books by Georges Sand but because the mystical charm of the book reminds him of this particular reading and its association with the night spent together with his mother. The book evokes by association a "pen" that conjures "a thousand trifling details of Combray which for years had not entered my mind." These thoughts "came lightly and spontaneously leaping, in follow-my-leader fashion, *to suspend themselves from the magnetised nib in an interminable and trembling chain of memories*" (RTP 3:920; emphasis added).[36]

At the same time, however, a negative association occurs related to death and his father:

> Imagine a room in which a man has died, a man who has rendered great services to his country; the undertaker's men are getting ready to take the coffin downstairs and the dead man's son is holding out his hand to the last friends who are filing past it; suddenly the silence is broken by a flourish of trumpets beneath the windows and he feels outraged, thinking that this must be some plot to mock and insult his grief; but presently this man who until this moment has mastered his emotions dissolves into tears, for he realises that what he hears is the band of a regiment which has come to share in his mourning and to pay honour to his father's corpse. (RTP 3:919)[37]

Like the "echo [that] never ceased" (RTP 1:40)[38] after his father had left him with his mother, this dream expresses the guilt of a (wishfully) incestuous son who has killed the father by assuming the mother's role.[39] The reading of *François le Champi* was, after all, strictly between mother and son, and its theme was how the boy got his girl: his mother. And in a dream about Proust's father, a theme for "intermittencies of the heart," the loss and return of the belief in death functions like the loss and return of feelings. "Absolute illusion of life. So you see that dead one is almost alive. Perhaps [Papa] would be mistaken in his responses, but at least there was a simulacra of life. Perhaps he is not dead."[40]

Unable to communicate with his father, Proust writes to his mother that he has thought so much about his father that he wants to write to tell him of his feelings: "At least, he consoles himself, my head writes."[41] But writing with the head (whether that means the intent to write or thought itself) does not suffice, because in the passage cited above, as he mourns his father he mourns himself: "The stranger, he explains, was none other than myself, the child I had been at that time, brought to life within me by the book, which knowing nothing of me except this child had instantly summoned him to its presence, wanting to be seen only by his eyes, to be loved only by his heart, to speak only to him" (RTP 3:920).[42]

Although the kind of dialogue between mother and son first envisaged in *Contre Sainte-Beuve* does not emerge in *Remembrance*, it is clear that from this scene on, the novel reads like an extended, if sometimes occulted, hymn to his mother. It is the story of their separation, which the hero mourns most acutely through others: his grandmother and Albertine. It is also the story of their reunification in Venice and the Guermantes' library through memory and art. Writing *against* Sainte-Beuve and *against* a certain kind of reading, the narrator nevertheless addresses his mother, picking out from the vicissitudes of life the "secret plan," the "tonality" of "what is." In its initial thrust, then, *Remembrance* is written to and for and perhaps even—in an act of identification—by the mother.

In the opening sentence of the preface to the *Contre Sainte-Beuve*, Proust writes: "Every day, I set less store on intellect." Next to the truth of feeling guaranteed by the sense of joy at privileged moments, and the revelations that these moments may bring, the truths of the intellect flatten and pale.[43] No matter how strenuous its efforts, the intellect cannot resurrect the past. Yet within the limited role assigned to the intellect, there resides a paradox that sets the stage for the narrator's quest for the truth in *Remembrance of Things Past:*

> Perhaps it will cause surprise that I, who make light of the intellect, should have devoted the following few pages precisely to some of these considerations that intellect, in contradiction to the platitudes that we hear said or read in

books, suggests to us . . . . Sainte-Beuve's Method is not, at first sight, such an important affair. But perhaps in the course of these pages we may be led to realise that it touches on very important intellectual problems, and on what is perhaps for an artist the greatest of all: this relative inferiority of the intellect which I spoke of at the beginning. Yet all the same, it is the intellect we must call on to establish this inferiority. Because if intellect does not deserve the crown of crowns, only intellect is able to award it. And if intellect ranks only second in the hierarchy of virtues, intellect alone is able to proclaim that the first place must be given to instinct.[44]

In the preface as published in both editions of *Contre Sainte-Beuve*, intellect and affect are clearly opposed. Proust suggests in an unpublished notebook version, however, that the intellect limits thought in its grasp of matter and the past:

> *It is not in [the intelligence] that we can find// this reality. . . . [The intelligence] retains nothing of reality* This reality which is matter.
> It is only by hiding itself, *outside the confines/outside the bounds/outside the limits of its light* outside of *its* its zone of light, that the artist can *perceive/refind* find lost reality and recreate it. *Seen/For the intelligence the past is lost* If we confine ourselves to intelligence, *the past, matter of our* our past, the matter of art, seems lost. In fact it is not, but each *day* hour *past* dead has become incarnated *in a material object, /in a* in an object *in a sensation entirely [material]* material and will remain there *unknown* unknown until.[45]

Prevented from moving beyond its own reach, intelligence appears incapable of making the past *live*: "*For the intelligence, the past is really the past* For the intelligence, the hours that we live die one after the other, *it is powerless.*"[46] Powerless to revive the past it may be, but the intellect nevertheless enables and empowers criticism. True, Proust attaches less importance both to the intellect and to criticism than to affect and art, but as he writes in another fragment, he will nevertheless give himself over to both in *Contre Sainte-Beuve*.[47] Because although intelligence is inferior to affect, and this is what is crucial, *only* the intelligence can comprehend this inferiority. And this means that one must always begin with the inferior faculty, a procedure recommended in *The Fugitive*: "The fact that our intelligence is not the subtlest, most powerful, most appropriate instrument for grasping the truth is only one reason the more for beginning with the intelligence, and not with an unconscious intuition, a ready-made faith in presentiments" (RTP 3:429).[48] Like the narrator, Proust wages his struggle against the limitations of the intelligence in the name of something higher: like Freud, he calls it the unconscious.[49] The generality of the unconscious works like the laws of physics for creation and operates through the work of memory; it provides art with the superior reality from which the varieties of experience and textual variants spring.[50]

In *Time Regained* the narrator announces his readiness to do away with the scaffolding of the work: "A work in which there are theories is like an object which still has its pricetag on it." This is not to be confused with the architectural structure. Rather, the conceptual use of language in the writing of theory, with its pre-set formulation and express ideologies (see Chapter 3), leaves no place for what is unique and tempts the writer "to write intellectual works—[which is] a gross impropriety" (RTP 3:916).[51]

Proust resisted writing a book of abstract analysis; he rejected traditional speculative thought as the articulation of a set of systematic laws because it differed from and was independent of both narrative and novelistic forms. What Proust wanted was to "recreate" the evolution of thought in the individual and to make it "live."[52] He could follow the "life of thought" only in its essential wandering through particulars. Generalities were to emerge as they were worked through in minute detail from a given point of view. It was in this way that Proust created from reminiscence, and the garden that was his mind, a new kind of speculative tool grounded in the knowledge that "our soul is never one."[53]

This struggle against intellect in one of the great analytic novels of the Western tradition may seem a paradox. It tells of the difficulty of forging a structure at the limits of rationality. But if that structure had not yet emerged clearly in 1914, the intense quality of the novel had. Proust quotes from a letter in which Francis Jammes pronounces the novel an unequaled highbrow model of analysis and form.[54] Jammes liked something in the abandonment of logic and structure; he sensed, and the rest of the text would bear this out, that there was another kind of theory, both concrete and logical, moving beyond the limits of reason. And Proust was clear: "[In] my literary theories, I find images born of an impression superior to the ones which serve only to illustrate the faculty of reason."[55]

Proust's reflection on the relationship between the affect and intellectual analysis was explicit. It was there that he elaborated the essential elements of his own "secret plan," the structure that would grant a retrospective order to the forthcoming work.[56] And the back-and-forth between exposition and narrative proved crucial in its structuring. In order to set up a framework within which the particulars of life and thought could take on meaning, Proust had to claim a firm structure. Memory—and the way memory organized experience in relation to matter—was to provide the founding principle of the work because, as he surmised, like memory the work was always the same yet perpetually becoming.[57]

Proust proclaimed the unity of the first and last sections of the book, and he had pointed to their simultaneous creation: "The last chapter of the last volume was written right after the first chapter of the first volume. Everything in between was written after that."[58] Although he had not actually written the first and last pages of the text, as he claims elsewhere to have done,[59] he had worked out a number of the key episodes of the novel: awakening disoriented in space and time, the sense of fluidity between dream life and consciousness, the experience of jotting down his perceptions.

Most important, Proust had sketched the sequence of experiences in involuntary memory that were to furnish the support, the inner structure of the total work.

It is an extremely real book, but borne up as it were . . . by a gift, by a peduncle of reminiscences in order to imitate involuntary memory. Thus a part of the book is a part of my life that I had forgotten and that suddenly I recall while eating a little bit of madeleine cake. . . . Another part of the book is recovered from sensations at waking, when one doesn't know where one is and believes oneself to be two years earlier in time or in another country. But all this is the stem of the book. And what it bears is real, passionate.[60]

What he calls the stem, those involuntary memories from which the memory of the past flowers, is to be found in the sketches for the preface. Unlike other prefaces, no text to which it alludes follows; in 1908 and 1909 that text remains virtual. Yet these sketches serve a crucial function by initiating the project.[61] In them, Proust juxtaposes sequences of involuntary memory: the first flush of joy when memories irrupt into consciousness ("a whole garden") as he drinks tea and dips toast, feels uneven paving stones, and hears a spoon drop on his plate. Mysteriously calling forth feelings of elation, of "pure life conserved pure,"[62] these very experiences begin and end the novel: in "Combray" the scene of the madeleine summons total recall of childhood amnesia; in *Time Regained* the same such memories repeat and amplify the experience of involuntary memory, preliminaries or rites of passage through Proust's ontology to his aesthetics, the subject of the next chapter.

2

E schewing reason as first principle, Proust plumbs the depths of thought through experiences so absolute as to constitute the ontological basis of the novel: the involuntary experiences of memory. When the hero discovers his vocation as a writer in *Time Regained,* he asserts that "the function and the task of a writer are those of a translator" (RTP 3:926).[1] Creation is the translation of memory. But who or what is translated, the roles of thought and feeling, and the language of truth all turn out to be tricky questions. Commanded by the image of the book, translation paradoxically allows newness to emerge from something presumed to be already there: "Certain obscure impressions . . . concealed within them not a sensation dating from an earlier time, but *a new truth*" (RTP 3:912; emphasis added).[2] The discovery of this "new truth" constitutes the core of Proust's project of a book of the self. This chapter deals with the basic logic that leads from involuntary memory, the essence of being, to the foundation of Proust's aesthetics in metaphor and its initial realization in music.

F rom the beginning, the narrator struggles to reconstruct the unity of the self; from the beginning, he raises the question of reading and the image of the book in that connection. Through the symbiotic reading of *François le Champi* by his mother (discussed in Chapter 1), the narrator presents an initial, albeit partial, model for reading which is at once concrete and abstract.[3] Because it is simultaneously suffused with feeling and riddled with gaps, the combination creates an overload of associations in memory. These associations so crisscross that they render the subject of the book virtually unimportant. Because "every reader is, while he is reading, the reader of his own self" (RTP 3:949), the text becomes meaningful only for what it triggers within the reader,[4] whether it be an advertisement for soap or Pascal's *Pensées* (the juxtaposition is Proust's). The narrator likens time to a library in which one recovers the past by requesting a book and remembers episodes by finding lost pages. These images thus come to stand for the possibility of making the self intelligible to itself through others. They serve as catalysts for discovery.

After his mother's death, Proust definitively gave up the translations of Ruskin that she had encouraged him to undertake, but he had not yet found the way to his own work.[5] If the structure of the work is, as it were, born at the empirical moment of his mother's death, it negotiates the certainty of loss against the hope of resurrection. Founded upon loss, translation turns out to be palliative.[6] Inscribing his mother from the very beginning of the project, Proust counters the effects of separation by sustaining a sense of connection with her in art. That connection is located in affect, its power to bind things past and present in the ability to forge the world anew. Dedicating himself to a notion of invention (at once old and new), the narrator of *Remembrance* vows to write what the bereaved young man could not: another kind of translation of the self.

Truth is there to be found by the writer: "The essential, the only true book, though in the ordinary sense of the word it does not have to be 'invented' by a great writer—for it exists already in each one of us—has to be *translated* by him" (RTP 3:926; emphasis added).[7] It is as though obscure and "precious image[s]" had been forgotten, as though "our finest ideas were like tunes which, as it were, come back to us although we have never heard them before and which we have to make an effort *to hear and to transcribe*" (RTP 3:912; emphasis added).[8]

Proust formulates the problem of finding newness in what is most archaic. In so doing, he brushes with Plato, whose philosophic project was founded on a concept of translation designed to circumscribe truth, whether truth was considered univocal or plurivocal. Within this project, truth could be translated as long as one defined meaning as the passage of one semantic element into another. It drew on the hypothesis that meaning was translatable.[9] For Proust as for Plato, translation depends upon knowledge as memory in relation to truth. But whereas for Plato the individual was merely the ventriloquist for universal truth, for Proust translation demands to be worked out in the infinite variety of individual experience. This also becomes the sticking point. Because Proust's sense of the self is fragmenting and fragmentary, translation provides a problematic general concept for what he seeks to generalize but cannot: the singularity of individual thought.[10]

Building on the general notion that every being is unique, Proust hypostatizes the concept of the book, bringing to life two principles crucial to his project. The first is *the principle of uniqueness:* "A new book," he writes, "was not one of a number of similar objects but . . . a unique person, absolutely self-contained" (RTP 1:44).[11] Proust's tropology, in which people resemble books and books people, displaces Sainte-Beuve's contention that books gain intelligibility from comprehension about the writer's life; here people reconstructed from books take on an essential quality that others lack. This asymmetry reverses the privilege traditionally granted to reality over fiction and partially explains why the narrator, having discovered his vocation as a writer at the end of the novel, prepares to write a book that cries out to be, yet has already been written. Access to the unique book of the self can be gained only through involuntary memory, the occurrence of which depends upon chance. The second principle is *the principle of insignificance.* Proust wrote in a letter dated 1909 that *"insignificance in an insignificant subject is the mark of its true originality."*[12] No object or person has absolute or objective meaning. Meaning can be conferred only by affect in memory. This means that if feeling carries with it the immediacy of instinct in the branding of truth, the foundation of Proust's aesthetics within *Remembrance* rests, contrary to the experience of the hero recounted by the narrator, on the necessarily relative value of all objects and events. They are inflected only by the feelings of the players who enact them.

Individuation emerges when life and art become coextensive through the images of the book, reading, and translation. In this literary program there are no guiding principles or established set of rules: "As for the inner book of unknown symbols . . . , if I tried to read them no one could help me with any rules, for to read them was an act of creation in which no one can do our work for us or even collaborate with us" (RTP 3:913).[13] As the repositories for experience, these two principles designate impressions as the locus of singular truth, even though the narrator hesitates about the status of such impressions. On the one hand, they alone convey truth: "Only the impression, however trivial its material may seem to be, however faint its traces, is a criterion of truth." (RTP 3:914.)[14] On the other, they cannot be grasped directly: only "its material pattern, the outline of the impression that it made upon us, remains behind as the token of its necessary truth" (RTP 3:914).[15] Such brute impressions must be deciphered as marks of signs.

The interior book turns out to be a myth because the original for any translation is unavailable.[16] Feeling occurs in one sphere, thinking and naming in another; between the two, one can at best establish a concordance, not bridge the gap.[17] The myth of interiority is flawed in the attribution of the translation of experience for the interpretation of signs.[18] Hence, the narrator-theoretician may view Marcel's life abstractly as the translation of a book internal to him, but nowhere does that original manifest itself in the writing. This means that since the singularity of the individual, this idiomatic quality, remains untranslatable, any translation implies loss of what is unique. The problem is how to generalize the ungeneralizable, translate the untranslatable.

Description never therefore renders a direct transposition of experience. At best, it translates a text that is always already there.[19] The artist cannot rely upon direct sense perception to reach the essence of things but must trust rather to the imagination, which is the only organ "for the enjoyment of beauty" (RTP 3:905). The imagination goes beyond transcription to interpret. "This book, more laborious to decipher than any other, is also the only one which has been dictated to us by reality, the only one of which the 'impression' has been printed in us by reality itself" (RTP 3:914).[20] The translation of impressions is not, however, an empiricist project, passing directly from the world to thought. Translation in this sense involves a complex process of which a part is hermeneutic, coming out of interpretation and the belief in meaning, and another part semiotic, dependent upon language. Deep and surface structures, roughly equivalent to involuntary and voluntary memory, intersect to salvage a particular sense of the absolute. Proust formulates an imperative for this in notes for *Time Regained,* suggesting that if all beings were eternal and the problems of the world resolved, the highest obligation would still remain to translate.[21]

Translation brings forth the language of a unique self in relation to the other through time and memory. The book toward which all this tends is a fable about literature as the translation of an "inner" world of thought. Not because a simple one-to-one relation may be established between a word and a feeling or thought, though Proust senses that Ruskin, like Carlyle, held such a belief: the poet was a sort of scribe of nature writing out something of its secret, to which the artist should add nothing.[22] What he or she conveys is something of the relationship of translation to language and the original with the reinstatement of past contexts. In this sense, individual works differ little from monumental works; single evocations restore a whole context without loss of what is unique: "A name read long ago in a book contains within its syllables the strong wind and brilliant sunshine that prevailed while we were reading it" (RTP 3:920).[23]

For Proust as for Walter Benjamin, the relationship of the translator to the original is one of survival: survival of one in the other through writing. Translation not only communicates meaning but, more important, operates according to a principle of growth from the original. Survival requires mutation and renewal of the living in which the origin is modified. "The intention of the poet is spontaneous, primary, graphic; that of the translator is derivative, ultimate, ideational," Benjamin wrote of the task of the translator.[24] Proust's text must perform both tasks: recover the original book of the self unprompted and simultaneously translate it. Whence comes a twofold imperative: first, translate "me"; then, "I" am untranslatable. The tension between the two defines the "truth of language" and the "language of truth" in an emerging pragmatics of writing.

Benjamin wrote, "While content and language form a certain unity in the original, like a fruit and its skin, the language of the *translation envelops its content like a royal robe with ample folds.*"[25] The ample folds of this royal robe suggest that translation is more than a simple transfer of meaning for Benjamin as for Proust, a subject to which I return in Chapter 6. For now, the question is how to bridge the passage between the language of memory and that of creation. As we have seen, conceptual thinking, as the realm of the intellect, goes only so far: intelligence may cleverly formulate generalities, while individuation in feeling appears for a long time impoverished and inarticulate. But the force of certain feelings demands articulation.

Early on in the novel, for example, the narrator remembers his reaction to a reflection on the water: "Gosh, gosh, gosh, gosh!" (RTP 1:170).[26] In groping to articulate the sensation through words, he understands that his "gosh," however enthusiastic and spontaneous, demonstrates a failure of language: "Thus it is that most of our attempts to translate our innermost feelings do no more than relieve us of them by drawing them out in a blurred form which does not help us to identify them" (RTP 1:169).[27] Beyond a diffused expression of joy, Proust sought to articulate *feeling of form:* the art of transmuting sensation into words.[28]

To do so, Proust had first to build a case for understanding thought. From the very first pages, his investigation of how the subject can know the self and the world incorporates a Cartesian element: doubt. In an attempt to find certainty, the narrator doubts everything: perceptions, dreams, thoughts, friendship, and social relations. Through this doubt and the experience of intense feelings of joy, however fleeting, Proust prepares the way for a description of the truth of the subject. In doubt, reason gives way to the *cogito* of sensibility; in doubt, suffering becomes interminable. But the effects of both ultimately prove to be positive: because the meaning of the interior book will not be reduced to thinking and the intellect, literature and *true* literary theory remain somehow outside the ken of reason.[29]

Proust equated books with dreams and a process of reading by association.[30] In their power to stir and provoke emotions, books are like "a dream more lucid and more abiding than those which come to us in sleep" (RTP 1:92).[31] Through the insertion of current events and feelings into archaic patterns, books like dreams afford the narrator a reading of the self. Indeed, the process of interpretation functions like that which one would give to a dream. Yet no dream recounted in the novel carries thematic privilege or demands special interpretation. Nor is the interpretation of these dreams any different from interpretation of the novel itself.[32] Because the fundamental structure of the novel is based on the association of ideas, Proust's equivalent to the basic rule in psychoanalysis, the entire novel calls for a kind of interpretation close to dream analysis in which associations create sense.[33] Through their paratactic power to level hierarchies of thought, books like dreams reorganize time, space, and the sequences of experience. What guides the narrator in this displacement is the belief that associations not only thicken and enrich objects; they bestow value.[34] "It is always an invisible belief that sustains the edifice of our sensory world and deprived of which it totters" (RTP 3:453).[35] But the one is finally within the other.

The withdrawal of associations accounts for the recurring sense of disappointment and let-down: "We try to discover in things, which become precious to us on that account, the reflection of what our soul has projected on to them; we are disillusioned when we find that they are in reality devoid of the charm which they owed, in our minds, to the association of certain ideas"(RTP 1:93).[36] Yet the result is equivocal: the "charm" of associations, roughly equivalent to the effect of Ruskin's pathetic fallacy, in which feelings are projected onto objects, at once enhances and threatens the subject. While the force of belief sustains thought through desire, privileging certain moments and people, this same force opens meaning to arbitrariness. Because associations come upon (befall) the thinker without hierarchical privilege, their apparent disorder puts the identity of the self at risk.

THE MEMORY OF MADELEINE

The first major reading of the "interior book" comes with the involuntary memory of the madeleine, the experience that brings childhood and Combray back in their entirety. Prior to publication of the final volume, in which Proust elaborates the theoretical significance of the scene, he stresses the importance of such unconscious memories as the foundation of his art. He reiterates the importance of his discovery that memory moves between and joins different levels of thought. But he vehemently defends himself against the suggestion that the power of involuntary memory comes from a mechanical notion of the association of ideas.[37] Neither causal nor habitual, involuntary memory is quintessential because it associates memories, not ideas; it is unique.

What prepares the extraordinary moment of the madeleine, and all the repetitions of involuntary memory thereafter, is a sense of resignation and sadness, a sense that it is perhaps necessary to accept the limits of rational thought. Perhaps the past was truly and irrevocably dead. But when he tasted the little cake dunked in tea, "an exquisite pleasure" invaded his senses, "something isolated, detached, with no suggestion of its origin" (RTP 1:48).[38] It is without apparent cause (Proust wrote "cause" not "origin" in French); the effects are nevertheless clear: difficulties become indifferent, and a precious essence fills him—"or rather this essence was not in me, it was me" (RTP 1:48).[39] Association of memory leads to the discovery of the essence of being from which three questions follow: "Whence did it come? What did it mean? How could I seize and apprehend it?" (RTP 1:48).[40] Setting aside his cup, he addresses himself: "The mind . . . is face to face with something which does not yet exist, to which it alone can give reality and substance, which it alone can bring into the light of day" (RTP 1:49).[41] Through the particularity of this epiphanic moment Proust raises the larger question of what constitutes thought, how such associations confer meaning. The narrator retraces the events to experience the moment anew. Something rises from within that allows the hero to "measure the resistance, . . . hear the echo of great spaces traversed" (RTP 1:49). Having initially been startled into extraordinary attention, thought now becomes vitiated through the labor to comprehend:

> Undoubtedly what is thus palpitating in the depths of my being must be the image, the visual memory which, being linked to that taste, is trying to follow it into my conscious mind. But its struggles are too far off, too confused and chaotic; scarcely can I perceive the neutral glow into which the elusive whirling medley of stirred-up colours is fused, and I cannot distinguish its form, cannot invite it, as the one possible interpreter, *to translate for me* the evidence of its contemporary, its inseparable paramour, the taste, cannot ask it to inform me what special circumstance is in question, from what period in my past life. [RTP 1:49–50; emphasis added][42]

Translation from image to concept cannot occur for the moment because the confusion is too great. Clarity is promised, however, as with the paper Japanese flowers which, when plunged into water, move from indistinct form to the forms of blossoms, boats, and people.[43] The image here plays a role analogous to thought, demanding translation through its heuristic—analytic—function. The narrator recognizes what Freud called "the co-existence of perception and memory, . . . the existence of unconscious mental processes alongside the conscious ones."[44] Successive efforts fail, however, to reevoke the force of the first moment.

Nevertheless, where before this moment the memory of Combray was partial and all efforts to retrieve the past voluntary, now Combray returns in its totality. In releasing a synecdochic effect, in which the part evokes the whole, the madeleine figures as the inaugural epiphany in the sequence of epiphanic experiences; it is the prototype or model for all others. In the final volume the narrator explains that "this being" had only come to him, "only manifested itself outside of activity and immediate enjoyment, on those rare occasions when the miracle of analogy" had made him escape from the present. "And only this being had the power to perform that task which had always defeated the efforts of [his] memory and [his] intellect, the power to make [him] rediscover days that were long past, the Time that was Lost" (RTP 3:904).[45] Taken as absolute, this power seems unrivaled, conferring essence through a total return of the past.

The struggle to recall the past by voluntary memory at moments other than these suggests a hierarchy in which the present moment appears to be the stronger, triumphing over the weaker one, though the weaker always appears more beautiful.[46] With the experience of involuntary memory, however, this relationship shifts, the weaker image comes back with a force hitherto unknown. Present and past rebalance themselves through juxtaposition in which, as Georges Poulet has suggested, time assumes "the form of space."[47] Opposed to the notion of seamless duration proposed by Henri Bergson,[48] Proust crosses space and time in memory, reshuffling temporal fragments through chance encounters. What Bergson had condemned as intellectual space, Proust rehabilitates by juxtaposing snippets of time and place. The association of memories forms a *contiguous* aesthetic space which becomes the principle of his art. Poulet argued convincingly that juxtaposition involves the simultaneity of elements, whereas superimposition involves the suppression of one by the other. Both imply contiguity, but only juxtaposition adequately renders the way in which previously simultaneous states reemerge in narrative. The model for memory work comes closer to the image of the glass panels described side by side, as though in a cathedral, than to the linear sequence of the *lanterne magique* or even the fresco :

> When I entered the room the violet sky seemed branded with the stiff, geometrical, fleeting, effulgent figure of the sun . . . lowering over the sea on the edge of the horizon like a sacred picture over a high altar, while the different parts of the western sky exposed in the glass fronts of the low mahogany bookcases that ran along the walls, which I carried back in my mind to the marvellous painting from which they had been detached, seemed like those different scenes executed long ago for a confraternity by some old master on a shrine, whose separate panels are now exhibited side by side in a gallery, so that the visitor's imagination alone can restore them to their place on the predella of the reredos. [RTP 1:860–61] .[49]

Poulet concludes that Proust's work is composed of distinct episodes that exchange information, mutually inform one another, and add on one by one to the whole collection.[50]

In *Time Regained,* Proust assumes that the whole may be reconstructed from the part, no matter how dispersed the elements: "Thus a connoisseur of painting who is shown one wing of an altar-piece remembers in what church or which museums or whose private collection the other fragments of the same work are dispersed and . . . he is able to reconstruct in his mind the predella and the whole altar as they once were" (RTP 3:1020).[51]

To accomplish the formidable task of reconstructing the whole of "what is" means encompassing the heterogeneous and inaccessible elements of experience, granting them at once a general form and life of particulars. The true miracle of analogy seems designed to resurrect the whole from the part without struggle, to hold together the entire theoretical fabric of the book on the peduncle of involuntary memory.

Proust thus elevates involuntary memory to a state beyond the limits of intelligence and reason. The narrator recovers not only the past but "perhaps very much more: something that, common both to the past and to the present," was perhaps "much more essential than either of them" (RTP 3:905).[52] As an experience without precedent, involuntary memory invents and enacts a law of creation. The association upon which it depends is at once singular and absolute.

The structure of involuntary memory functions—like translation—according to a principle of growth at work both in the life story of the narrator and in the models for the work of art. But if growth suggests change, the sequences of involuntary memory that constitute the project remain the same. All are preceded by discouragement and despair (the past is dead; he has no talent), after which an apparently inconsequential sensation follows: tasting the madeleine "soaked in [a] decoction of lime-blossom" (RTP 1:51), feeling uneven paving stones underfoot (RTP 3:898), and so on. Then, suddenly, an "exquisite pleasure" (RTP 1:47, 899) wells up; the sense that there is more than the mere coincidence of two moments at stake (RTP 3:872) renders "a joy which [is] like a certainty" (RTP 3:900).[53] In the end the narrator realizes that involuntary memory has less to do with content than with the "life of the mind" as a species of "logical reasoning" (RTP 3:904). The transposition of sensation to essence has to do with the passage from absolute singular event to analogical thinking (RTP 3:869, 870): the need to discover what is unique "by analogy" (according to another logic) becomes the primary catalyst for writing a novel.[54]

Yet whether renewal comes through resurrection in the miracle of analogy or reconstruction in the effort of the will, it depends upon deferred action or "aftering" in which two moments connect. By combining what is at once archaic and recent, these rare events cause us "suddenly to breathe a new air, an air which is new precisely because we have breathed it in the past" (RTP 3:903). This is no utopia—"that purer air which the poets have vainly tried to situate in paradise"—but a renaissance, profound because it has "been breathed before," and true because "the true paradises are the paradises that we have lost" (RTP 3:903).[55] Through affect, this joy of certainty or feeling of form, involuntary memory confers the recognition of an essential being at once unique and universal.[56]

Since the publication of the novel, there is perhaps no single scene that has received more attention from critics and readers than that of the madeleine.[57] The question I would ask about this attention is not so much, why the privilege of this scene (the answer seems clear, given the importance that Proust attributed to it), but rather, why did the scene of the madeleine dominate critical discourse for so long and then disappear? From a place of centrality it fell into the category of Proust's outmoded metaphysics. But as such, it still retained its privileged status. Serge Doubrovsky, for example, argued that the madeleine served as a screen memory for a scene of masturbation in *Contre Sainte-Beuve* and that the function of the narrative within the novel is maternal: sudden retrieval of this memory generates the story and engenders the book.[58]

Whether one agrees with this kind of teleological reading, in which everything leads from or comes back to one scene, it is the transformation of such insignificant moments into something significant and original that constitutes the extraordinary power of the novel.[59] I would contend that if the scene of the madeleine is indeed, as Proust would have it, the fundamental stem of the work, it brings with it more than the guarantee of the essential quality of being. It brings with it the restoration of a context, Combray—the very one to which the narrator's mother belonged—as replacement of loss. In addition to the name of a tea cake, "Madeleine" was the name of a mother—François le Champi's adoptive mother. The relationship between the cake and the reawakening of Combray may be arbitrary. But the revelation of determinism, in the displacements of thought and their metaphysical consequences, comes back to the mother.

Feeling privileges insignificant events inscribed in memory. But through involuntary memory, feeling does not link the "mind" with things; rather, it links the present and past. Thus, to the question "What does involuntary memory mean?" one answer will be that it means the forging of an essential, creative power through a rigorously determined associative structure. Association in the scene of the madeleine differs little from other kinds of association. It differs little, that is, except for the force of belief, the sense of absolute ontological priority, that the moment enacts. The moment of involuntary memory performs belief in the encounter between two moments and leads from memory to art, from association to metaphor, in an analogical process. But before going on to Proust's notion of metaphor, as the foundation for his aesthetics, let us pause to follow some queries about where this belief in involuntary memory might have arisen.

The availability of the Proust manuscripts and the publication of the correspondence have revived certain questions that were swept aside during the structuralist period: the status of the autobiographical "I" in its authorial as well as its narrative function; the question of how and when ideas are generated. For example, in both the *Contre Sainte-Beuve* and in his correspondence, Proust at times appropriates the "I" of his character and narrator, albeit with disclaimers, to speak of his novel.[60] This may have been what motivated Anthony Pugh in his analysis of the manuscripts to investigate the autobiographical basis for involuntary memory. To his own question "Is there a difference between what the narrator says he does and what he does?" Pugh answers: "For Proust there was no doubt an element of poetic justice in giving the involuntary memory a key role in the dénouement of the novel. He had long hoped that involuntary memory would be the answer. It was not to be, but in his fictional version he could have his way. He had indeed already alluded to it, with one example (the *madeleine*) given prominence."[61]

Pugh concludes then that "all of [Proust's] choices operate on the level of composition; they are questions of structure, not of experiences happening in Proust's daily life."[62] The decisive illumination comes not from a lived experience of involuntary memory but from Proust's discovery of the idea for the two ways (Swann's, the Guermantes'), out of which "a deep structure developed."[63] So the question of what relates the work to the life within the manuscripts brings Pugh back to the question of structure. But he has perhaps not stayed long enough with the more fundamental question that has been out of favor for some time: what is it that bridges the gap from life to work? For it is indeed this question that the narrator poses through the transition from involuntary memory to creation.

In the move to transcend experience through memory and (later) art, literature seems never to be a literary description of experience but always a description of the literary experience.[64] Indeed, Proust turns surprisingly to precedents, examples of involuntary memory in the works of Chateaubriand, Nerval, and Baudelaire:

> And in one of the masterpieces of French literature, Gérard de Nerval's *Sylvie*, just as in the book of the *Mémoires d'Outre-Tombe* which describes Combourg, there figures a sensation of the same species as the taste of the madeleine and the warbling of the thrush. Above all in Baudelaire, where they are more numerous still, reminiscences of this kind are clearly less fortuitous and therefore, to my mind, unmistakable in their significance. Here the poet himself, with something of a slow and indolent choice, deliberately seeks, in the perfume of a woman, for instance, of her hair and her breast, the analogies which will inspire him and evoke for him
>
> l'azur du ciel immense et rond
>
> and
>
> un port rempli de flammes et de mâts.
>
> I was about to search in my memory for the passages in Baudelaire at the heart of which one may find this kind of transposed sensation, in order once and for all to establish my place in so noble a line of descent and thus to give myself the assurance that the work which I no longer had any hesitation in undertaking was worthy of the pains which I should have to bestow upon it, when . . . [RTP 3:959][65]

If the force of involuntary memory had seemed to lie in its unpredictability and power of illumination, it was because no cause could be found to account for the complete resurgence of events in their context. Although the origin of involuntary memory remained without explanation, there was a sense that intelligibility was possible because of the accompanying pleasure, its "joy of certainty," as the inauguration of a cognitive conquest. To invoke literary precedence, however, domesticates this empowering force and reduces the principles of insignificance and individuation to derivatives of literary examples. In principle, involuntary memory cannot imitate; it can only evoke. Therefore, if by integrating the stem of the novel into literary history the narrator retrieves the novel from arbitrariness, at the same time involuntary memory no longer constitutes a unique event.

The liberation from arbitrariness, as experience comes to reveal a determined system, already occurs with the passage into writing in the description of the Martinville steeples.[66] As the narrator describes how he "transcribed" experience into words, the act of writing puts an end to random thought and creates through the force of will a joy similar to the one experienced in involuntary memory. Taking pleasure away from objects and even conceptual thought, the discovery of writing seems to lie "behind" sensation: "Without admitting to myself that what lay hidden behind the steeples of Martinville must be something analogous to a pretty phrase, since it was in the form of words which gave me pleasure that it had appeared to me, I borrowed a pencil and some paper . . . and in spite of the jolting of the carriage, to appease my conscience and to satisfy my enthusiasm, composed the following little fragment" (RTP 1:197).[67]

If writing seems to arise from experience, it is because pleasure and a sense of well-being function as the unifying elements between perception, memory, and creation. It is also because although there is no explicit concession to or recognition here of the importance of language, such unique scenes do nevertheless have linguistic counterparts.

A text by Bergotte brings a similar kind of pleasure, particularly the sense of dissolving difference. This unity cannot be identified with a given passage in a book; it comes rather from an "ideal passage" which, while common to all of Bergotte's books, remains particular within each one.[68] Here a pattern is repeated: contrary to any federating tendency, going from the many to the one, [69] the narrator takes off from an idealized form of singular experience within a model and looks to its pluralization in the performance of the text. In this way, Proust questions how the model relates to the *experience* of art, whether in creation or reception. The narrator's discovery, at the end of the novel, of his vocation as a writer and his determination to write a book exemplify the problem: it is neither the particular book that we are reading nor any book that we may read. Just as the space of this book is not the not same thing as its places, so *the* book maintains a status between the ideal and the real, unequivocal as a model only because unrealized in the form of extant books. The joyous destiny of the narrator's "invisible vocation," after useless years of sterile intellect, is survival in translation.[70]

Translation conveys a model for the tension between the "unifying powers of memory and the imagination and the corresponding, substitutive errors of . . . 'idolatry.' "[71] In these terms Proust named the poles of the "severe construction" of his art. They were close to but moving away from Ruskin's position on these issues. Lodged within Ruskin's otherwise intellectually sincere project, Proust had discerned the paradox of a splendid and tempting deception. No one had defined more accurately than Ruskin a certain kind of idolatry. But Proust sensed that all art would somehow harbor a kind of enslavement through the love of self-made images.[72] The real tension between Ruskin's idolatry and his sincerity could not simply be played out at certain moments in certain parts in his work; rather, it played itself out at every moment in those deep regions where the self receives images, where intelligence and memory combine to form a spiritual and moral life. Proust writes that Ruskin himself never stopped committing the sin of idolatry; his doctrines were not aesthetic but moral, even though he appeared to have chosen them for aesthetic reasons. Proust argued that it was because Ruskin presented his doctrines as true rather than beautiful that he could not be honest with himself about why he had chosen them.[73]

And what of Proust's moralism? If Proust counts idolatry as an error, idolatry opens the way to otherness on the road to self-knowledge in art: "There is no better way to become aware of what [one] feels oneself than by trying to recreate what a master has felt. In this profound effort it is our thought itself that we bring out into the light, together with his."(ASB, 193).[74] This is why Bergotte as the model for the writer, Elstir for the painter, and most especially Vinteuil for the musician all serve the heuristic itinerary of a progressive interiorization of art. They provide a link in the chain between involuntary memory and creation. In passing from reader, listener, or spectator to writer, the narrator must separate himself from artistic models. This detachment marks the end of one kind of translation (emblematized through reading as an act of reception) and the beginning of another—one that sensation and memory combine to create. Whatever errors the senses induce, they present no obstacle to the ultimate ambition of the narrator: to write a book that will "transcribe a universe which had to be totally redrawn" (RTP 3:1104).[75] As the quest for art moves from analogy in the models of other artists to the experience of writing, however, the narrator does not escape the pitfalls that Proust attributed to Ruskin's thinking. At the very moment when models should cease to matter and authorities are no longer needed for the creative process to begin, at the very moment when he is ready to embark on the project of writing the book, the narrator returns to the models Chateaubriand, Nerval, and Baudelaire for involuntary memory. It is a surprisingly regressive move, for any analogy here—especially in the form of outright recourse to literary authority—threatens to obliterate the idea, so carefully developed, that the work must be unique.

It is in the passage from the doctrine of the metaphor to metaphors, the passage from the one to the many, that the problem occurs. Elstir provided an example of metaphor in his paintings: he was "unable to look at a flower without first transplanting it to that inner garden in which we are obliged always to remain. . . . So that one might say that [in this case, the roses] were a new variety with which this painter, like a skilful horticulturist, had enriched the rose family" (RTP 2:975).[76] His transplants extended nature through art, a feat the narrator believes to be transferable to writing: "I was able to discern from these that the charm of each of them lay in a sort of metamorphosis of the objects represented, analogous to what in poetry we call metaphor" (RTP 1:893).[77] Thus Proust renders the passage from ontology to aesthetics by moving from a substantive to a metaphorical style:

> Truth will be attained by him only when he takes two different objects, states the connexion between them—a connexion analogous in the world of art to the unique connexion which in the world of science is provided by the law of causality—and encloses them in the necessary links of a well-wrought style; truth—and life too—can be attained by us only when, by comparing a quality common to two sensations, we succeed in extracting their common essence and in reuniting them to each other, liberated from the contingencies of time, within a metaphor. [RTP 3:925].[78]

Yet, the concept of the metaphor confounds rather than founds Proust's aesthetics. Since metaphor is to art what reminiscence is to life and, most crucial to the argument here, what associations are to analogy, metaphor was meant to transport the artist from feeling through thinking, then on to a higher realm:

> Whether I was concerned with impressions like the one which I had received from the sight of the steeples of Martinville or with reminiscences like that of the unevenness of the two steps or the taste of the madeleine, the task was to interpret the given sensations as signs of so many laws and ideas, by trying to think—that is to say, to draw forth from the shadow—what I had merely felt, by trying to con-

vert it into its spiritual equivalent. And this method, which seemed to me the sole method, what was it but the creation of a work of art? [RTP 3:912][79]

Still articulated in abstract terms, Elstir's painting rendered metaphor an intellectual act, equivalent to renaming: "If God the Father had created things by naming them, it was by taking away their names or giving them other names that Elstir created them anew. The names which designate things correspond invariably to an intellectual notion, alien to our true impressions, and compelling us to eliminate from them everything that is not in keeping with that notion" (RTP 1:893).[80]

The problem, as Proust raises it in his preface to Paul Morand's *Tendre Stocks,* is that the criterion of singularity in the work of art remains at odds with the concept of a unified style. That is, Proust asks how the style of the artist can be at once radically new and universally true.[81] As a partial answer, he recounts Anatole France's question "What is your canon?"—a question to which he responds unequivocally by refusing the very notion of a canon because it imposes a universalizing style on the singularities of heterogeneous thought.[82]

Proust chose Flaubert as a model for style, a writer in whose work he found the lack of all metaphors.[83] The difficulty of passing from ideal to realized form raised obliquely by this choice admits to no ready formula and renders the comparison between experience and art—contrasting, say, a living flower to a sculpted one—somewhat superfluous.[84]

What is not superfluous is that the much celebrated definition of metaphor at the end of the novel furnishes the general principle upon which to base art, though concrete examples of such metaphors in the novel are remarkably scarce.

METAPHOR AND METONYMY

Proust called all figures of analogy metaphor.[85] Yet most of the metaphors in the novel lie within a sequence of extended comparisons. Involuntary memory may appear at first to function as pure metaphor devoid of all metonymic relations, but it alone initiates metonymic contagion or irradiation.[86] Genette concludes that when Proust describes the two objects joined in metaphor, conceived as essence, it is on the condition that both elements figure in the place described. In other words, metaphor is constructed from two terms that have already been related by spatiotemporal contiguity. And Proust pushes contiguous association to the limits of substitution: "This dim coolness of my room . . . presented to my imagination the entire panorama of summer" (RTP 1:90.)[87] The "sense-signal" in the madeleine becomes the equivalent of the context to which it is associated, as a synecdochal substitution. Metaphor thus comes out of metonymy: metaphor finds lost time; metonymy revives it. The story for Genette begins only through metaphor in metonymy.

However, in his analysis of the dominant figures in the text, Genette points to a growing discontinuity.[88] He views the difference between the fluidity and discontinuity of the successive states not as a difference of order but as a difference of emphasis, with the discontinuous elements subordinated to fluidity and continuity largely through rhetorical control. Genette emphasizes the metonymic level (which prior to his important study had been largely neglected), but he leaves undisturbed the hierarchical relationship in which the miracle of metaphor (epiphany) appears; metaphor takes priority over metonymy. In order to bridge the gap from theory to practice, from the ideal to its working-out within the novel, the narrative at once maintains and yet questions this hierarchy. Proust maintains the hierarchy at the most explicit level by placing involuntary memory at both the beginning and the end of the novel, as discussed in Chapter 1; he maintains it further by opposing "true" memory work to all other relations. He questions the hierarchy, however, by recognizing its inability to transform the growing discontinuity of knowledge, especially in love and jealousy, into the continuous certainty of feeling.[89]

Pierre Zima takes the narratological argument in another direction, contending that Proust's novel is unified through a principle of association that no longer divides according to the opposition between metaphor and metonymy. He analyses Proust's text, as well as the texts of Franz Kafka and Robert Musil, in light of an ambivalence manifest within the narrative structure. He argues that narrative transformations need be understood as textual reactions to social, existential, and cognitive ambivalence. Meaning found within a universe dominated by appearance and ambivalence is constantly deferred and remains incomplete. Consequently, there is a duplicity, splitting, and then doubling of characters, with the two great exceptions of the narrator's mother and grandmother. Zima's argument rests on a clear opposition between conscious mental activity (the intelligence) and the unconscious. To the mediated, false word of social life Proust opposes a form of writing that issues forth from the unconscious; founded upon association, it is paradigmatic, paratactic, and dreamlike.[90] In this way, conscious life (the intelligence) is subordinated to the unconscious (artistic instinct) which expresses itself through association. The unconscious is involuntary, evoked only by chance. It is not causal logic but unconscious association that guarantees the truth of discourse and the elimination of arbitrariness. Paradigmatic writing, issuing from association, must be radically distinguished from logical thought of communication, due to its *figural and nonconceptual nature*.[91] But Zima's theory does not overcome the dichotomies of unconscious and conscious, society and art.

The complexity of Proust's aesthetics results from the desire to link such opposites in an inextricable relationship. The art to which he aspires opposes boorish art; it is, he says, like that of the architects who place a carving behind a statue where no one but a terribly curious scholar could see it,[92] or the fashion designer who lines pockets with the same color silk as the dress itself. In art, it is the detail that leads to universalizing particulars. Music is in this sense the true model for art, for there metaphor and metonymy operate synonymously, touching off a reaction akin to involuntary memory: music comes out of the depths of being, as its effects rejoin beings.[93] Art thus finds temporal ways of performing within the world. In music, change may be grasped through sound: "When [the] vision of the universe is modified, purified, becomes more adapted to his memory of his inner homeland, it is only natural that this should be expressed by a musician in a general alteration of sonorities, as of colours by a painter" (RTP 3:259).[94]

FROM SONATA TO SEPTET

Music guides the artist away from the pitfalls of idolatry and intellectualism. It establishes a process of growth in art as translation, such that if reading leads to the threshold of spiritual life in association and memory, music takes the listener beyond. Thus Vinteuil's little phrase from the sonata comes to be the "national anthem" of love between Swann and Odette, irrupting with each hearing into the present. As a fragment within the whole of the piece, this phrase is the only part Swann wishes to know. When the sonata begins, the return of the past is instantaneous in what the narrator calls *the cloakroom of his memory*;[95] as the images of Swann's love for Odette wash over him, the narrator likens the phrase to a protective goddess who has donned (*revêtu*) a sonorous appearance.[96] These memories separate the Swann of the past from the Swann of the present; they are a painful reminder that his love for Odette will never be reborn.[97] Swann has in fact so interiorized the passage that he regrets any meaning it might have for others, as though its private meaning would be lost were others to be privy to it. He longs for a private language as proof of a uniquely possessed love.[98] But the significance of the phrase no more inheres within the music itself than it did within books; its significance depends upon associations of memory.

The musical encoding of "true ideas" goes beyond reason, and the effect of the five notes of the sonata, in which two repeat insistently, makes one thing clear: this music can provide no more than a faded translation of the revelation of the "divine" world. Only music, as the first universal form, takes on the "inflection of being." Of the arts, only music appears without thematic message. And it alone returns without having been heard, like an idea in need of transcription, like some invisible creature whose previously unknown language is nevertheless understood: the only one ever encountered with immediate recognition.

Listening to the septet, the hero finds himself "in a strange land" where the road, unfamiliar at first, suddenly becomes recognizable. "It was into a rose-red daybreak that this unknown universe was drawn from the silence and the night to build up gradually before me" (RTP 3:252).[99] This strange and remote air composed on seven notes promises an ideal world. The work interpellates only him in the same way that Vinteuil's phrase was addressed only to Swann. This time it is the monumental, great, though as yet unpublished work by Vinteuil that no one had known existed. What distinguishes the septet from the sonata is the sense of growth and amplification in a promise fulfilled, the translation of a dialogue, from a "timid question to which the little phrase replied, from the breathless supplication to the fulfillment of the strange promise that had resounded" (RTP 3:256).[100] One could put together Vinteuil's music "note by note, stroke by stroke," as the expression of an "unsuspected world, *fragmented by the gaps between the different occasions of hearing his work performed*" (RTP 3:257; emphasis added), just as in Elstir's world, paintings were scattered into galleries and private houses. In the "intermittencies" of music the sonata forms a "continuous line with brief calls," whereas the septet welds "together into an indivisible structure a medley of scattered fragments."[101] Both convey the same prayer to create anew, and the narrator frames his pursuit in similar terms, "free from analytical forms of reasoning as if it were being carried out in the world of the angels, so that we can gauge its depth, but [not] translate it into human speech" (RTP 3:258.)[102] He concludes: "Each artist seems thus to be the native of an unknown country, which he himself has forgotten" (RTP 3:258).[103] It is his "inner homeland" (RTP 3:259).[104] While "composers do not actually remember this lost fatherland, . . . *each of them remains all his life unconsciously attuned to it*" (RTP 3:259; emphasis added) in the transposition from the depths of being into sound.[105]

As the music of the septet moved toward the cadenza, and the description toward its end, "the joyous motif was left triumphant; it was no longer an almost anxious appeal addressed to an empty sky, it was an ineffable joy which seemed to come from paradise, a joy as different from that of the sonata as some *scarlet-clad Mantegna archangel sounding a trumpet* from a grave and gentle Bellini seraph strumming a theorbo" (RTP 3:262; emphasis added).[106] The figure is a *robed archangel* whose trumpet rings with triumphant joy: "I knew that this new tone of joy, this summons to a supra-terrestrial joy, was a thing that I would never forget. But would it ever be attainable to me?" he asks (RTP 3:262).[107] This exceptional moment is experienced as one of those "starting-points, [those] foundation-stones for the construction of a true life: the impression I had felt at the sight of the steeples of Martinville, or of a line of trees near Balbec" (RTP 3:263).[108] No idol here. Mlle Vinteuil's friend had deciphered this unknown work "from papers more illegible than strips of papyrus dotted with cuneiform script, the formula, eternally true and forever fertile, of this unknown joy, the mystic hope of the crimson Angel of the Dawn" (RTP 3:264).[109] It was thanks to her that he "had been able to apprehend the strange summons which [he] should henceforth never cease to hear" as the promise of something beyond the futility experienced in pleasure and even love (RTP 3:265).[110]

This summons and promise offer the possibility of passing from the ideal model to a plural creative performance, but they raise serious questions about the establishment of a sense of the absolute. The images of aesthetic epiphany—the madeleine, the septet—have not bridged the gap from ontology to aesthetics. They have only evoked the possibility of such a passage. The following chapter deals with the relationship between principles of thought and their enactment in the sociopolitical world in the absence of certainty.

PART TWO: THE TEXT

3

Man desires a world where good and evil can be clearly distinguished. . . . This "either-or" encapsulates an inability to tolerate the
essential relativity of things human, an inability to look squarely at the
absence of the Supreme Judge. *This inability makes the novel's wisdom
(the wisdom of uncertainty) hard to accept and understand.*—Milan Kun-
dera, *The Art of the Novel*

R ight up to the last volume, it is as though Proust's novel
were suspended on two "if" clause questions: if one can
never know the truth behind phenomena, but only relations
among things, what is the nature of truth? if there are no absolutes, what bond can function in place of universal laws in the
modern world?[1] The ideal transfer from involuntary memory to
metaphor, discussed in Chapter 2, involves the workings of
thought, which remain at a remove from the social world. The
two operate in parallel throughout the novel, however, because
of the need to relate aesthetics to ethics. The problem is how to

distinguish the forms of moral evaluation with a view to establishing more than the absolute in the name of which one judges, which the structural composition of the book was meant to provide; beyond that, it is necessary to know *how to judge* at a given time and place.

The Dreyfus case provided Proust with an event whose literary transformation linked ethics to the aesthetic theory of the first and final volumes of the novel. It was an event that imposed choice and judgment upon individuals, cleaving France at the end of the nineteenth century in a way that no other affair has done since, and setting the stage for many issues that remain unresolved at the end of the twentieth century: What is the role of nationalism in the definition and development of the individual? Where is the borderline between necessary distinctions in social and ethnic categories and racism? Where does diplomacy stop and compromise begin?

Remembrance of Things Past does not merely illustrate reactions to the Dreyfus case, distributed in bits throughout the novel. As the narrator chronicles the characters' reactions to the case, he inscribes something that seems radically impossible at many given moments in time: a shift in position. He shows that any theoretical formulation of relativism will be reductionist when confronted with the problem of freedom and change through time—atavisim and opinion, in more Proustian terms. For Proust, there were no shortcuts to abstraction with respect to these questions: the only access to them was through a description of people and places in their relation to ideas.[2] He summed up the dilemma this way:

> When we find that the systems of philosophy which contain the most truths were dictated to their authors, in the last analysis, by reasons of sentiment, how are we to suppose that in a simple affair of politics like the Dreyfus case reasons of that sort may not, unbeknownst to the reasoner, have ruled his reason? Bloch believed himself to have been led by a logical chain of reasoning to choose Dreyfusism, yet he knew that his nose, his skin and his hair had

been imposed on him by his race. Doubtless the reason enjoys more freedom; yet it obeys certain laws which it has not prescribed for itself. [RTP 2:307][3]

This chapter deals with the question of how the narrator as future writer makes and describes an identity for which one takes responsibility in a world where the personal is necessarily political and ethical.[4] What traditionally underlies the opposition between good and evil is the opposition between right and wrong. In general, Proust avoids that polarization. Rather, he poses the problem of the relationship that a writer establishes with respect to her or his characters, less with the "possible analogy between the ethical choices of characters within novels and the ethical acts of readers of novels"[5] in mind than with the possible analogy between the positioning of the writer-subject with respect to the characters. In this way, the Proustian notion of individual subject joins the contemporary reactivation of the concept of agency, demanding that any theoretical construction be exceeded by its historical and contextual portrayal.[6]

It is because Proust recognizes the paradox of insignificance, making of it a principle of his art, that he is able to seize on concrete examples, attach them to an abstraction, and make both example and idea "live" in the interaction. He thus opens a chain of thought that leads from the question of freedom to the question of responsibility as the locus of ethical problems. By suggesting that even overtly political themes become comprehensible only when passed through the stages of "experience," Proust takes a more political stand than he is usually given credit for. The remark "no form of action exterior to oneself has any importance" does not suggest a radical form of quietism.[7] True, Proust approaches neither Kant's universal law nor Heidegger's "original ethics" lying distantly beyond the reach of the untutored—if reachable at all. But taking a leaf from Kant, Proust plunges into the predicament of human thought, twisting the tail of the philosopher as he who reaches its limits: the freedom to think beyond the determined. Through literature, Proust diverts ideas in his own particular way to political ends.

To recall the affair to mind: Alfred Dreyfus was a Jew, a French military officer who was accused and convicted of treason in 1894 on the basis of a similarity of handwriting. The evidence presented included a handwritten dispatch, sent to the military attaché, Major Schwartzkoppen, of the German Embassy in Paris: the famous *bordereau*, which listed confidential documents about French national defense. Dreyfus was sentenced for life to Devil's Island in French Guiana. At the time, the military establishment was permeated with anti-Semitism, and the army wished to contain its embarrassment over the case. Initially, the French public applauded the conviction, relieved that a threat of treason had been quelled; then it quickly lost interest. But three years later the young and brilliant Colonel Georges Picquart, director of intelligence, received an anonymous *pneumatique* (the *petit bleu*) to a young French officer, Captain Esterhazy, whose handwriting ultimately revealed him to have been the author of the *bordereau*. Picquart was silenced by his superiors, but Dreyfus's brother persisted in demanding revision of the case. Esterhazy was acquitted 1898, and Picquart condemned. The same year, Emile Zola published his famous letter to President of the Republic Félix Faure: *J'accuse,* accusing the judges of obeying orders—for which he was tried and sent to jail. By this time, France was divided between the anti-Dreyfusards, who tended to be royalist, militarist, and nationalist, and the Dreyfusards, who were republican, socialist, and anticlerical. Only much later was it discovered that Dreyfus had been convicted on the basis of documents forged by Colonel Henry. In 1899 a military court, which would not admit to error, found Dreyfus guilty once again and sentenced him to ten years in prison. It was not until 1906 that he was reinstated to his rank in the army and ultimately acquitted.

In three chapters of his first novel, *Jean Santeuil*, Proust deals directly with the Dreyfus trials. In the chapter, titled "Truth and Opinions," the main character, Jean, is elated because truth shines through opinion when an expert testifies that the handwriting on the *bordereau* could not possibly have been that of

Dreyfus: "It was thrilling to hear such things said because one felt that they were simply the outcome of a train of reasoning conducted on scientific lines, and had nothing to do with mere opinion about the rights and wrongs of the case."[8] Truth "was really something that existed in itself and had nothing to do with opinion, . . . the truth to which a man of science owes his loyalty is determined by a series of conditions which are brought about, not by social prejudices—no matter how fine and noble— but by the very nature of things. . . . And the more such men's opinions may differ from what we had been led to expect, the more delightedly do we feel that Science is something wholly divorced from every other human and political activity."[9]

Such a dichotomy could only be the stuff of naiveté, as Proust would demonstrate in *Remembrance of Things Past*. The "nature of things," at least with respect to the Dreyfus affair, was clearly political. Julien Benda summed up the effects this way: "I have often thought that this affair was a good fortune for the men of my generation. . . . One rarely has such an occasion to make a clear-cut choice, at the threshold of life, between two fundamental ethics, and to know immediately who one is."[10] The good fortune of the men has to do with the simultaneity of choice and ethics with self-knowledge. Proust, however, put forth no such simple equation of political position with self-knowledge. Emphasizing the problem of belief in opinions and the need to scrutinize a question from every side, he wrote: "We feel we ought not to rely on our own opinions and range ourselves on the side of those whose opinions are the least favourable to our own attitude. If we happen to be Jews, we make a point of trying to understand the anti-Semite point of view: if believers in Dreyfus, we try to see precisely why it was that the jury found against Zola."[11] Accordingly, the duty of the novelist might be to understand those who opposed his or her position. For Proust was an avowed Dreyfusard, as his letters show.[12] He confided to Mme Straus: "Do not believe that I have become anti-Dreyfusard. I write at the dictate of my characters and it happens that many of them are anti-Dreyfusard."[13] And he queried Sydney Schiff: "Were you a Dreyfusard back then? I was, passionately."

But opting for comprehension, not partisanship, the novelist has not wandered outside ethics: "*Now, as in my book I am absolutely objective,* it happens *The Guermantes Way* seems anti-Dreyfusard. But *Cities of the Plain 2* will be entirely Dreyfusard and rectifying."[14]

Truth would need to be understood and formulated in opposition to opinion, *doxa*.[15] Proust writes in *Jean Santeuil* that in listening to Picquart ("a philosopher whose thoughts . . . were ceaselessly employed in trying to get a clear view of the problems"),[16] one has the same feeling "of which we are chiefly conscious, which moves us so deeply, in reading the *Phaedo,* when following Socrates' argument we are suddenly overwhelmed by the realization that we are listening to a process of logical reasoning wholly undebased by any selfish motive, as though nothing, nothing at all, could have any meaning except truth in all its purity."[17]

Although in *Remembrance of Things Past* there is an attempt to bring such truths forth, idealism disappears. And when the difficulties of authentification of truth and being in relation to handwriting recur in *Remembrance*, their political content replaced by the passion for women (Gilberte, Albertine), Proust reveals both the irony and tragedy of such a belief. Like the Socrates whom Plato portrays, Proust yearns to describe (and hence implicitly judge) the acts of man in order to gain a measure of reliability in human thought. But the condition for such diversion would have to be the application of absolute norms to human affairs, in which—and this is the paradox—transcendent criteria seem always to remain relative.[18]

Formulated in the adage "know thyself," Delphic wisdom means for Proust as for Plato, that truth can emerge only through the individual; no matter how clear-cut the attempt to distinguish between truth and opinion, as in the passage above, truth must be teased out of the singularity of individual existence, leaving to the individual the job of disentangling one from the other. In this instance, the truth starts with maternal love, which is then complicated by the familial relationships, all involving political conviction at some level. What is at stake is the relationship of atavism to opinion.

Several concerns overlap in Proust's presentation of Judaism: it is first an autobiographical referent, where questions of origin and filiation put into motion the ideological determinations of opinion; then a formal narrative strategy, a potential move toward disengagement through writing. Finally, through the genesis of the versions, the text charts change.[19]

With respect to his family of origin, Proust's father was Catholic and his mother Jewish. In the novel, the narrator announces his own position indirectly (and it happens only once, to the best of my knowledge) by alluding to the difference in opinion between himself and his father: upon learning that he is a Dreyfusard, his father does not speak to him for a week. On the maternal side, his grandmother shows benevolent ambivalence (whenever anyone mentions Dreyfus's possible innocence, she nods her head like someone preoccupied with serious thought); his mother, caught between love for her husband and hope for her son's intelligence, maintains an undecided silence. But his maternal grandfather is more complicated. The versions of "Combray" differ as to who the anti-Semitic character in the family is: the grandfather or the maternal grand-uncle, with whom the narrator meets the future Mme Swann early in the novel. In the final draft the grandfather takes on this function and sides with the pro-army faction (the Dreyfusards had turned violently antimilitary in the course of the affair). The persona who assumes the brunt of the anti-Semitic jokes also migrates from Bloch to Swann.

In the early drafts Swann is noticeably more Jewish, the grandfather noticeably more anti-Semitic. In a notebook version of early 1909, the narrator makes himself accomplice to the grandfather, playing down the importance of his anti-Semitic remarks, and creates in Swann his own double: "Although much younger, [M. Swann] was the best friend of my grandfather who however did not like Jews. It was one of these little weaknesses in him, one of these absurd prejudices, as there are *sometimes* precisely in the most upright natures, those most firmly for what is good. For example, the aristocratic prejudice in Saint-Simon, the prejudice against dentists that certain doctors harbor, or the feeling against actors in some of the bourgeois."[20] As the variations disappear after 1911 (the grandfather replaces the granduncle once again, and Bloch takes over his function as negative Jew), the revisions of the discourse on Judaism serve neither a purely referential nor a purely formal end; they serve the needs of a developing aesthetics based on an intricate relation between determinism and freedom.

The narrator runs through a series of other minor characters, stating each of their positions. Some, like M. de Norpois, seem to go first one way, then another: "There, he's a Dreyfusard, there's not the least doubt of it, " yet only a page later, "no, he's definitely an anti-Dreyfusard; it's quite obvious" (RTP 2:247-48).[21] The same problem occurs with Charlus, whose attitude is difficult to penetrate: in his view, Dreyfus had not committed a crime; had he done so, it would have been a betrayal of Judea rather than France, or else an infraction of French hospitality, so little did he consider Dreyfus to be French. Odette worries that Swann's Jewish origins would be turned against her; she begs Swann not to speak of his convictions and in his absence even professes to nationalism. Saint-Loup is initially Dreyfusard; Marcel's mother and Mme Bontemps are anti-Dreyfusard. Proust accounts exhaustively for the positions of his characters, right down to the Guermantes' *maître d'hôtel*, who is for Dreyfus, and his own, who is against him—showing how even households divide against themselves.

The narrator takes a proleptic view of the hero's life, a strategy that both allows for irony and gives protection to the unfolding of the lives of his characters, measuring the distance between what is said on the moment and its implications for the future. Within the spectrum of characters and in view of the changes that occur, there is an unsettling kind of ambiguity, a deliberate interference or jamming of positions about Jews and Judaism in the presentation of reaction to the case. Three elements collide: the Jewish conscience, a Christian discourse, and the personal problems described by the narrator. The way in which characters play upon and sometimes invert anti-Semitism shows the "elasticity, the mobility that a change in milieu demands ... this flexibility of the organism."[22]

What concerns us here is the connection between opinion and disinterested truth, evoked first in relation to Plato in *Jean Santeuil* and later in relation to Kant and Dreyfus in *Remembrance of Things Past*. This connection provides the bridge from the fixed ideals embodied in the project (to intuit a world beyond phenomena and reason) and the sinuously moving story of change and betrayal within the characters.

To the narrator, as to the admirers of Mme de Guermantes, the social world seems both absolutely fixed and infinitely arbitrary. It is through analogy, and the association of small details, that the narrator comes to understand the principles of freedom. Visiting Gilberte for an afternoon snack, the narrator generalizes from an anticipated pleasure in the details of her household: Mme Swann's perfume and the special plates of chocolate cake surrounded by the petits fours that were *de rigueur* at the Swanns'. "This ordered and unalterable design seemed, like Kant's necessary universe, to depend on a supreme act of free will" (RTP 1:545).[23]

The analogy to freedom, however—specifically freedom of choice within the workings of the social world—is fragile because of the lack of firm ground. It leads to contradictions that although frivolous on the surface reveal a serious inability to formulate ethical problems. Thus the narrator, recounting that Mme de Guermantes would allow herself the freedom to refuse hundreds of invitations, comments: "The fashionable world was stunned, and, without any thought of following the Duchess's example, derived nevertheless from her action that sense of relief which one has in reading Kant when, after the most rigorous demonstration of determinism, one finds that above the world of necessity there is the world of freedom" (RTP 2:495).[24] Rather than guide moral choice, the evocation of a Kantian notion of freedom introduces the conundrum of quietism: The Duchess of Guermantes was "*anti-Dreyfusard (while believing Dreyfus to be innocent, just as she spent her life in the social world while believing only in ideas)"* (RTP 2:495; emphasis added).[25] It is this very disjunction between the so-called world of ideas and their enactment in social life that prevents consistent ethical thought.

With the ostensible knowledge of hindsight, the narrator writes in the final volume: "I had seen everybody believe, during the Dreyfus affair . . . that truth is a particular piece of knowledge which cabinet ministers and doctors possess, a Yes or No which requires no interpretation, thanks to the possession of which the men in power *knew* whether Dreyfus was guilty or not" (RTP 3:953).[26] This then is the danger of a false notion of singular truth: each possesses it and judges human affairs accordingly. What shines through is not the truth of ideas but the herd mentality of people who empower social authorities to judge for them.

In a letter to Mme Straus dated July 21, 1906, Proust describes the rectification of Dreyfus's situation in curiously envious terms:

> But for Dreyfus and Picquart . . . life has been "providential" after the fashion of fairy tales and serial thrillers. That is because our suffering was founded on facts—on truths—physiological truths, human and emotional truths. For them, suffering was founded on error. Fortunate, indeed, are those who are victims of error—judicial and otherwise! They are the only human beings for whom there are redress and restitution. But [Dreyfus] is incomparable and even moving. And it is impossible to read this morning's latest scene: "In the courtyard of the Military College with five hundred participants," without having tears in one's eyes.[27]

The ability to believe that truth is a matter of a Yes or No, that errors can be corrected, is at the basis of the unitary vision of the novel: there is a truth; it can be revealed. In some sense, then, Jean holds out the hope that everyone might have his or her "day in the courtyard," a metaphor for the representation of truth that allows pathos its day and innocence its reward. In *Remem-*

brance the narrator gets his day, as it were, at the Guermantes' with the final moments of involuntary memory.

If such an ideal were opposed to the description of a frivolous social world, unaware of and—more disturbing still—without ground in truth, the task of writing would be clear: to uncover truth and separate it from opinion. But things are not so simple. A constantly unfolding malaise emerges within the novel: the sense that the comprehension of error, and a potential ethical sense, may come only through interpretations provoked by temporal dislocation; the sense that whatever the subject at hand, something else is always at stake.[28]

Proust shows how that social and political attitudes remain immobile until, as in a kaleidoscope reshuffling fragments of color, some unpredictable change of criterion produces a new alignment of positions.[29] Had a war been substituted for the Dreyfus affair and had the Jews shown their patriotism, Proust argues, things would have been totally different. Although one of the lessons of the affair is that whatever appears fixed in immobile structures may be reversed only a little later on, this analysis still does not account for the discovery of constant, absolute values by which to explain the vicissitudes of history. Within the novel the narrator yearns to make of the question of ethics, and of "who one is," more than a question of belief, more than a sequence of disjunctive fragments and patchwork of associative thinking.

One passage in particular opens up the the possibility of moving from opinion to truth, when Swann recounts "word for word" a revelation to the narrator. It is a passage on which I dwell now at some length, a passage in which Swann assumes the position of narrator and tells how the Prince of Guermantes changed his thinking about Dreyfus. But just before the narrator passes interpretive responsibility to Swann, he judges Swann, who is Jewish, to have failed a test of judgment through inflexibility. It is as though Swann had discovered an invariant to human behavior: "He subjected all his admirations and all his contempts to the test of a new criterion, Dreyfusism" (RTP 2:605).[30] Just as Swann equates anti-Dreyfusism within the social world to anti-Semitism, he equates Dreyfusism with Judaism. Theoretically, through atavism this grants him the ability to see what those in the "fashionable" world could not: that Dreyfus really was innocent. But his story obliges Swann, who himself believes that atavism determines opinion, to drop this argument in order to account for change.

"THE REVOLUTION WROUGHT BY A POLITICAL CONVERSION"

S wann's narrative concerns the Prince of Guermantes, who confesses to a change of heart about the Dreyfus case. Thus framed, a story unfolds. Swann recounts how the Prince apologizes for avoiding him, having heard that Swann opposed his position in this affair "which is splitting the country" (RTP 2:731). To have discussed the issue would have been very painful—as painful, he confesses, as when the brother-in-law of the Princess (the Grand Duke of Hesse) pronounced Dreyfus innocent two years before. The plot of Swann's story begins to thicken. Some time later the Prince comes to believe that grave illegalities have been committed during the Dreyfus trial. Doubts about the proceedings and a newfound conviction about Dreyfus's possible innocence haunt him—all of which he hides from the Princess because "Heaven knows that she ha[d] become just as French as [himself]" (RTP 2:734). When the Henry document is proved a forgery, however, the Prince no longer has any doubts. He begins to read two Dreyfusard papers, *Le Siècle* and *L'Aurore*,[31] without telling the Princess. One day he catches the maid sneaking something to his wife; when questioned, she refuses to answer.

In isolation, the Prince decides to unburden his moral distress to l'abbé Poiré, a friend who to his surprise holds the same conviction. The Prince asks him to say a mass for Dreyfus the next day but is told that a mass has already been requested. Astonished that a kindred soul exists in the parish, the Prince presses the abbé, learns that the convictions of the other person predate his own change, and asks to meet "him" in order "to unbosom [himself] to this rare bird" (RTP 2:737). But to his query "What is his name?" he receives the answer "The Princesse de Guermantes" (RTP 2:737).[32] So, like the characters in Ionesco's *The Bald Soprano (La Cantatrice chauve)* who have lived at the same address, slept in the same room, and raised the same daughter, though they don't seem to know it, the Prince and Princess of Guermantes run similar parallel lives.

The Prince reasoned thus: while he had feared offending his wife's "nationalistic opinions, her faith in France, she had been afraid of alarming [his] religious opinions, [his] patriotic sentiments" (RTP 2:737). What the maid had been slipping into the house was the copy of *L'Aurore* that she bought daily for the Princess. Now, he tells Swann of his pleasure in the kinship of ideas; Swann will perhaps understand from this story how deep was the difficulty in bringing his feelings to light. He concludes: "It is a relief to me not to have to keep away from you any longer, and above all a relief to make it clear to you that if I had other feelings it was because I hadn't a shadow of a doubt as to the soundness of the verdict. As soon as my doubts began, I could wish for only one thing, that the mistake should be rectified" (RTP 2:737).[33] Swann, recognizing the extent to which the Prince has transformed himself, is moved by this admission.[34]

But there is nothing *disinterested* about the act of positioning here. Swann now indiscriminately finds both the Prince and the hero's friend Bloch intelligent because of their allegiances. And Bloch, upon learning of the Prince's change of opinion, immediately wants to enlist his signature on a circular for Picquart. Swann, ever the diplomat and protector of the social hierarchy, points out how impossible this would be for the Prince and suggests that such a proposal might even drive him back to his former position. Then Swann too balks at the idea and refuses to sign, suggesting that his name, being too Hebraic, might create a "bad effect." If he approves of the revision, he adds, he nevertheless wants to stay far away from the anti-militarist campaign; so much so that he has changed his will requesting to be buried with the military honors awarded his "rank as Chevalier of the Legion of Honour" (RTP 2:739). This scene, orchestrated with pauses at dramatic moments and a series of hints leading up to the revelation, reads like good comedy.

Underlying the Guermantes' inability to communicate is a difference of *identity*. The Princess is an adopted (and professed) French national. When the Royal Prince of Sweden confuses her with the Empress Eugénie, who was a Dreyfusard, expressing his happiness at their mutual sympathy for the case and suggesting that this was no surprise, since he knew the Princess to be Bavarian, she retorts that *she knows who she is:* "Sir, I am now a French princess. I share the views of all my fellow-countrymen" (RTP 2:731).[35] But because personal identity cannot rest on a unified national identity, even by choice, in this affair, hers is a contradictory stance: overtly nationalistic, covertly Dreyfusard. In both the Duchess's and even Swann's position, there is a suggestion that ideas operate on two levels: one necessary (without choice), the other contingent (with choice). Yet for the Princess, *everything* involves choice: the choice to be French, nationalistic, and Dreyfusard. In each case (for Swann, the Duchess, and the Princess), albeit with variation, it is in the discrepancy between private belief and public action that Proust signals the (comic) malaise.

The discovery of a hidden political sympathy on the part of the Princess, revealed simultaneously with her husband's change, raises the question of sexual identity, both of which have social repercussions. The Princess has fallen in love with the character Charlus. Rumors of his homosexuality reveal certain positions to be invisible and others to be visible: invisible when it comes to believing in Dreyfus's innocence, visible when it comes to sexual mores. So a shrill voice, Proust writes sardonically of Charlus, a smile, and a way of gesturing might lead to the same kind of certainty of opinion as "enables a judge to sentence a criminal who has not confessed, or a doctor a patient suffering from general paralysis who himself is perhaps unaware of his malady but has made some mistake in pronunciation from which it can be deduced that he will be dead in three years" (RTP 2:999).[36] And in the judgment of the character Charlus, whose virile ideal was matched by his particularly feminine nature (RTP Gall. 2:614), there lies a comparison—which Proust makes explicit—between the solitude of homosexuals, who he says are without anything but precarious honor and provisional freedom (until the discovery of this "crime" of homosexuality), and the solitude of victims, alone except on the days of great misfortune when great numbers rally round, as the Jews had done with Dreyfus.[37] Nothing, however, is said about the woman's change and the Princess's solitude as a Dreyfusard. Contrary to the view of the Duke de Guermantes—"Women never understand a thing about politics" (RTP 3:35)[38]—the Princess has distinguished herself within her social context. But even her position of privilege can not protect her from the mortality of succession; soon another will carry the name of Princess of Guermantes: Mme Verdurin, whose own Dreyfusism for a time slowed her own social ascension.

What this story tells, then, is the way in which *who one is* (self-identity) emerges and dies through both program and event: the way in which a narrative, drawn toward an empirical moment, splits unities (households, couples, the sense of national identity) in order to reconstitute itself, only to be subsumed into a greater loss. The Dreyfus affair became a catalyst for change; not only of opinion but of position within the social hierarchy. "This was a time when in the aftermath of the Dreyfus case an anti-Semitic trend had arisen parallel to a growing trend towards the penetration of society by Jews. The politicians had not been wrong in thinking that the discovery of the judicial error would be a severe blow to anti-Semitism. But, temporarily at least, a form of social anti-Semitism was on the contrary enhanced and exacerbated thereby" (RTP 3:586).[39]

Referring to the Duchess of Guermantes and the inability to change, the narrator states that "it is difficult, when one's mind is troubled by the ideas of Kant and the yearnings of Baudelaire, to write the exquisite French of Henri IV, so that the very purity of the Duchess's language was a sign of limitation and that, in her, both intelligence and sensibility had remained closed against innovation" (RTP 2:521–22).[40]

The expression *bel et bien* provides an example of the way in which language becomes fixed, the way in which it comes to be associated with the affair in the specific context of the Jockey

Club and the Duke of Guermantes: "Whenever anybody referred to the Dreyfus case, out would come 'well and truly.' " The Duke would protest: "Dreyfus case, Dreyfus case, it's easy to say, and it's a misuse of the term. It's not a question of religion, it's *well and truly* political" (RTP 3:33; emphasis added).[41] Five years might go by, but the moment the affair came up, out would pop the expression *bel et bien*. Meaning "all right" or "no doubt," the term combines notions of beauty and goodness which are neutralized in banality; now only vacantly emphatic, the phrase is emptied of thought.[42] But it does curiously signal a connection that Proust will make in his narrative recapitulation of the affair: how, with the passage of time, contingency becomes a past given; here, how uncertainty turns into certainty. "That shocking crime," exclaims the Duke of Guermantes, "is not simply a Jewish cause, but *well and truly* an affair of vast national importance which may bring the most appalling consequences for France, which ought to have driven out all the Jews" (RTP 3:35; emphasis added).[43] The positioning through linguistic association signals the context in which the comment occurs but remains ungrounded by any kind of truth value; this arbitrariness serves in the description of the social destiny of the characters, but cannot lead to any universal guarantee of a subject in the world: "We have of the universe only inchoate, fragmentary visions, which we complement by arbitrary associations of ideas, creative of dangerous illusions" (RTP 3:586).[44] It was this kind of association that linked the Jews during the Dreyfus trial and its aftermath with antipatriotism and anarchy, and allowed some to establish a hierarchy of the races—between Aryans and Semites—according to which behavior ostensibly became predictable.

In an apparently more benign fashion, the narrator one day reminds the Duchess of a red dress that she had worn at the party given by her cousin, M. de Breauté. Searching for something to say, Breauté comes up with an obscure and unwelcome association. "Twisting his tongue about between his pursed lips: 'Talking of the Dreyfus case . . . ' (why the Dreyfus case?—we were talking simply of a red dress)" (RTP 3:33).[45] From these twists of the tongue, the subject of conversation slips from Drey-fus to a dress by way of the connection with red. The association is not Breauté's but links passion, as a subject to be suppressed, with red dresses or coats (see Chapter 6). Such maneuvers of language, as the expression *manœuvrer sa langue* also suggests, demonstrate how the argument inches toward guilt by associa-tion. After some meandering, the conversation turns to what might have motivated Zola to go to court over Dreyfus and be condemned, and his bad faith in fleeing before being arrested. Then the Duke and the Duchess assert that the Jews necessarily supported Dreyfus because "if he hadn't been a Jew people wouldn't have been so ready to think him a traitor *a priori*" (RTP 3:35).[46] It is then that the narrator deflects the discussion, re-turning to his own transition: "I felt that the conversation had taken a wrong turning and reverted hurriedly to the topic of clothes" (RTP 3:35).[47] In so doing, he does not simply refuse the shift of the argument; he shows by this forced benign depoliti-cization of association how political association can be.

The only comfort comes from a process of forgetting through time, in which Dreyfusism becomes integrated into thought through a series of habitual ideas retrospectively award-ed respectability. And the pardon through forgetting granted to Dreyfusism also extended to the Dreyfusards. "*As for asking one-self whether intrinsically it was good or bad, the idea no more entered anybody's head, now when it was accepted, than in the past when it was condemned. It was no longer 'shocking' and that was all that mattered*" (RTP 3:747; emphasis added).[48] The extension of the pardon could occur because of the relativism built into all social and political opinions, and it is that sense of relativism which leads from ethics to aesthetics here. The parodic freedom glimpsed in the actions of a Mme de Guermantes (an anti-Drey-fusard believing in the innocence of Dreyfus who exercises her options by refusing invitations) finds its serious counterpart in the choices of the Prince and Princess of Guermantes. The com-pelling question for the characters as for the narrator is one of responsibility in the exercise of freedom of choice.

It was fashionable to say that the prewar period was separated from World War I by something "as profound . . . as a geological period" (RTP 3:748).[49] So the narrator chronicles how one event succeeds another, and frivolity becomes so widespread and systematic that the only thing considered to last within the social world is birth and beauty tied to other privileges. In this perspective the war, like the Dreyfus case, was considered a vulgar and evanescent fashion.

The narrator sweepingly generalizes about the relationship of thought to politics, taking up the post-Kantian position separating aesthetics and ideology, and his observation comes couched in a parenthetical aside:

(The truth is that this profound change wrought by the war was in inverse ratio to the quality of the minds which it affected, at least above a certain level. At the very bottom of the scale the really stupid people, who lived only for pleasure, did not bother about the fact that there was a war. But, at the other end of the scale too, people who have made for themselves a circumambient interior life usually pay small regard to the importance of events. What profoundly modifies their system of thought is much more likely to be something that in itself seems to have no importance, something that reverses the order of time for them by making them contemporaneous with another epoch in their lives. And that this is so we may see in practice from the beauty of the writing which is inspired in this particular way: the song of a bird in the park at Montboissier, or a breeze laden with the scent of mignonette, are obviously phenomena of less consequence than the great events of the Revolution and the Empire; but they inspired Chateaubriand to write pages of infinitely greater value in his *Mémoires d'Outre-tombe*.) [RTP 3:748–49][50]

Again Proust emphasizes, here as elsewhere, that the subject of art is not ultimately what counts the most. As for the literary theories developed at the time of the Dreyfus affair, they tended to dictate that "the artist must be made to leave his ivory tower"

and that the themes chosen by the writer "ought to be not frivolous or sentimental but rather such things as great working-
class movements or—in default of crowds—at least no longer as
in the past unimportant men of leisure . . . but noble intellectuals or men of heroic stature" (RTP 3:915).[51] But if these theories troubled the narrator at one time, as he admits, his attitude
at the end of the novel is unequivocal: "Authentic art has no use
for proclamations of this kind, it accomplishes its work in silence" (RTP 3:916).[52]

As for the question of literacy, Proust writes: "The idea of a
popular art, like that of a patriotic art, if not actually dangerous
seemed to me ridiculous. If the intention was to make art accessible to the people by sacrificing refinements of form, on the
ground that they are 'all right for the idle rich' but not for anybody else, I had seen enough of fashionable society to know *that
it is there* that one finds *real illiteracy* and not, let us say, among
electricians" (RTP 3:917).[53] He confides to Jacques Rivière that
he hates ideological works and in one of the sketches for *Time
Regained* argues for the accessibility of art to everyone, in form
as well as content.[54]

At the beginning of the war, Maurice Barrès had suggested
that the artist (Titian was his example) must serve the glory of
his country.

> But this he can do only by being an artist, which means
> only on condition that, while in his own sphere he is
> studying laws, conducting experiments, making discover-
> ies which are as delicate as those of science, he shall think
> of nothing—not even his country—but the truth which is
> before him. Let us not imitate the revolutionaries who out
> of "civic sense" despised, if they did not destroy, the
> works of Watteau and La Tour, painters who have brought
> more honour upon France than all those of the Revolu-
> tion. [RTP 3: 917–18][55]

Proust rejects empirical moralism and its corollary in art,
"the falseness of so-called realist art,"[56] on the grounds that
there is an other, presumably higher, order in art. He would have

subscribed to Oscar Wilde's comment that "ethical criticism cannot be divorced finally from political criticism. When we talk about persons we are also talking about changing societies."[57] Already within *Contre Sainte-Beuve,* the distinction between the different levels of the subject suggested a move in that direction: "A book is the product of an other self than that which we display in our habits, in company, in our vices."[58] What the discussion of change in the Prince of Guermantes shows is that although "our social personality is a creation of the thoughts of other people" (RTP 1:20),[59] narrative still provides a corrective. The question is at what level politics operates, and what it is that one calls political. When it is reduced to fashion, politics constitutes only a distraction: "Every public event, be it the Dreyfus case, be it the war, furnishes the writer with a fresh excuse for not attempting to decipher this book: he wants to ensure the triumph of justice, he wants to restore the moral unity of the nation, he has no time to think of literature. But these are mere excuses, the truth being that he has not or no longer has genius, that is to say instinct" (RTP 3:913).[60]

The Dreyfus affair certainly changed the "accepted values of people and brought about a new configuration of parties . . . since later they had again disintegrated and re-formed" (RTP 3:1042).[61] But the social reshuffling, its disintegration and reformation, confirms more than relativism within the social realm. For Proust it confirms both the need for a structure grounded in some truth and at the same time a process in the world through which it might be worked out. These are the terms of what constitutes a political frame for the development of an ethics of the subject.

Relativism is the diffused philosophic term for what association does in language: putting one thing in relation to another. Because one is unable to know anything more than the relations between thoughts and memory, to understand the value of an event except in terms of change in language and society through the narrative sequences, Proust demonstrates a relativizing principle with the Dreyfus case, a corollary to the principle of insignificance discussed in relation to involuntary memory: without intrinsic value, even significant events become banalized.

The narrator meets many of the characters of the novel in the *Bal des têtes*, and he sees time engraved on their faces, much as one sees it in the stones of churches; they appear in the connectedness of perspectives: healing wounds, annulling the divisions and conflicts of the past.[62] "The diversity of the points in my life through which, like so many interwoven threads, those of each of these personages had passed had in the end brought into conjunction even those that seemed the furthest apart from one another, as though for the execution of infinitely varied patterns life possessed only a limited number of threads" (RTP 3:1019).[63]

In reliving the particular memories of people, the narrator reflects that circumstances enclose them "finally on every side" and restrict his view of them, preventing him "from discovering their essence. For between us and other people there exists a barrier of contingencies" (RTP 3:1023).[64] The effect of this barrier is that heterogeneity and change within the characters become easier to comprehend than any concept of unity. Referring to World War I, Proust maintains that "it is difficult to speak of things which have no precedent and of the repercussions upon an organism of an operation which is being attempted for the first time." He adds that "generally, it is true, novelties which people find alarming pass off very well" (RTP 3:824).[65] The comment applies more generally. Change cannot be tracked without precedents and repetition.

In a work where many have noticed that the will has almost no place, change within these characters assumes a particularly important function. The ability to change voluntarily signals an exercise of freedom that counters the nationalist, anti-Semitic philosophy developing at the time, in which everything (in both individual and collective life) is said to be determined (Taine's "race, milieu, moment" sums it up). Further, if only the collectivity matters, leaving no room for individual freedoms, then the determination of social life rests on matrices anterior to individual reason (instinct and race). According to such an argument, only heredity matters. As the Duke of Guermantes remarks: "When one goes by the name of 'Marquis de Saint-Loup' one isn't a Dreyfusard. I'm sorry, but there it is" (RTP 2:242).[66] This was the very argument that Maurice Barrès had invoked to condemn Dreyfus, whose culpability, he claimed, followed from the mere possibility of guilt.[67]

It is thus against this notion of determinism, a kind of determinism for which Swann had argued, though for reasons totally opposed to those of the "revolutionary right,"[68] that Proust portrays the lack of consensus and the possibility for change within individuals. He goes further: he shows change to be possible where it is least suspected. Saint-Loup, whose background would have led him to be anti-Dreyfusard, chooses Dreyfusism—and then switches back. But while still in his Dreyfusard phase, he repeats word for word what the narrator affirms: "Why, yes; environment is of no importance . . . . The real influence is that of the intellectual environment! One is conditioned by an idea!" (RTP 2:119).[69] Though the man of his own ideas is, as the text in French suggests, free to choose, Saint-Loup ultimately chooses what heredity might otherwise have dictated. And when the narrator abandons the social and political world to enter the world of art, where there is an imperative to rewrite life, it is for reasons that are profoundly consonant with his Dreyfusard position and the maternal side of his heritage.

The subject of the work of art turns out then to be both important and unimportant. What counts for the question of ethics is not so much that Proust analyzes the moral positions of the characters but that he poses his problem as a writer of literature rather than as a writer of philosophy or criticism—an operational distinction—in terms of the futility of judging his characters. If, before he understood and created these characters, Proust had had to judge them, there might well have been no novel, just as there might well be no psychoanalysis if the analyst had to judge the patient in advance. Proust enacted his writerly freedom by revising the novel until the time of his death. The interminable proliferation of texts confirms the always unfinished process of choice for Proust, in which change cannot be overcome or transcended but only reined in and interpreted. By delegating authority to Swann (in the passage evoked earlier), with whose intractable stance he is known to sympathize, he frees the narrator from constituting the narrative self on any single issue and at the same time grants him the stance of future author.

If the determinations of chance and fate change at the level of political positions and social hierarchy, they do not excuse the kind of inconsistency (however amusing) to which a Mme de Guermantes' so-called freedom gives rise. But they do allow for a principle of individuation in which the subject constitutes itself from self-questioning and choice. In that process, forces beyond the will play a great part. "Even mentally, we depend a great deal more than we think upon natural laws, and our minds possess in advance, like some cryptogamous plant, the characteristic that we imagine ourselves to be selecting. For we grasp only the secondary ideas, without detecting the primary cause (Jewish blood, French birth or whatever it may be) that inevitably produced them, and which we manifest when the time comes" (RTP 1:953). Still the power to change in characters like the Prince and Princess reveals a measure of freedom in the exercise of judgment where politics and ethics are concerned. The narrator adds:

> I knew that, as deep, as ineluctable as Jewish patriotrism or Christian atavism in those who imagine themselves to be the most emancipated of their race, there dwelt beneath the rosy inflorescence of Albertine, Rosemonde, Andrée, unknown to themselves, held in reserve until the occasion should arise, a coarse nose, a protruding jaw, a paunch which would create a sensation when it appeared, but which was actually in the wings, ready to "come on," unforeseen, inevitable, just as it might be a burst of Dreyfusism or clericalism or patriotic, feudal heroism, emerging suddenly in answer to the call of circumstance from a nature anterior to the individual himself, through which he thinks, lives, evolves, gains strength or dies, without ever

being able to distinguish that nature from the particular motives he mistakes for it. [RTP 1:952–53][70]

Invoking the names of the blossoming girls, the narrator conjures up a shadowy area of feeling and thought: the relation to women. It is with the question of passion that the interweave between chance and fate replays scenarios in strikingly new forms. They put into question the truth of the subject and any corresponding unitary vision of the novel, a subject that the next chapter explores.

4

As for our sentiments, we have said so too often to repeat it here, as often as not love is no more than the association of the image of a girl (whom otherwise we should soon have found intolerable) with the heartbeats inseparable from an endless wait in vain and her failure to turn up at the end of it.—Marcel Proust, *The Captive*

Whereas in politics, opinion leads to general associations, and involuntary memory—the most profound association—gives unique value to the encounter of past and present, desire in love leads to the pursuit of knowledge through association. The following chapters look at how love unsettles the pursuit of truth. In this chapter, I analyze three sequences in which the irruption of newness disrupts certainty: in the first, the narrator tracks the way memory skews truth through desire in his inaugural encounter with Gilberte; in the second, the "blossoming girls" attract by their very anonymity and indistinctness; in the third, Proust suggests his own theory of relativity. These stories portray incipient love and show how memory and perception guide the subject to singular and perhaps even dangerously new theories.

In *Swann's Way* the narrator writes that the accidents of life come when and where they are least suspected: "from inside, from the heart" (RTP 1:678.)[1] This means that the contingencies of life, stirred by contact with people, places, and things, reveal the structure of being in its immutability. To put it another way, present contingencies reveal past givens that could not have been perceived as such upon the moment. Nowhere is this more evident than when the narrator describes the pitfalls of love as an apprenticeship in epistemology.

MISTAKEN IDENTITIES: GILBERTE'S EYES

The first sequence has to do with the narrator's meeting Gilberte along Swann's Way and falling in love with her. In describing the encounter, Proust writes one of the most perplexing sentences of the novel. In it and in scenes that follow, the reader is alerted to a curious turn of memory. Taken together, these scenes activate the question "How can the subject perceive any sort of truth at all?" Memory plays such extraordinary tricks in the process of association that it is only long after an event, only after a long series of events, that reason and logic intervene to "correct" mistakes. In order to follow the operation of these mistakes in the construction of the self as writing subject, I deal with a specific incident in which association determines love.

Out walking one day with his father and grandfather through Swann's Way, Marcel wishes that their calculation could be foiled: they had suggested this path because Mme and Mlle Swann, Odette and Gilberte, were to be gone for the day. He wishes that by some miracle Mlle Swann and her father would appear so near to them that they could not avoid being introduced to her.[2] Just following an overwhelming experience of the hawthorns and their perfume, and the vague and obscure feeling with which they leave him, he peers over the hedge, looks into the park, and his wish is fulfilled:

Suddenly I stood still, unable to move, as happens when we are faced with a vision that appeals not to our eyes only but requires a deeper kind of perception and takes possession of the whole of our being. A little girl with fair, reddish hair, who appeared to be returning from a walk, and held a trowel in her hand, was looking at us, raising towards us a face powdered with pinkish freckles. Her black eyes gleamed, and since I did not at that time know, and indeed have never since learned, how to reduce a strong impression to its objective elements, since I had not, as they say, enough "power of observation" to isolate the notion of their colour, for a long time afterwards, whenever I thought of her, the memory of those bright eyes would at once present itself to me as a vivid azure, since her complexion was fair [*she was blond* (my translation)], so much so that, *perhaps if her eyes had not been quite so black—which was what struck one most forcibly on first seeing her—I should not have been, as I was, so especially enamoured of their imagined blue.* [RTP 1:153; emphasis added][3]

Seeing the girl, whose hair is reddish blond (the translation neglects the most important aspect here, which is blondness), he is marked indelibly by the strong impression that her eyes make upon him, so indelibly that—*because* he says he lacks the discernment of observation—he does not retain the color of those eyes. When the memory comes back to him, it is in a vivid azure, not because she was fair, as the English version would have it, but, the narrator maintains, because she is blond ("puis qu'elle était blonde").[4] That is, *he asserts a causal relationship where a general association is at work: blonds have blue eyes.* This is of course less a comment on the objective state of all blonds than a statement about the power of habit. Habit facilitates practical life with a kind of mechanical memory or automatic thought. At the same time, by dulling perceptions, it reduces thought to a common denominator, some general aspect. So strong is the power of habit that it can hide almost the entire universe.[5] For truth resides not in the generic association of blond with blue but in the specific affect that may give access to the essence of being through the singular impression. Habit at once defends and prohibits knowledge of what takes place at another level. It is, the narrator states, because her eyes are so startlingly black that he falls so in love with their imagined blue.

In its structure, the hero's love for Gilberte prefigures the loves to follow; specifically, it forecasts his love for Albertine, which becomes more desperate and intense (see Chapter 5). In the movement from one object to another, from Gilberte to Albertine, the process is amplified but remains unchanged: desire in love is always accompanied by anxiety and unrest, whereas certainty leads quickly to indifference. Identities merge—first in time, through succeeding generations, and then in space, through the association with places.[6] Just as Marcel's mother grows more and more to resemble his grandmother, so Gilberte comes to resemble Odette and is mistaken for her toward the end of *Time Regained*.[7] And Gilberte's daughter, Mlle de Saint-Loup, ultimately incarnates the "transversals" of the two ways, those ways that seem so irrevocably separate at the beginning of the novel, when she is compared to a crossroad in a forest where paths from the most distant points meet. The walks through the diverging ways of his childhood seem ultimately to lead to her: one, through her mother (Gilberte) and the Champs-Elysées, by association with Swann and the evenings at Combray, leads to Swann's Way; the other, through her father (Saint-Loup) and memories of the beach at Balbec, to the Guermantes' Way.

The memory of Gilberte's eyes, however, is not the sole example of error. Repeated instances of mistaken identity throughout the novel do more than merely illustrate the difficulty of locating truth. They perform a complicated operation by showing the way habit lures the mind away from individuation in association. A reading of one scene bears this out. At the end of the novel, as the narrator works through the process of forgetting Albertine, he reflects that our "impressions, our ideas, have only a symptomatic value" (RTP 3:572).[8] When he stopped seeing Gilberte, the "love of women arose within . . . [him], relieved of any exclusive association with a particular woman already loved, and floated like those essences that have been liberated by previous destructions and stray suspended in the springtime air, asking only to be reunited with a new creature" (RTP 3:572).[9]

It is at this time that he sees a group of three young women whose elegance and energy remind him of the young girls with whom Albertine was associated.

> The [blond] had a rather more delicate, almost an invalid air, which appealed to me less. It was she, nevertheless, who was responsible for my not contenting myself with gazing at them for a moment, having stopped dead, with one of those looks which, by their fixed absorption, their application as to a problem, seem to be concerned with something far beyond what meets the eye. I should doubtless have allowed them to disappear, as I had allowed so many others, if . . . [the blond] had not darted a furtive glance at me and then, turning round, after having passed me, a second one that set me aflame. . . . My ardour would doubtless have subsided, had it not been increased a hundredfold by the following discovery." (RTP 3:573–74)[10]

What he discovers is that her name is Mlle Déporcheville, a name easily changed to Mlle d'Eporcheville. The latter, he believes, is a girl of "excellent family," somehow connected with the Guermantes, whom he remembers that Robert had met in a "disorderly house [*maison de passe*] and with whom he had had relations" (RTP 3:574). He has often tried to imagine what she is like from the way Robert has spoken of her. But now that he has seen her, she seems just like the others except for her sly glance. It has made her appear accessible—almost partly his; he can imagine them spending hours together, as if she has already given him permission for a rendezvous. In short, though he cannot remember exactly what she looked like, the thought of her evokes in a vague sort of way a blond-haired girl; and *voilà*, he is madly in love with her. He realizes, however, that his love is based on the assumption that of the three girls, Mlle d'Eporcheville was in fact the blond who turned to look at him twice.

Having no objective verification of which one she might be, he returns to ask the concierge, who must in turn ask his wife; savoring the uncertainty of her identity, he reflects on the kind of error to which a purely verbal portrait can lead, and the sort of intuition or breath of chance that is yet sometimes at work in these situations. However, a number of *if* clauses are now considered. *If* it turns out that Mme d'Eporcheville, whom he believes in and already loves and who makes him think now only of possessing her, is one of the brown-haired girls, then the existence of her fabricated being will be put to an end. *If* this turns out to be the case, then the two elements that he has *arbitrarily associated* (the blond and the girl about whom Robert has spoken) would be separated into two distinct elements. He has associated them like a novelist plucking elements from reality to create an imaginary being; what matters is the way in which the elements are combined in association, since no element signifies by itself. *If*, then, it turns out that she has brown hair, clearly all his arguments will be destroyed. Consequently he is buoyed when the concierge returns to report that Mlle d'Eporcheville is indeed the blond.

With this evidence in hand, he peremptorily and fatefully excludes the possibility of a homonym. It is too much of a coincidence, he reasons, that one of the girls is named Mlle d'Eporcheville, and that she has given him this kind of look, for her not to be the one described by Saint-Loup in the *maison de passe*.

Now sure of his object, he prepares with agitation to see her again at the Guermantes' home, where he plans to ask for a rendezvous. As an extra precaution he decides to telegraph Saint-Loup to ask for the exact name and description of the young woman, not so much because he has any doubt at all about the identity of this person or because the girl he saw and the one Saint-Loup had spoken of were in any way distinct for him—he has no doubt that they are one and the same person—but because it is in some way pleasurable to receive word of her, details about her, in secret. As he writes the note to Saint Loup, he is pleased with his progress in dealing with Mlle d'Eporcheville, compared to the "savage" way he had loved Gilberte with "impotent desires." All the knowledge accumulated from Saint Loup about Mlle d'Eporcheville will be put in the service of the "novel" which he has just begun with her.[11] Nothing must get in the way of his meeting this girl again.

Contrary to experience, the narrator declares, "certain philosophers assert that the external world does not exist, and that it is within ourselves that we develop our lives. However that may be, love, even in its humblest beginnings, is a striking example of how little reality means to us"(RTP 3:577).[12] Had he been asked to draw her picture from memory, give her description, or even recognize her in the street, he could not have done so. He could not say more than that she was pretty, simple, tall, and blond. The combination of desire, anxiety, and fear of an absence suffice to bring associations to bear upon this fragmentary memory and to constitute "love."

But the next morning the narrator receives his answer in the telegram from Saint-Loup: " 'De l'Orgeville, *de* particle, *orge* barley, *ville* town, small, dark, plump, is at present in Switzerland.' He states: It was not the girl" (RTP 3:578).[13]

What this scene shows is that the life of thought has its own peculiar rhythms. Put on a certain course, however erroneous, it simply carries out commands automatically. And only a moment later, he repeats the process in another context. In the mail that his mother leaves him he finds a copy of *Le Figaro* with an article bearing the same title as the one he has submitted to the paper and which, he knows, has not been printed. It is only when he sees his own signature that his thoughts collect, and he recognizes the article as his own. He has been like "an old man who is obliged to complete a movement that he has begun even if it has become unnecessary, even if an unforeseen obstacle, in the face of which he ought at once to draw back, makes it dangerous" (RTP 3:579).[14]

To return to the story line: when Marcel enters the Guermantes' living room, he sees the same blond young woman whom he thought he had recognized with Saint-Loup during the preceding twenty-four hours. She asks to be "represented" to him. He feels that he has met her until the Duchess of Guermantes says that she would like him to meet Mlle Forcheville. He is quite convinced that he has never met any young woman of this name, since it is not a name he could have forgotten, given all he knows retrospectively about Odette's loves and the jealousy of Swann.

> In itself, he says, my twofold error as to the name, in having remembered "de l'Orgeville" as "d'Eporcheville" and in having reconstructed as "d'Eporcheville" what was in reality "Forcheville," was in no way extraordinary. Our mistake lies in supposing that things present themselves as they really are, names as they are written, people as photography and psychology give an unalterable notion of them. But in reality this is not at all what we ordinarily perceive. We see, we hear, we conceive the world in a lopsided fashion. We repeat a name as we have heard it spoken until experience has corrected our mistake—something that does not always happen. [RTP 3:585][15]

No extraordinary event, then, this. The mistake came from a false association around the name. All that was needed, or so it would seem, was correction through experience. But that is not given to all:

> This perpetual error, which is precisely "life," does not bestow its countless forms merely upon the visible and the audible universe, but upon the social universe, the sentimental universe, the historical universe, and so forth. . . . *We have of the universe only inchoate, fragmentary visions, which we complement by arbitrary associations of ideas, creative of dangerous illusions.* I should therefore have had no reason to be surprised when I heard the name Forcheville . . . had not the fair girl [the blond girl] said to me at once, anxious no doubt to forestall, tactfully, questions which would have been disagreeable to her: "Don't you remember that you knew me well long ago . . . you used to come to our house . . . your friend Gilberte. I could see that you

didn't recognise me. I recognised you at once." [RTP 3: 585–86][16]

Only after she leaves does he learn that her name is Forcheville because Odette married Forcheville following Swann's death. Forcheville had adopted her out of "charitable" feelings so that she would be more eligible to marry in name as well as in wealth. Through inheritance from one of Swann's uncles, Gilberte has already become one of the richest heirs in France.

These "inchoate, fragmentary visions," which we complement by "arbitrary associations of ideas," are creative of "dangerous illusions" when measured against a reality to which they have no relation, as in the foregoing example. They are errors only because the "intellectual armature" has dictated a course that must align desire with its object. But the life of the affect has never been duped: all scenarios, like all the walks through the two ways, lead to a structure of desire. "More often than not when I thought of her [Gilberte], I would see her standing before the porch of a cathedral, explaining to me what each of the statues meant, and, with a smile which was my highest commendation, presenting me as her friend to Bergotte. And invariably the charm of all the fancies which the thought of cathedrals used to inspire in me . . . would be reflected in the picture I had formed in my mind's eye of Mlle Swann" (RTP 1:108).[17]

Thus, the novel is not about the women the narrator has loved, or the reality of their being. The novel is about the way in which desire emerges repeatedly in seemingly arbitrary configurations—early drafts of the manuscript show the name of the blond changing from Courgeville to Chaussecourt to Ossecourt.[18] It is also about the way in which the intellect must, by virtue of the powers of analysis vested in it, comprehend the force of these perpetual errors in order to constitute thought. The number of missed occasions—women never loved, novels never written—all go to prove that the production of truth emerges from a combination of chance and a determined structure in desire for the other. [19]

The narrator writes in *The Fugitive:* "Everything starts from an initial error. . . . A large part of what we believe to be true (and this applies even to our final conclusions) with an obstinacy equalled only by our good faith, springs from an original mistake in our premises" (RTP 3:671).[20] What the mental misfire in this scene shows is not so much that the world is a mental construct in which blue might just as well be black—what solipsists might call truth because the material world does not exist—or that Marcel made "wrong" associations. What it means is that all meaning is subject to interpretation and the force of desire; for art to appear there must be an intertwining of both the revelations and the habits of thought, on the one hand, with so-called "objective reality" and the arbitrary system of signs, on the other. Rewriting the world as word can happen only if the process is at once hermeneutic and semiological, an operation through which thought de-forms and re-forms the world otherwise in order to inhabit it.

THE BLOSSOMING GIRLS

Like involuntary memory, the mistaken fragmentary memory of Gilberte's eyes evokes the inaugural moment in the hero's love for her and the analysis that follows. Unlike involuntary memory, however, it brings no epiphany. What the love for Gilberte sets in motion is a craving for knowledge predicated upon the uncertainty of memory and perception.

The second sequence concerns the young "blossoming girls" and the narrator's first perceptions of them in *Within a Budding Grove.* Haunted by the inability to unify his perceptions and thoughts concerning his past and to rehabilitate the areas of memory unavailable to rational thought, the narrator finds himself fascinated with the indistinct, almost anonymous character of the young girls to whom he is drawn and of whose group he wishes to become a part.

With the appearance of the adolescent girls at Balbec, the narrator continues his investigation of desire. Until then, two invariable models have dominated in the life of the narrator: his mother and his grandmother.[21] His grandmother is the important one in Balbec; his thought gravitates toward her in a relationship that appears to be unmediated: "My thoughts were continued and extended in her without undergoing the slightest deflection, since they passed from my mind into hers without any change of atmosphere or of personality" (RTP 1:718).[22] Like his mother, the grandmother provides a fixed reference point in the affective life of the hero by which he is able to situate himself. In the sequence with the girls, the focus shifts. The sight of the girls makes explicit a process of change and repetition: change within the girls whose forms the narrator perceives; repetition of his own patterns of desire. All this the narrator understands by analogy.

The moment preceding the encounter with the girls is filled with expectation. Searching for some beautiful object, his thought projects desire into the emptiness of space. Then, as he waits in front of the Grand Hotel for his grandmother, the girls turn up:

> At the far end of the esplanade, along which they projected a striking patch of colour, I saw five or six young girls as different in appearance and manner from all the people one was accustomed to see at Balbec as would have been a flock of gulls arriving from God knows where and performing with measured tread upon the sands—the dawdlers flapping their wings to catch up with the rest—a parade the purpose of which seems as obscure to the human bathers whom they do not appear to see as it is clearly determined in their own birdish minds. [RTP 1:846][23]

The "patch" turned "flock" moves with inscrutable resolution; it is separate from anyone else on the beach. And while the group stands out, no individual characteristics allow the eye to distinguish one girl from another. They meld in the seascape.[24] He is filled with desire in the anticipation of a kind of pleasure achieved only in dreams, loving all the young girls and none. The fascination with this group then eclipses the preoccupation with his grandmother, who, no longer fixed in his thought, becomes just another player in the seaside scene.

In their second appearance, the "beautiful procession of young girls" (RTP 1:881)[25] turns into the "mountainous blue

undulations of the sea, the outline of a *procession* against the sea"
(RTP 1:891; emphasis added).[26] Still undifferentiated (not only
to him at the time but later even to themselves in a photograph),
they now loom in the "congealment of a single cluster, scintil-
lating and tremulous," "a sort of vague, white constellation,"
an "indistinct and milky nebula" (RTP 1:881).[27] Eyes stand
out—some black, some green—in the passage from organismic
to cosmic images, but without connection to a particular person. It is in fact the "want . . . of the demarcations" that "permeated the group with a sort of shimmering harmony, the
continuous transmutation of a fluid, collective and mobile beauty" (RTP 1:847–48).[28] So although as a whole their luminescent
unity attracts him, individually they offer neither distinguishing
marks nor especial appeal.

It is the quality of wholeness that leads him on, with the mis-
ty promise of envelopment, beside the images of birds and cos-
mos, in the sea itself. In a variant, Proust speculates that perhaps
what we love, what gives pleasure during so many evenings,
making us leave parents and torture mistresses, is something not
so very different from what we believe: something causing longing and turmoil because it had been "denatured" or transformed. That is, "something which is not a being and which
momentarily lends beings their value, a cathedral, a valley, in
this case, at the edge of blue mountains of the sea, the sun, the
beach."[29] It is not, then, because the young women possess intrinsic value—any more than, say, cathedrals or even the fate of
the Dreyfus affair—that they attract. *It is what they borrow from
the sky and sea by analogy in association that turns them into a locus
of desire.*

Other images too confer value. The young girls in their early
years, says the narrator, like "primitive organisms in which the
individual barely exists by itself, is constituted by the polypary
rather than by each of the polyps that compose it . . . were still
pressed one against another" (RTP 1:882).[30] It would require a
number of intervening years, and "all the transformations possible during girlhood," for him to perceive a process among and
within the girls. The "distance traversed in a short interval of

time by the physical characteristics of each of these girls" made of them "a criterion too vague to be of any use" for recognition (RTP 1:882).[31] Only later would he be able to individualize and disjoin "the spores . . . of the pale madrepore" (RTP 1:883).[32] For the moment, it is their aura of indistinctness, in which attributes overlap and enhance one another, that is so appealing. It is as though association had materialized in visual form and been compared to music: "The most different aspects were juxtaposed, because all the colour scales were combined in it, but confused as a piece of music in which I was unable to isolate and identify at the moment of their passage the successive phrases, no sooner distinguished than forgotten" (RTP 1:847).[33]

The girls embody the problem of the one and the many like the image that *lends* them an enigmatic philosophical status, the polyp. As an intermediary being that grows by division and sectioning, the polyp became one of the great entities of speculative biology in the nineteenth century. Since each cutting produces a head, the polyp or hydra presents the model of a composite entity whose overall individual identity constitutes a problem. So the question of the unity of the girls in the relationship of the whole to the parts, as with the polyp, poses a theoretically new problem. The polyp is a being whose parts regenerate and reconstitute other identical beings. At the same time, one can consider the polyp to be formed out of the array of polyps constituted in the sectioning. On this model, one can conceive of the living organism either as infinitely composed of itself or as the totality that embraces a homogeneous plurality in its minute parts. The fascinating image of a multiple whole is what strikes Marcel. The girls appear as a single body, synchronized like a good waltzer, though their position relative to the narrator remains unclear. Johann Fichte allowed that "the man who sees the whole in each part always knows where he stands,"[34] but the narrator's desire to close the distance and join in with the girls renders such clarity impossible in the novel:

> The supposition that I might some day be the friend of one or other of these girls, . . . might ever, by some mirac-

ulous alchemy, allow the idea of my existence, some affection for my person, to interpenetrate their ineffable particles, that I myself might some day take my place, among them [*dans la théorie qu'elles déroulaient le long de la mer*]—that supposition appeared to me to contain within it a contradiction as insoluble as if, standing before some Attic frieze or a fresco representing a procession, I had believed it possible for me, the spectator, to take my place, beloved of them, among the divine participants. [RTP 1:853][35]

To become a part of their flow or *theory* (as the French text puts it) is something the narrator feels he can do only by arresting the movement of the girls. Yet it is the desire for stability that translates itself: either linguistically through naming, as was the case with Gilberte, or visually through painting and architecture. In an effort to find his bearings, the narrator fixes the moment by invoking the frieze, where motion is frozen in art. In the world of the girls, however, no stoppage occurs. Even when the procession slows and individuals emerge, their motion remains elusive.[36] Befriending the girls seems as impossible as if the young girl in Benozzo Gozzoli's frieze—the girl with *the rose-colored tunic,* green eyes, and a mysterious look—were to know his name and, most especially, *to know that he was looking at her.*[37] Yet they materialize association for him because only the hero can bring these images together as an integral if incongruous part of the whole.[38]

For a time, Albertine appears with the band of young women whom he mistakenly thinks come from a shady milieu. They retain for him "a preliminary glamour which they would never now lose," thanks to the "vacuity of seaside life" (RTP 1:903). He cannot distinguish her among the others in the early encounters and is "unable to confer on her retrospectively an identity which she did not have for [him] at the moment she caught [his] eye" (RTP 1:905).[39] But the need to transfer his love to one object finally wins out. The inability to see difference among the girls, or continuity within their images, negates their existence for him.[40] Even though Albertine begins to differentiate herself little by little from the others, this difference does not as yet grant her a singular identity; like Gilberte, though the details of their stories diverge, Albertine is fragmentary from the beginning.

She appears several times, each time changed: first, in a black "polo" pushing her bicycle and spouting tough slang, [41] then in Elstir's studio, totally transformed in a silk dress.[42] Perhaps the most disconcerting change of all is her language, so that when he hears her say *parfaitement* instead of *tout à fait*, he is almost unable to match her with the other images: now a well-brought-up Baccante with bicycle (RTP 1:933).

> Each time, a girl so little resembles what she was the time before (shattering, as soon as we catch sight of her, the memory that we had retained of her and the desire that we had proposed to gratify), that the stability of nature which we ascribe to her is purely fictitious and a convention of speech. . . . As for the successive facets which after pulsating for some days the roseate light, now eclipsed, presents to us, it is not even certain that a momentum external to these girls has not modified their aspect, and this might well have happened with my band of girls at Balbec. People extol to us the gentleness, the purity of a virgin. But afterwards they feel that something more spicy would please us better, and recommend her to show more boldness. In herself was she one more than the other? Perhaps not, but capable of yielding to any number of different possibilities in the headlong current of life. [RTP 3:59][43]

The very mobility of the girls differentiates them from the rest of humanity and makes them inscrutable:

> In themselves, what were Albertine and Andrée? To know the answer, I should have to immobilise you, . . . I should have to cease to love you in order to fix your image, cease to be conscious of your interminable and always disconcerting arrival, O girls, O successive rays in the swirling vortex wherein we throb with emotion on seeing you reap-

pear while barely recognising you, in the dizzy velocity of light. We might perhaps remain unaware of that velocity, and everything would seem to us motionless, did not a sexual attraction set us in pursuit of you, O drops of gold, always dissimilar and always surpassing our expectation! [RTP 3:58-59][44]

The exquisite and rare vision of the volatile young girls occasions reflection upon the role of chance: "Chance seems to us then a good and useful thing, for we discern in it as it were the rudiments of organisation, of an attempt to arrange our lives" (RTP 1:883).[45] He goes on to explain how contingency turns into a given and "makes it easy, inevitable, and sometimes . . . painful for us to retain in our minds images for the possession of which we shall come in time to believe that we were predestined, and which but for chance we should from the very first have managed to forget, like so many others, so easily" (RTP 1:883).[46] Chance encounters demonstrate that little in life can be organized by the will and that in time, through forgetting, these events become the givens of the past. That is because in passing from a chance encounter to some as yet undefined necessity, these rudiments of organization ensure that newness will emerge. They personify a *theory* scrolled out before him at the edge of the sea ("dans la théorie qu'elles déroulaient le long de la mer").[47] The omission in the English translation of the word "theory" in relation to the girls (see the first of the three passages just quoted) suggests how unfamiliar and intriguing is this pairing of the two. Indeed, what theory could the girls possibly suggest? Could there be a hidden premise?

PROUST'S SPECIAL THEORY OF RELATIVITY

The third and final sequence, illustrates how the allure and perils of his desire to melt into the seemingly amorphous, unstructured universe of the young girls lead to the discovery of an order hitherto unperceived by the narrator.

After the apparition of the girls, the narrator discovers a sense of "new pleasure" in the restaurant at Rivebelle, "finding [himself] in that different zone into which the exceptional introduces us after having cut the thread, patiently spun throughout so many days, that was guiding [him] towards wisdom" (RTP 3:867).[48] The opening of an "exceptional" meaning seems to nullify the patient search for meaning in the labyrinth of perceptions. Casting off his coat, the narrator shrugs away life's vicissitudes and with them the "fear of falling ill, the necessity of not dying, the importance of work" (RTP 1:867). Then, gypsies play a "warlike march," and the narrator and his group cut a swath through the tables like a "path of glory." Feeling "a happy glow" from the rhythms of the music, as though military honors were being bestowed upon them, their stride and demeanor remain serious enough to avoid the ridiculous.

It is from this moment on that he declares himself a "new man," no longer the grandson of his grandmother but the fleeting brother of those waiters there to serve him. It is then that a new conception of the relationship among beings unfolds. At first, the narrator attributes this sense of novelty to too much wine, but the images soon take on their own logic: tables become like planets figuring in the allegories of old in which the force of attraction between the stars (*les astres*) is so great that the diners have eyes only for the other tables. But it is the movement of the waiters that is most extraordinary: "The incessant revolution of the countless waiters who, because instead of being seated like the diners they were on their feet, performed their gyrations in a more exalted sphere. No doubt they were running, one to fetch the *hors d'oeuvre,* another to change the wine or to bring clean glasses. But despite these special reasons [*ces raisons particulières], their perpetual course among the round tables yielded, after a time, to the observer the law of its dizzy but ordered circulation*" (RTP 1:868).[49]

Like the procession of young girls against the sea, the waiters move in a fast track, different from the likes of the bathers and diners. Like the girls, the waiters function according to their own system, one whose laws seem to emerge from the observation of their behavior, while for the others "the round tables were not planets and . . . they had not cut through the scheme of things in such a way as to be delivered from the bondage of habitual appearances and enabled to perceive analogies" (RTP 1:869). Proust appropriated in his own way Einstein's formulation of the special theory of relativity for the question of human value.[50] Demonstrating that movement is always relative to a system of reference, the unenlightened (bathers, diners, and others) remain ensconced in their own banality, unable to see beyond, and leave it up to the gifted to see and act.[51] Proust approaches Einstein's theory when he suggests that people exhibit deterministic behavior. But within the novel he differs from Einstein because although observations from shifting referent points show something different, the laws one may derive from them are not the same. The lament that follows the scene at Rivebelle suggests that those who are thus able to understand, to discern by analogy, may well be doomed to suffer.

In discussing the passion to know in 1950, Einstein wrote about an attitude that is illustrated in his theories of relativity but goes far beyond them:

> There exists a passion for comprehension, just as there exists a passion for music. . . . Time and again the passion for understanding has led to the illusion that man is able to comprehend the objective world rationally, by pure thought, without any empirical foundations—in short, by metaphysics. I believe that every true theorist is a kind of tamed metaphysicist, no matter how pure a "positivist" he may fancy himself. The metaphysicist believes that the logically simple is also the real. The tamed metaphysicist believes that not all that is logically simple is embodied in experienced reality, but that the totality of all sensory experience can be "comprehended" on the basis of a conceptual system built on premises of great simplicity.[52]

Like the axioms of theoretical physics, which cannot be deduced from experience, Proust's "theory" of the blossoming girls cannot be deduced from experience alone. But like them too, his theory cannot be the invention of pure thought. It was at the juncture of these two imperatives that Einstein turned to a "system built on a premise of great simplicity."[53] Now if the restaurant scene offers a prototypical example of relativity for the narrator, his encounter with newness still remains confused. What is cause and what effect? The cause may be attributed to drink in the restaurant (as an escape from rationality), or to the pubescent state of indeterminacy in the girls (as the object of the narrator's scrutinizing desire). But in the itinerary of this epistemological *bildungsroman,* neither suffices. Through the movements of the girls and the waiters, the narrator glimpses the incommensurability of otherness in love. He struggles to reconstruct a world of meaning and value. As movement and the intelligibility of perceptions become confused in the encounter with the young girls, as heterogeneous perceptions, memories, and thoughts beset the narrator, he flags here as elsewhere: "The insoluble problems which I set myself . . . made me more exhausted and unwell" (RTP 1:100).[54] Comparing the clarity with which the girls, like the waiters, seem to operate, the narrator despairs of finding his own formula for simplicity.

In the process of perceiving, remembering, and transferring erotic energy to a particular object, the subject of the chapter to follow, the narrator—nowhere near leaving his labyrinth—reflects: "Philosophy distinguishes often between free and necessary acts. Perhaps there is none to the necessity of which we are more completely subjected than that which, by virtue of a climbing power held in check during the act itself, brings back (once our mind is at rest) a memory until then levelled down with all the rest by the oppressive force of bemusement and makes it spring to the surface because unknown to us it contained more than any of the others a charm of which we do not become aware until the following day" (RTP 1:881). It is this process that we call association, and it leads, as with Freud, to a determined mental scheme: "Perhaps, too, there is no act so free, for it is still unprompted by habit, by that sort of mental obsession which, in matters of love, encourages the invariable reappearance of the image of one particular person" (RTP 1:881).[55]

That one particular person is Albertine. In understanding the relationship between chance and necessity, little has changed from Gilberte, whose entire being was captured in the mistaken memory of her eyes, to Albertine, whose capture will preoccupy the narrator for more than two volumes. What one can say is that it was no accident at all that the spelling of the two names overlap: "It is thus that the letters of the name of the woman that I was going to love had been given to me by the woman I had so loved, like the game in which one draws on a wooden alphabet. A circular chain crosses our life, linking what is already dead to what is full of life."[56] We know that the love for Albertine was always already inscribed within the love for Gilberte.

In the process of life and death, the resurrections and intermittencies of love, the hero moves into a world in which the emergence of the blossoming girls signifies the death of the grandmother, as absolute model or point of reference. From his inability to mourn her physical being upon the moment, the narrator gleans the awareness that the organization of thought, like that of the living organism or system generally, is the result of antagonistic processes.[57]

The narrator equates the experience of music with the experience of women, and he suggests that the cruelty of music ("arrangements of waltzes, of German operettas, of music-hall songs") "ogled [him], came up to [him] with lewd or provocative movements, accosted [him], caressed [him] as if [he] had suddenly become more seductive, more powerful, richer" (RTP 1:869–70). This kind of untoward force attracts like a whirlwind pulling him away from the presumed stability of the past. The narrator has already described the cluster of girls in the image of the harmonious waltzer. Yet here girls seem more dangerous: they threaten established meaning through the relation of order to disorder.[58] They belong to the "whirl of destiny" associated with the death of the nineteenth century.[59] Any "new theories" that the girls harbor come through analogy in the form of stories or tunes of jealousy. Jealousy is the key to interminably deferred meaning to which Proust's interim novels are dedicated: these tunes "are the most merciless of hells, the most gateless and imprisoning for the jealous wretch to whom they present that pleasure—that pleasure which the woman he loves is enjoying with another—as the only thing that exists in the world for her who is all the world to him" (RTP 1:870).[60] To understand that these worlds may never intersect, as Proust's special theory suggests, in no way wards off the craving for knowledge—the topic to be explored next.

5

Within the volumes entitled *The Captive* and *The Fugitive*, the narrator of *Remembrance* spins an excruciating, unending tale of jealousy. In the course of telling this tale, a theory of knowledge emerges in which nothing anywhere is ever certain. Jealousy is born before the intellect, rendering the intelligence unable to console the lover, who is as defenseless against jealousy as against sickness and death.[1]

One might think that the ostensible choice of art over life (evoked in Chapter 2) would diminish the ravaging effects of jealousy by establishing the separateness of art and life. That is not the case. This chapter deals with how Proust develops a poetics hewn out of the entanglement of the two, and how jealousy in love becomes the condition both of possibility and of impossibility for realizing the work of art. As art leads beyond the intellect, so does love, and the compulsion to which it gives rise is what I explore here.

Jealousy is inseparable not merely from love but from the work of art as well; all three coexist by a kind of analogy that allows any one to be forerunner to the others: "This first work of his must be considered simply as an unhappy love which fatally presages others of the kind: his life will resemble his work and in future the poet will scarcely need to write, for he will be able to find in what he has already written the anticipatory outline of what will then be happening" (RTP 3:941–42).[2]

From the first to the final volume the repetitions of experiences with women, the attempts to exhume past events, all trigger creativity. "A novelist might, in relating the life of his hero, describe his successive love-affairs in almost exactly similar terms, and thereby give the impression not that he was repeating himself but that he was creating, *since an artificial novelty is never so effective as a repetition that manages to suggest a fresh truth*" (RTP 1:955).[3]

Within the novel the association between love and art comes from Swann, himself a failed artist. The narrator points to Swann as the source of knowledge for the material of his future novel. Swann had inspired the desire to go to Balbec and all that followed:

> But for this I should never have known Albertine. . . . Had I not gone to Balbec I should never have known the Guermantes either, . . . nor should I have made the acquaintance of Saint-Loup and M. de Charlus and thus got to know the Duchess de Guermantes and through her her cousin, so that even my presence at this very moment in the house of the Prince de Guermantes, where out of the blue the idea for my work had just come to me . . . had come from Swann. A rather slender stalk, perhaps, to support thus the whole development of my life, for the "Guermantes way" too . . . had emanated from "Swann's Way." [RTP 1:954][4]

The presence of Swann in the life of the narrator is a given from the first pages of the book. It is he who by his presence at dinner "creates" the scene in which the narrator first writes (the letter to his mother), he who inspires the desire to travel.

"Swann in Love" provides the story to which and through which the narrator associates his memories and experiences. Swann does not, cannot, for all his sensitivity, realize an artistic creation. Swann's love is the first in a series of loves fraught with and dependent upon jealousy. An understanding of art, society, and love will begin to make sense in relation to Swann: "I thought then of all I had been told about Swann's love for Odette, of the way in which Swann had been tricked all his life. Indeed . . . the hypothesis that made me gradually build up the whole of Albertine's character and give a painful interpretation to every moment of a life that I could not control in its entirety, was the memory, the rooted idea of Mme Swann's character, as it had been described to me" (RTP 2:832).[5] It is this prototype that later gives form to the narrator's love for Albertine, not so much because of the fulfillment of any prophecy but because of the power and ruses of the narrative as it unfolds in time.[6]

The passage from "Combray" to "Swann in Love" comes about by an "association of memories" (RTP 1:203).[7] The story, which preceded the narrator's birth, was rendered with a precision more likely to be found in accounts of people "who have been dead for centuries" than in those of best friends. Though these memories "superimposed upon one another" formed a "single mass," the narrator could still distinguish the old from the new, those of another person from his own (RTP 1:203).[8]

Because "every reader is, while he is reading, the reader of his own self" (RTP 3:949),[9] the question is, how does Marcel interpret Swann's text? What does he learn from one text to another by analogy?

He learns first that the desire for knowledge inheres in love. Swann confides to the narrator in *Cities of the Plain*: " 'I have never been curious, I have never been inquisitive, except when I was in love, and when I was jealous.' 'Are you jealous?' " (RTP 2:728).[10] Marcel replies that he has never been jealous, doesn't even really know what the word means. This benign comment kicks off Marcel's free fall into jealousy, such is the power of the all-knowing narrator's ironic stance: everything from then on operates to prove this statement wrong.

Swann instructs him in two things: first, that jealousy is not entirely unpleasant, since it arouses interest in the lives of others and sweetens the feeling of possession; second, that to be jealous means to live by desire and the insatiable need for possession. For Swann, jealousy gives value to love. For Marcel, the two are so inseparable that the rival turns out to be a benefactor. It is not even necessary that the rival really exist: "The progress of our work requires only that they [rivals] should have that illusory life which is conferred upon non-existent rivals by our suspicion, our jealousy" (RTP 3:943).[11]

However positive these formulas, the narrator experiences jealousy as a constantly spreading pain: "He who desires knowledge, suffers nevertheless from knowing and seeks to learn more" (RTP 3:51).[12] Neither partial nor divided, its compulsion is exclusive. The drive toward totality in jealousy creates and destroys love from its inception. Hopelessly complicitous, the feelings of happiness and suffering (as the two aspects of love) lead to an untenable epistemological position: all love, like all theory, "requires to be stated as a whole" (RTP 1:606).[13] According to this postulate, love must be a function of a totality greater than any of its parts; it is a function of that which is unknown and inaccessible. "One only loves that in which one pursues the inaccessible, one only loves what one does not possess" (RTP 3:391).[14] This means that even though love demands totality, "it is born and it survives, only if some part remains for it to conquer" (RTP 3:102).[15] In this world, love thrives upon the paradox of incompleteness: jealousy "is a thirst for knowledge thanks to which, with regard to various isolated points, we end up by acquiring every possible notion in turn except the one that we require" (RTP 3:80–81).[16]

The unknown quality that all pursue—such is the Platonic hypothesis and the dream—must be Beauty itself. The idea would come from seizing upon incomplete impressions in fortuitous encounters:

> If night is falling and the carriage is moving fast, whether in town or country, there is not a single torso, disfigured

like an antique marble by the speed that tears us away and the dusk that blurs it, that does not aim at our heart, from every crossing, from the lighted interior of every shop, the arrows of Beauty, that Beauty of which we are sometimes tempted to ask ourselves whether it is, in this world, anything more than the complementary part that is added to a fragmentary and fugitive stranger by our imagination, overstimulated by regret. [RTP 1:766][17]

Proust adds, in a note to *Time Regained*:

Every individual who makes us suffer can be attached by us to a *divinity* of which he or she is a mere fragmentary reflection, the lowest step in the ascent that leads to it, a divinity or an Idea which, if we turn to contemplate it, immediately gives us joy instead of the pain which we were feeling before—indeed the whole art of living is to make use of the individuals through whom we suffer as a step enabling us to draw nearer to the *divine form* which they reflect and thus joyously to people our life with divinities. [RTP 3:935][18]

The search for beauty in its divine form goes beyond successive images of the person; to possess the other means to possess his or her essence. The lover does not focus on this or that changing part of another, as he does in Hardy's *Well-Beloved*. What the hero loves is the "invisible person who set all this outward show in motion" (RTP 2:60).[19] It is this *unique quality* of an *unfamiliar world* that the narrator will taste only when he hears the great unpublished work by Vinteuil, the septet whose "life" he wishes to capture.[20]

Increasingly, the jealous lover's interest becomes focused on the relationship between chance and necessity, between the moment when feelings are aroused in events and their subsequent insertion into a determined structure. To see how this works, I examine one moment, a decisive one in which the vague desire to love transforms itself and becomes the exclusive desire for one person. In Swann's case, two moments precede what might be called the crystallization of his love for Odette. First, the performance of the sonata by Vinteuil, in which the little phrase holds the power to evoke their love; second, the moment when Swann notices the similarity between Odette's face and the face of Zephora, Jethro's daughter, as shown in a Botticelli fresco in the Sistine Chapel. These two moments prepare Swann's passion for Odette through their association with music and painting. The event that triggers the passion takes place one evening when Odette leaves the Verdurins' earlier than usual, and Swann spends the rest of the evening in search of her. It is then that he "discovers" he needs Odette and indeed loves her. This is the turningpoint that kicks off the love affair, which ends well before their marriage with a phrase that is perhaps so well-known because it is so terrible: " 'To think that I've wasted years of my life, that I've longed to die, that I've experienced my greatest love, for a woman who didn't appeal to me, who wasn't even my type' " (RTP 1:415).[21]

For Marcel, the contingency of any love is even more evident. One day, while observing Albertine, he awaits another woman: Mme Stermaria. When she cancels the rendezvous, he realizes that if the circumstances had been only slightly different, his love might have settled on her rather than Albertine. But when Albertine cancels a visit to Marcel one day, no longer can he escape the need to possess her. What this event, like so many others, shows is the part that chance plays in love. Love is not absolutely necessary and predestined, as the hero desires and needs to believe; it is an individuating process in which the singular event leads to a determined structure of the self.

Lovers turn out to be no more than accomplices to a structure. And prior to the discovery of art the uniqueness of each experience can be understood only within the generalizing language of a system. The language of love has not been formed for this or that lover. Nor is it destined expressly for any particular being. This language has served and will serve for others. Woman is not unique; she is legion—which means that however irreplaceable she may seem in the eyes of the one who loves her, "the truth is that [she] has merely raised to life by a sort of magic countless elements of tenderness existing in us already in a fragmentary state, which she has assembled, joined together, bridging every gap between them, and it is we ourselves who by giving her her features have supplied all the solid matter of the beloved object" (RTP 3:513).[22] Love is greater than the woman in that it envelops her, but it does not know her. And suffering, in summoning a portion of the soul larger than the whole, shows the immensity of love and how it is governed by laws. This means that total love emerges neither from the sum of successive "I's" nor from the sum of women loved, but rather from this "portion of our mind more durable than the various selves which successively die within us and which would, in their egoism, like to keep it to themselves, a portion of our mind which must . . . detach itself from individuals so that we can comprehend and restore to it its generality and give this love, the understanding of this love, to all, to the universal spirit, and not merely first to one woman and then to another" (RTP 3:933–34).[23]

Although the need for knowledge now proves to be an integral part of love, it will never be clear why this is so. It is "best to make no attempt to understand, since in so far as these [contrasting situations relating to love] are as inexorable as they are unlooked-for, they appear to be governed by magic rather than by rational laws" (RTP 1:539–40).[24] Yet throughout the entire novel the narrator struggles for control through analysis and comprehension.

But does Marcel learn anything from the Swann story? Quite the opposite, for having quoted Swann as the source of his work (through all the intermediaries), he will go on to repeat many of the same mechanisms.

Toward the end of the novel he adds a short narrative, isolated from everything around it, in which he reviews the way jealousy operates. The fragment begins with a general statement: "Jealousy is a good recruiting-sergeant who, when there is a gap in our picture, goes out into the street and brings us in the desirable woman who was needed to fill it" (RTP 3:955). The agenda for this anonymous vignette includes the rhythm, the workings, and the provenance of jealousy. The narrator hypothesizes that jealousy could arise just about anywhere: in perusing a telephone book, in intercepting a look between two people, or just in an afterthought. In this case, it comes from the "Tout-Paris" and for the country the "Chateau Directory." The story is as follows: the narrator remembers absentmindedly having heard a beautiful girl, who had since "become indifferent," say that she was to go see her sister in the Pas-de-Calais region near Dunkirk. He had, still absentmindedly, thought that "perhaps the beauty had formerly been pursued by Monsieur E—, whom she had ceased to see, since she had ceased to go to the bar where she used to meet him. . . . Now suddenly, opening the *Annuaire des Châteaux* at random we find that Monsieur E— has his country-house in the Pas-de-Calais, near Dunkirk" (RTP 3:956). He supposes, without verification, that the sister is a chamber-maid, and then several hypotheses come to mind. First, E— took the sister to work for him as a chambermaid to please the beauty. Since they no longer see each other at the usual bar, this would mean that they meet at his house, and the narrator concludes that they cannot do without each another. There is no end to what can be imagined: "Drunk with rage and love, we paint furiously away at the picture." Still, if this hypothesis proved false, it would not be inconceivable— such is the second hypothesis—that Monsieur E— recommended the sister to one of his brothers out of pure "obligingness," in which case the conclusion would be that they are indifferent to each other. Yet a third hypothesis: if the sister were not a chambermaid, and if the beauty simply had relatives in the area, there would be no reason to fear. This last hypothesis calms the anguish (jealousy) and concludes the story, which ends, as did Swann's, in indifference. "And the whole composition takes shape, thanks to the presence, evoked by jealousy, of the beauty of whom already we are no longer jealous and whom we no longer love" (RTP 3:957).[25] So jealousy repeats the ternary structure inherent in all love: from indifference to desire, in which it reaches full expression and then subsides again in indifference. In every case, the narrator associates indifference with certainty and desire with distress. Love seems locked into the adage that there is no desire without anguish, no certainty without indifference.

Proust attaches special significance to this scene, writing in the margins of his manuscript "capitalissime." Not only is this story framed by a beginning and end, but it is all the more perfect, as the moment *par excellence* of jealousy, that "we never dream how small a place in it the real woman occupies" (RTP 1:917).[26] It is not the woman who is important but *the means of knowing her*. The moment a woman barely known to him comes into focus, jealousy arouses anxiety as the mobilizing force of love. Then love disappears at the moment he ceases to be anxious. The vignette unfolds as though the narrator could remain a kind of impersonal spectator, as though by summarizing and objectifying the painful stages through which jealousy moves (rehearsed in the proliferation of hypotheses), he could provide a general theory for it. By providing an outline of the anguish that thought inflicts upon itself and containing it within narrative limits, the generalization through an example should respond to the need for a totalizing structure. But such a speculative move is destined to fail here because it disregards what Proust never ceases to write about throughout the novel: the narrator cannot withdraw to a position outside the scene because he plays a part within the whole. This means that the desire to maintain distance, as a defense, is translated into the compositional structure of the fragment, as its condition—one that requires a beginning and an end.

There is only one moment in Marcel's often desperate love for Albertine which corresponds to the speculative tranquillity of this scene: the moment when she sleeps. Alone, he thinks about her easily, but in her absence he does not possess her; when she is present, he can speak to her but is far too distracted to be able to think, whereas while she sleeps, she no longer eludes him: "She was animated now only by the unconscious life of plants. . . . Her personality was not constantly escaping, as when we talked, by the outlets of her unacknowledged thoughts and of her eyes. She had called back into herself everything of her that lay outside, had withdrawn, enclosed, reabsorbed herself into her body. In keeping it in front of my eyes, in my hands, I had an impression of possessing her entirely which I never had when she was awake" (RTP 3:64).[27] It is only then that Marcel feels a "pure" and "spiritual" love, an oasis from jealousy.

The search for this absolute resting spot is nothing short of an attempt to identify once and for all the singularity of an individual's existence within a region of transcendental being. The greatest fear comes from the sense that out of the multiplicity of discrete places and moments, nothing of what preceded would subsist in what followed, and that he might come to the end of his life bereft of the sense of an individual and permanent self. For this reason, death constitutes the foundation of being as the temporal boundary of life. For this reason too, separation from the loved one is the only real death. Although a "resurrection" occurs in each of these "intermittencies of the heart," each time it is within a new self: "I was not one man only, but as it were the march-past of a composite army in which there were passionate men, indifferent men, jealous men—jealous men not one of whom was jealous of the same woman" (RTP 3:499).[28] The "desperate and daily resistance" to a death of "successively fragmented parts" must now make room for the growth of a new being: this "aggregate" of "newly formed cells." In this way, new selves are born all throughout life by putting to death the shreds of old ones.

The experience of the death of others awakens the struggle between survival and nothingness within the self. When the narrator's grandmother dies, he senses nothing at all. It is only many years later, as he is taking off his shoes, that he "learns" through the delayed action of memory that she is dead. The experience is the same, though reversed, with the death of Albertine, who, in confirming to what extent thought functions anachronistically, prohibits the calendar of facts from coinciding with that of feelings. To kill Albertine, it would be necessary to kill each of the sufferings of which this love is composed, and kill them not only, as he says, in the region where Albertine was accidentally killed on a horse but kill them "in him." Once that had been accomplished, it would then take more than biological regeneration for her to come alive again within him. Just such a strange experience is tested when, upon reading a telegram he believes to have come from Albertine after her death, he is unable to resuscitate any "previous self," and the news that she lives does not move him at all: "Albertine had been no more to me than a bundle of thoughts, and she had survived her physical death so long as those thoughts were alive in me; on the other hand, now that those thoughts were dead, Albertine did not rise again for me with the resurrection of her body" (RTP 3:656).[29]

The structure of jealousy described in the fragment above corresponds to the program of the work of art because it channels desire and memory into the formal structures of writing. In this program, art wins out over life and keeps them ever separate. But the disappearance of love in the work of mourning combines with an obsession that makes this disentanglement difficult, long before the "decision" to write a book.

What I examine next is how a passage about forbidden desire leads to reinterpretation throughout the rest of the novel. Although the narrator takes the reader through the scene and a sequence of associations that follow, these associations neither solidify a meaningful interpretation of the event nor allow it to fade out. To establish the importance of such a moment within the work, the narrator will fall back on phylogenetic reminiscence. As Freud suggested, the structures inherited from phylogeny are like the categories of philosophy whose function it is to articulate how impressions derived from actual experience emerge. From this "mental thing" that one calls love, in the linking of facts and perceptions, the individual takes his or her place within the system of language and society.

MONTJOUVAIN

Life is composed of an infinite number of books if not already read at least already written: "But each past day has remained deposited in us, as in a vast library where, even of the oldest books, there is a copy which doubtless nobody will ever ask to see" (RTP 3:554).[30] Every day remains catalogued within

the self like a book within a library, but when a certain book—
that is, a certain day—reappears, there is no ready-made theory
to explain it. The narrator recalls one such day, a day he will
never forget because it becomes pivotal to the understanding of
his relationship with Albertine. It is the day when, hidden behind a bush at Montjouvain, Marcel peers through a window
and sees Mlle Vinteuil receive her friend, a young woman with
a bad reputation in the area.

Here is what happens: Mlle Vinteuil is in full mourning because of the recent death of her father, and, awaiting her friend,
she looks for his portrait and places it where they will be able to
see it and it them. A desecration of the father's portrait becomes
the condition for the scene of seduction between the two wom-
en. When Mlle Vinteuil shows the portrait to her friend, she
does it with a gesture reminiscent of the one her father used to
make when he would put musical scores (which he wanted to
play for Marcel's parents) on the piano. Offhandedly, she says
(as her father used to say) that the portrait is not "in its place."

Physically and mentally, Mlle Vinteuil is a paradoxical being.
Androgynous in her allure, she has both rough "man-like" features and those, more finely wrought, of a "distressed" girl with
a "soft" and "delicate" expression. She takes pleasure in being
"treated with tenderness by a woman who had shown herself so
implacable towards the defenceless dead" (RTP 1:178),[31] playing
the child by sitting on the knees of her friend.[32] The roles of all
three (Mlle Vinteuil, her father, and her friend) also change.
Though M. Vinteuil had been taken up with the responsibilities
of "having to play mother and nursery-maid to his daughter"
(RTP 1:174),[33] one cannot predict who in this scene plays which
role or what value may be attributed at any given moment. What
is known is that the father's passion for his daughter knew no
limits: " 'Poor M. Vinteuil,' his mother would say, 'he lived and
died for his daughter, without getting his reward.' " (RTP
1:175).[34] Her question is whether he would receive it after his
death, and if so in what form, for she knew that it could come
only from his daughter. The response to this question begins in
this scene and is related later in the novel to the complete work

of his music, which he had given up trying to transcribe into clean copy, for at this point no one imagined that it might have any value.

Mlle Vinteuil is a sort of artist of evil but no less natural for it; this kind of sadism, we are told, is so "purely" sentimental, so "naturally virtuous," that sensual pleasure appears to be associated with harm. But as important as sadism may be for this argument, it is not what matters most in the scene. What matters is that the scene constitutes a first experience and a first impression that set the stage for a long sequence of associations: "We shall see, in due course, that for quite other reasons the memory of this impression was to play an important part in my life" (RTP 1:173).[35]

Like the fragment about jealousy from *Time Regained*, this scene has no structurally meaningful position within the volume; it is disconnected from the context in which it is situated. Its force comes from its power to evoke memory. Although it does not resemble the experience of involuntary memory, because it cannot evoke the totality of a context when it is revived in the narrator's thought, it serves as another "cornerstone" for the experience and the analysis of jealousy. It is a fragment to which the narrative refers and without which *The Captive* and *The Fugitive* cannot be understood. Proust writes: "By suppressing it . . . I would have caused two entire volumes, for which it is a cornerstone, to collapse on the reader."[36] Whereas the fragment on jealousy set up an ideal of containment through the description of jealousy, the scene at Montjouvain begins a narrative process that is coextensive with the psychic process of association. It is the negative paradigm of how understanding emerges when meaning is glimpsed in the interval that separates the (textual) *event* from what follows. It was for this reason that he could qualify the work as a *suite coupée de lacunes*.

Two moments are thus necessary for meaning to emerge: the time of the event, whether real or imagined, and its subsequent elaboration in "delayed signification" (*nachträglicheit*). Because the imagination is not constitutively able, upon the moment, to understand its own structure and the principles of its organization, the work of interpretation can unfold only in time. Albertine puts the process in motion: "Albertine was merely, like a stone round which snow has gathered, the generating centre of an immense structure which rose above the plane of my heart" (RTP 3:445).[37] And Montjouvain functions within the novel as a primal scene.[38] "*My feeling for Albertine, my jealousy, stemmed . . . from the irradiation, by the association of ideas, of certain pleasant or painful impressions, the memory of Mlle Vinteuil at Montjouvain, the precious goodnight kisses that Albertine used to give me*" (RTP 3:657; emphasis added).[39]

It is the few words spoken by Albertine about Mlle Vinteuil in *Cities of the Plain* which trigger a series of fantasies so overwhelming that only certainty about facts could put them to rest: Albertine admits that the friend with whom she traveled to Trieste, who had been like a mother and sister to her and whom she is to see again, is Mlle Vinteuil's best friend, and she knows Mlle Vinteuil almost as well. At the moment of this confession the image of Montjouvain, which had been completely lost from thought until then, returns to haunt the narrator with a force of disruption hitherto unknown. It becomes imperative that he know whether Albertine was or was not a lesbian. Seeking the cause of this resurgence, he feels as though he were being punished, tortured, for having let his grandmother die—whence the association between the crime that he, as insensitive grandson, may have committed (out of the blanks of his mind) and the initiation rites of this scene into sensual knowledge. In his guilt, as both insensitive child and oversensitive voyeur, the lacunas of thought become analogous to "bad actions" that cause "fatal consequences": now Marcel, spectator to the scene at Montjouvain, will be punished forever (although the same kind of knowledge had been gained from the story of Swann) because he can never now be innocent of a certain kind of knowledge. "The notion of Albertine as the friend of Mlle Vinteuil and of Mlle Vinteuil's friend, a practising and professional Sapphist, . . . was a terrible *terra incognita* on which I had just landed, a new phase of undreamed-of sufferings that was opening before me" (RTP 2:1153).[40] The narrator forces himself to confront what he neither could nor would recognize prior to this: the image of Albertine in the room at Monjouvain as "she surrendered herself, [with her] strange, deep laugh" (RTP 2:1157).[41] As the sun rises in Balbec, where he has previously always been so happy, the narrator experiences a first unhappiness, an unhappiness that will continue to swell within, for such is the ambivalent law of suffering: "At that moment, Albertine—my sickness—ceasing to cause me to suffer, left me—she, Albertine the remedy—as weak as a convalescent" (RTP 2:1156).[42] Only a lack of creativity prevents him from going deeply enough into his suffering, the narrator states, for alongside any terrible reality there is a joy in the discovery of a form that is new.

Formally, the positions of the various actors cannot be fixed in the scene at Montjouvain. All one knows with certainty—although even this certainty has no guarantees—is that the scene "itself" is not anymore in *its place* than the portrait and the musical scores of Vinteuil. What the narrator-voyeur and his rival, the portrait of the father, witness is a scene in which the possibility of the project, as total work, is played out in the search for meaning in writing. Thus, searching for a euphemism to describe what they are doing, Mlle Vinteuil exclaims: "When I say 'see us' I mean, of course, *see us reading*" (RTP 1:176; emphasis added).[43] The question is, who reads? how and when? For the interpretation of the scene, which comes only much later, will be made by the one who seems most disinterested of all: the narrator. As witness to the "actual" scene, he knows empirically that the friend was not Albertine. But that does not stop his associations from substituting her for the friend. Because jealousy never leaves anything intact, it is he who becomes unhinged, plagued by obsession, hounded by the necessity of giving meaning to this scene; his life becomes an excruciating performance of the way in which the origin of a fantasy integrates itself into a structure of constant displacement.[44] Propelling forbidden desire through fantasy (for his mother through Vinteuil, Albertine, and the young girls), the narrator makes homosexual love the origin of all nonoriginary truth. The amalgamation of shifting figures designates this event as a constitutive scene in the work, one different from and similar to the sequence of involuntary memories. The event differs in its consequences from involuntary memory because no revelation of absolute truth will emerge from it, and is similar in its reliance upon the association of memories.

Through Montjouvain two series are associated in parallel: his mother, music, and Albertine; then his father, Vinteuil, and himself. To these two series, divided by gender, Proust adds the couple Adam and Eve. In the very first pages of the novel, the narrator's sense of time and space becomes dislocated. Finding himself awake contrary to his habits, and thus freed from the constraints of reason and contingency, he begins to doubt who he is. While he is in this state, "more destitute" than Plato's cave dweller, a woman is born from a dream:

> Sometimes, too, as Eve was created from a rib of Adam, a woman would be born during my sleep from some strain in the position of my thighs. Conceived from the pleasure I was on the point of consummating, she it was, I imagined, who offered me that pleasure. My body, conscious that its own warmth was permeating hers, would strive to become one with her, and I would awake. The rest of humanity seemed very remote in comparison with this woman whose company I had left but a moment ago; my cheek was still warm from her kiss, my body ached beneath the weight of hers. If, as would sometimes happen, she had the features of some woman whom I had known in waking hours, I would abandon myself altogether to the sole quest of her, like people who set out on a journey to see with their eyes some city of their desire, and imagine that one can taste in reality what has charmed one's fancy. And then, gradually, the memory of her would dissolve and vanish, until I had forgotten the girl of my dream. [RTP 1:4–5][45]

The matrix of a treacherous betrayal in love begins in this kind of fantasmatic interaction with a woman whose existence is internal to thought: the only woman available, the only one the lover will ever possess. Eve is second in the order, the woman who, in aspiring to the knowledge of good and evil, transgresses the law of God. As Adam's double, Marcel carries then the possibility of "becoming-woman" that is already within man (the *devenir-femme de l'homme*). Indeed, Marcel identifies himself with a suffering and weakened Adam: "The mist, from the moment of my awakening, had made of me, instead of the centrifugal being which one is on fine days, a man turned in on himself, longing for the chimney corner and the shared bed, a shivering Adam in quest of a sedentary Eve, in this different world" (RTP 2:358).[46] Like an androgynous amputee, Marcel feels in his body the painful lack of the one whom he no longer possesses in waking life: "O mighty attitudes of Man and Woman, in which there seeks to be united, in the innocence of the world's first days and with the humility of clay, what the Creation made separate, in which Eve is astonished and submissive before Man by whose side she awakens, as he himself, alone still, before God who has fashioned him!" (RTP 3:74).[47]

Homosexuality becomes the truth of love because of what Gilles Deleuze calls the law of the divergent series.[48] Because a work is made of up the memories of past loves out of which develop the prediction of new ones, it is a question not only of ontogenesis, in the development of an individual passion, but of phylogenesis as well: "The race of inverts, who readily link themselves with the ancient East or the golden age of Greece, might be traced back further still, to those experimental epochs in which there existed neither dioecious plants nor monosexual animals, to that initial hermaphroditism of which certain rudiments of male organs in the anatomy of women and of female organs in that of men seem still to preserve the trace" (RTP 2:653).[49]

Following natural law, the laws concerning love would be confirmed not so much in the substitution of homosexual for heterosexual partners as in the sexual inversion and exchange of roles which follow. Adding something more general, more disinterested, these laws seem to suggest that it is wiser to attach oneself to thought rather than to people who exist. A kind of

Platonist utopianism holds out the hope that finding what is hidden within the loved one will reveal some unifying principle of being. For example, from every village and city, the women of Gomorrah (having been dispersed for so long) tend to come together to reform the biblical city destroyed by God. The same tendency may be found, always intermittently, in the exiles from Sodom.

In a rhythmic movement of intermittencies, the work of art supposes and proposes a form of redemption. The proper biblical name governing this process changes ("Just as all men die in Adam, so all men will be brought to life in Christ"), [50] but within the novel it remains consistently the same: as all die in Marcel, all must relive in him. Within Marcel, however, what separates love and the work of art is that art presupposes a revelation where love demands analysis and interpretation. The essence of love sought by the jealous lover can be found only in the hermeneutic work of meaning: the jealous lover is a hermeneut for whom the signs of love, like the objects of the world, are hieroglyphs. [51] Whether in moments of joy or of pain, comprehension will never be entirely disconnected from what intelligence adds, so that even if one can separate affect and intellect for purposes of argumentation, one cannot do so and arrive at truth.

Reconstituting the unity of the other—in this instance, Albertine—implies the grasp of a truth not yet revealed: is she or is she not of Gomorrah? What the answer to this question would bring, as the revelation of meaning, is the maintenance of sexual difference in a hierarchy. The significance of woman remains enclosed like the meaning encapsulated in objects, dreamed of only in the form of sensual possession. Jealousy might become the transcendent element conferring a unified meaning on a plurality of experiences, resulting in the concept of a total person in contact with the world, but Daniel Lagache recognizes that the presumed unity of jealousy itself would become then an object of knowledge. [52]

The analogy between a work of art and love shows a rule of growth operating in each case. Just as one love is inscribed in another—as Gilberte's body and name migrate to Albertine (RTP

2:503, 548)—in which weaker loves call forth or demand greater ones (RTP 3:252), so Vinteuil's septet becomes the triumphant amplification and completion of his sonata (RTP 3:255). The narrator suggests that this weakness is a point of departure not only for love and music but also for writing: "If we were not obliged, in the interests of narrative tidiness, to confine ourselves to frivolous reasons, how many more serious reasons would enable us to demonstrate the mendacious flimsiness of the opening pages of this volume" (RTP 3:189).[53] The septet is the model for the completed work of art, the fruit of genius.[54] It is the retrospective apotheosis toward which art tends: "I wondered whether music might not be the unique example of what might have been—if the invention of language, the formation of words, the analysis of ideas had not intervened—the means of communication between souls. It is like a possibility that has come to nothing; humanity has developed along other lines, those of spoken and written language" (RTP 3:260).[55]

Swann was mistaken in having associated the little phrase with the pleasure of love, and he could not have known the septet, this bit of revealed truth, because he had died before its inaugural performance. It was, in any case, "a truth that . . . he could not have used, for though the phrase perhaps symbolised a call, it was incapable of creating new powers and making Swann the writer that he was not" (RTP 3:911).[56] Having known Swann, the narrator understands what it means to love a woman in an artistic way. Marcel does not repeat this mistake: for him, love for Albertine is not mediated through a work of art. Nevertheless, during the performance of the septet, two ideas simultaneously absorb him: everything else seems extraordinarily insignificant by comparison with this vast work; at the same time, in an uncomfortable association, Albertine, the sole person whose memory is mingled with this music, comes to mind. No longer are her sexual tastes an issue; rather, the question is how it is that this "revelation"—the strangest one he has ever received, a form of joy as yet unknown—came from Vinteuil, Vinteuil who at his death had left a work of "illegible" nota-tions. How could Vinteuil have passed from this "empty form" to the "frame of a *chef d'oeuvre*" which is the plenitude of life?

However routine, banal, and insignificant the story of an individual's life may appear, compared with the ideal of aesthetic unity and transcendence, unexpected relations crop up between the two. Just as the network of relations leading to the experience of the hero's discovery of a vocation can be traced back to Swann, so Vinteuil's work was redeemed by the young woman present in the scene at Montjouvain. She spent years "unravelling the cryptic scroll left by him, by establishing the correct reading of those illegible hieroglyphs, she had the consolation of ensuring an immortal and compensatory glory for the composer over whose last years she had cast such a shadow" (RTP 3:263; see Chapter 2).[57] Thanks to her labor, what had become possible was the knowledge of the complete work of Vinteuil, [58] a work whose future glory was now assured. What also became possible through this work was the strange calling which now the narrator never ceased to hear: "the promise and proof that there existed something other, realisable no doubt through art" (RTP 3:265).[59] It is this promise that he longs to fulfill; it allows him to measure, in pleasure as in love, the distance left to go in his still unfinished work.

Beyond the scene at Montjouvain, beyond the fantasies of Albertine in the arms of Mlle Vinteuil, the substance of the book comes neither from the accumulation of diverse perceptions, facts, and feelings nor from a causal explanation of the transformation of random events into a necessary structure. It comes from "readings" of the scene. The first took place on a day at Monjouvain when the narrator found himself hidden behind a bush. It was then that the voyeur had "dangerously" widened the fateful path to knowledge, just as he had done in listening to Swann's tale of love. Thereafter, he had to admit that jealousy was not only love's shadow; more important, it was the condition upon which the realization of the work depended. So in a sense Albertine too becomes the redeemer of a work, not of Vinteuil's but his.

What this scene shows, as a model for so many others, is that the way leading to the writer's vocation is strewn with interpretations that can never fix the meaning or the essence of what is unique: "Everything [is] so interwoven and superimposed in our inner life" (RTP 3:255).[60] Remembering people, places, and events is at once a highly individual act and one of the most common of all. Within the novel, reminiscence gives access to a past hitherto closed off and stages the encounter between program and event; the associations surrounding each of these singular memories create the possibility of displacing the basis of knowledge.

The abandonment of love may seem to allow for the passage from incompleteness to the whole in the absorption with the work of art. But it does something else as well. The author, the one who lays the foundations of the work and makes it grow, leads a double life: in love and in art. Since jealousy is "a demon that cannot be exorcised, but constantly reappears in new incarnations" (RTP 3:98–99),[61] what tortures the narrator is not so much imagining Albertine's infinite "inner" inaccessibility (she is "a person who inwardly reached to infinity" [RTP 3:393]);[62] what tortures him most is *his own desire to give shape to new novels*. Although he decides only in the final volume (but perhaps also from *Within a Budding Grove* on) that it was with her that he wanted to have his work (RTP 3:915),[63] to have done with Albertine was, contrary to the theory of the work of art, to have done with the work itself and, beyond that, with himself as subject. "As there is no knowledge, one might almost say that there is no jealousy, save of oneself" (RTP 3:392–93).[64]

IN PURSUIT OF KNOWLEDGE

Because subject and object (like love and art) cannot be separate, there is an instability in the hermeneutic function of jealousy. At times, meaning comes about through comprehension, and reading renders a quasi-transparent metaphor for the completeness and finality of writing. Errors can be corrected in this view, texts revised in contemplation of some definitive version. At other times, as with Albertine's false resurrection in a telegram (which cleverly transforms the name Gilberte to Albertine), everything "springs from an original mistake in our premises" (RTP 3:671).[65] In this view, there is no first truth to be found, and all reading is constitutively misreading.

Jealousy, as an incipient theory of knowledge, allows us to address this problem. Jealous love is not a single, indivisible, and seamless passion; it is composed of an infinity of successive loves and ephemeral jealousies which, because of their vast uninterrupted number, lend an illusion of continuity and unity. Arranging facts, stories, and events in a hierarchy that distinguishes between true and false is a necessary step in the process of knowing and interpreting the other. But the greatest error, Proust maintains, is to assume that everything in the loved one's life is identical to the part that the lover knows; for example, Swann deludes himself into believing that what is visible to him is the whole truth about Odette, as a part leads to a whole. Inversely, though still within the same logic, one might believe that the signs of love lie only in that they hide what they express, which means that the truth of language can be found systematically behind the lies, and there is a truth. M. de Guermantes conveys this process parodically when he sends a telegram, the prototype for all who wish to cancel a date: "Cannot come, lie follows" (RTP 3:721).[66]

Odette has a system for lying that follows a similar formula. Into every fabricated story she tells Swann she inserts a small, innocuous—but also incongruous—truth. This little fact, which is meant to authenticate the fiction by anchoring it in "reality," ends by having the opposite effect: it betrays her. No matter how true the fact, it is like excess material that detaches itself from the logic of the fiction and draws a line between truth and falsity: the recourse to truth, intended to authenticate the lie, shows up difference within the story. What Swann understands when his mistress Odette lies to him is not only that she is lying but that there is a truth hidden behind the lie. The key to Odette's discourse comes from understanding the hierarchy of thought in which falsehood remains separate from truth.

Albertine lies differently. Plausibility is what counts for her, and truth emerges only involuntarily because her ruses are impenetrable. Over and over, Marcel is thwarted in his ability to "know" Albertine's "truth" and to possess her totally. From her, Marcel learns not to look for "real life and thought . . . in the direct statements" with which others "suppl[y] him with their own free will." He has come "to attach importance . . . only to disclosures that are not a rational and analytical expression of the truth; the words themselves [do] not enlighten [him] unless they [are] interpreted" (RTP 3:83).[67] Whereas Odette's truth can be found by reading her statements backward, because interpretation presupposes the return to a fixed system of meaning, Albertine appears unknowable in her changeability, and her ruses seem as innumerable as his jealousy is insatiable: both without end. "When she was lying, her story erred either from inadequacy, omission, implausibility, or on the contrary from a surfeit of petty details intended to make it seem plausible" (RTP 3:176).[68]

Thus, when Albertine reverses her confession about her relations with Mlle Vinteuil and her friend, revealing that she hardly knew the young women, all evidence of an empirical sort seems to crumble. Rather than invalidating everything that has happened until then, her admission confirms the completely "mental" structure of jealousy as the vain pursuit of a final form of knowledge. Albertine's argument appeals to values: lying had only one objective—to bring her, through Mlle Vinteuil, closer to music as the most important of artistic forms. Through this attempt to essentialize love through art, more clever than Swann's, she had "as so often happens, reached the truth by a different road from that which she had intended to take" (RTP 3:342).[69]

Her error of interpretation comes from misjudging the effect of the confession: what compulsively occupies Marcel has nothing to do with her lack of musical culture and everything to do with her "disreputable associations." "What had abruptly drawn me closer to her—far more, fused indissolubly with her—was not the expectation of a pleasure . . . but the grip of an agonising pain" (RTP 3:342).[70] Where pleasure indicated the path to truth, now pain and suffering draw him into a labyrinth in which the alternation between avowal and disavowal does not lead back to a first truth. This alternation seems to come from another order, one far more troubling, which is neither that of universal principles nor that of an essential structure.

The way in which each of these women lies, however, determines the nature of truth in each case. The question that arises from Albertine's form of lying is this: what would it mean and what would happen if there were no overall system of lying? What kind of truth could there be, how would one interpret the signs of love, and what status would jealousy have in the work?

In the 1987–89 Pléiade edition, *The Fugitive* is a work in which even syntax disintegrates, so corrosive is the inability to know. In it, the interpretive powers of the subject (Marcel), which require the culmination of meaning in comprehension by the intelligence, fail. This is why the impasse created by Albertine's lies is so painful. "It is . . . one of the most terrible things for the lover that whereas particular details—which only experiment or espionage, among so many possible realisations, would ever make known to him—are so difficult to discover, the truth on the other hand is so easy to detect or merely to sense" (RTP 3:83–84).[71] How to go beyond the impasse—in which truth and lying cannot immediately be placed in hierarchic order, and thought understood according to an enveloping meaning—is a question exacerbated by the separate 1987 Grasset edition of *Albertine disparue*. In this volume there is a major change: Proust makes an important addition that I deal with in this chapter, and some important deletions that I take up in the next. He adds a fact concerning Albertine (and Montjouvain, indirectly) in a telegram from Mme Bontemps. In the Pléiade edition, this telegram reads: "My poor friend, our little Albertine is no more. Forgive me for breaking this terrible news to you who were so fond of her. She was thrown by her horse against a tree while she was out riding" (RTP 3:485). To this, in the separate edition, Proust adds that Albertine was riding *near the Vivonne*.[72] Albertine's denial that she was a friend of Mlle Vinteuil's and her

death in proximity to Montjouvain do not add up to a fortuitous contradiction. The narrator reconstructs: it was the night
that he had gone to see the Verdurins, the very night he told her
he wanted to leave her, that she had lied about her relations with
Mlle Vinteuil. From the "insolent and blossoming cortège"
(RTP 3:61),[73] the memory of Albertine now is associated with the
Guermantes' Way, the Vivonne, and the water lilies (RTP 1:166,
169). As the narrator comments in a part that is cut from the
Grasset version, "Every event is like a mould of a particular
shape, and, whatever it may be, it imposes, upon the series of
incidents which it has interrupted and seems to conclude, a pattern which we believe to be the only possible one, because we do
not know the other which might have been substituted for it"
(RTP 3:519).[74] The suggestion that events belong to an irrevers-
ible history in individual thought is contradicted by the publication not only of the separate volume of *Albertine disparue* but
of the many variants in the other editions as well. Each text is
like an event and a series that might have been.

The question is, then, what does that brief addition *change*?
Must one now rethink all of Proust because a line has been
added? Does it tighten the unity of the work, as the editors of
the Grasset edition would have it, demonstrating the force of
the project to dominate even in the afterlife of the text? The
answer comes, in a sense, in the very next paragraph when the
narrator points out the force of any gap in memory or thinking.
Trying to recall suddenly how Albertine had reacted when confronted, whether she had blushed, he realizes that he cannot call
up the image at will. "And when later on, eager to discover a
truth, we work back from deduction to deduction, leafing
through our memory like a sheaf of written evidence, when we
arrive at that sentence, at that gesture, we find it impossible to
remember, and we repeat the process a score of times, in vain:
the road goes no further" (RTP 3:520).[75] Each text constitutes an
endpoint and a link with others. As an endpoint, it cannot be
generalized beyond its appearance within the text. Taken in a
chain of other events, its meaning can be generalized.

The proximity of the Vivonne to Montjouvain leads to the conclusion that there could no longer be any doubt about the nature of the friendship between Mlle Vinteuil and Albertine. But if this "discovery" leads to certainty by association (of places, names, and people), it does not erase the relativity of all spatiotemporal coordinates:

> Distances are only the relation of space to time and vary with it. We express the difficulty that we have in getting to a place in a system of miles or kilometres which becomes false as soon as that difficulty decreases. Art is modified by it also, since a village which seemed to be in a different world from some other village becomes its neighbour in a landscape whose dimensions are altered. In any case, to learn that there may perhaps exist a universe in which two and two make five and a straight line is not the shortest distance between two points would have astonished Albertine far less than to hear the driver say that it was easy to go in a single afternoon to Saint-Jean and la Raspelière. [RTP 2:1029][76]

Thus, for many opposed towns, "prisoners hitherto as hermetically confined in the cells of distinct days as long ago were Méséglise and Guermantes" (RTP 2:1029),[77] the "absolute" limit would be crossed, their absolute value displaced into a relative series. From Vinteuil on the Méséglise side to the Vivonne on the Guermantes' side, where Albertine will land in Gomorrah, the future work (whose discovery is made on the side of the Guermantes) emerges in the revisions of a self-displacing program. To understand what this means in terms of the overall project and the deletions from *Albertine disparue* requires another take on the relationship to Albertine, the subject addressed in the final chapter.

6

P roust puts an image through successive states by *an associative process* that comes to define the artist's mode of thinking and asserts that a writer reasons—that is to say, he goes astray—only when he has not the strength to force himself to make an impression pass through all the successive states that culminate in its fixation, its expression. This process, repeated throughout the novel, allows events to emerge as new experience, to develop and pass through various stages and then be relived in memory. Because of this, the experience of love, no matter how exceptional it may seem, is subjected to an inexorable law of memory and forgetting. There is only one moment that prepares an involuntary memory, the moment when in Venice with his mother the narrator experiences the sensations of the uneven paving stones. Within the whole novel only this passage, to the best of my knowledge, undergoes the kind of radical excision that the Grasset edition of *Albertine disparue* presents. What is the importance of this passage? And why, one wonders, would Proust cut a passage that he had so carefully prepared? To begin to answer these questions, I examine a sequence of letters and texts that lead up to, describe, and then return to this event.

From the initial description in the preface of *Contre Sainte-Beuve* to the courtyard of the Guermantes mansion at the end of *Remembrance*, little has changed in the recounting of the moments of involuntary memory. Marcel puts his foot "on a stone which was slightly lower than its neighbour" and feels the same flush of joy as when he saw trees, viewed the twin steeples of Martinville, and tasted the flavor of a madeleine dipped in tea. The emotion is the same; only the images have changed: "a profound azure intoxicat[es]" his eyes (RTP 3:899), and he recognizes the vision: it is Venice. "The sensation which I had once experienced as I stood upon two uneven stones in the baptistery of St Mark's had . . . restored to me complete with all the other sensations linked on that day to that particular sensation, all of which had been waiting in their place—from which with imperious suddenness a chance happening had caused them to emerge—in the series of forgotten days" (RTP 3:900).[1]

A few preliminary comments are necessary to a reading of the pages of those forgotten days, described in *Time Regained*. In a letter of February 6, 1916, to Maria de Madrazo, one of Reynaldo Hahn's older sisters and a relative of the Venetian clothes designer Mariano Fortuny, Proust writes: "Many times I have wanted to ask you questions about feminine clothes, not for any mistress, but for the heroines of the book. . . . Do you know . . . if in Venise there are paintings (I would like some titles) in which there are coats or dresses from which Fortuny might be or might have been inspired. I would like to find a reproduction of such a painting, and I would see if it could inspire me."[2]

Proust learns that it was Vittore Carpaccio's work the designer had copied, and he writes again in a letter dated several days later, February 17, that he would like to know exactly which painting and which coat in the painting might have inspired Fortuny. He requests a book about him, or any precise information concerning a given dress or coat, and then he asks in passing whether Fortuny ever did shoes, hoping perhaps to enhance the scene in which the paving stones bring Venice back to him in involuntary memory. Proust explains that these questions concern the creation of his character, his Albertine, and outlines the sequences of the story:

> This desire to adorn her . . . with the memory of her finery, during a trip to Venice, after she is dead and where the sight of certain paintings will be painful for me; it is thus that I have constructed things (but don't speak about it except to Fortuny if you wish). In the beginning of my second volume, a great artist, whose name is fictive and who symbolizes the great painter in my work just as Vinteuil symbolizes the great Franckian musician, says in front of Albertine (who I do not yet know will one day be my adored fiancée) that from what they say, some artist has discovered the secret of ancient Venetian fabrics, etc. He [the Venetian artist-designer] is Fortuny.
>
> When Albertine (third volume) is engaged to me, she speaks to me about Fortuny's dresses, . . . and I surprise her by giving her several of them. The very brief description of these dresses illustrates our love scenes . . . and since as long as she is living I do not know to what extent I love her, these dresses evoke Venice for me: the desire to go there, to which she is an obstacle . . . etc. The novel follows its course: she leaves me; she dies. A long time later, after great suffering followed by a fading of memory, I go to Venice, but in the paintings of xxx (let's say Carpaccio, since you tell me that Fortuny was inspired by *Carpaccio*), I rediscover a certain dress that I had given her. Before, this dress evoked Venice for me and made me want to leave Albertine; now the Carpaccio in which I see the dress evokes Albertine and makes Venice painful.[3]

He declares that the Fortuny leitmotif, by turns sensual, poetic, and painful, plays a "capital" role in the book, although he has not as yet developed it extensively. He declines the offers of both Madame Straus and Madame de Madrazo to show him their Fortuny coats. On March 9 he borrows a book on Carpaccio.[4] He cannot exactly remember the colors in the life of Saint Ursula cycle and asks Maria de Madrazo in a letter written the same day if she would request that Fortuny give a very unimaginative description of the coat in the Carpaccio painting—colors, design, material—and verify that it is the figure with back turned whose coat he copied.[5]

Venice becomes important early in *Swann's Way*. Marcel plans to go there during Easter week. A few words from his father about the weather suffice to put him into such a state of ecstasy that a feeling of miraculous disembodiment comes over him, followed rather quickly by a vague desire to vomit. He is then sent to bed and forbidden by the doctor to go either to Venice or even to the theater to see the actress he had longed to see: La Berma. The feelings of anticipation of these separate events, going to Venice and going to the theater, are related by a common sense of pleasure. Seeing the Carpaccio paintings in San Giorgio dei Schiavoni would, he is sure, give him a feeling as exquisite as hearing La Berma recite the lines from Racine's *Phèdre*.[6] However, the feelings of anticipation and pleasure depend on the specifics of each association: it could not be Carpaccio in any gallery that would catch his imagination, or La Berma reciting her lines in any play; it would have to be Carpaccio in Venice and La Berma in *Phèdre*.[7]

In like manner, Fortuny's dresses and coats would mark off the singular brilliance of artistic creation in clothes design related to his Venetian imaginings, because they were not only "faithfully antique but markedly original" (RTP 3:376).[8] They bring back a Venice, long since perished, "where everything was being reborn, evoked and *linked* together by the splendour and the swarming life of the city, in the *piecemeal* reappearance of the still-surviving fabrics worn by the Doges' ladies" (RTP 3:376; emphasis added). Fragments from the past come together in the links established by the sight of the clothes.

As promised in the epistolary sketch, the narrator buys a Fortuny dress for Albertine while she is imprisoned in his apartment. One in particular is blue and gold; it is so reminiscent of

Venice that it reminds him of a trip he has sacrificed for her. Afraid to take Albertine with him to Venice because he fears her sexual inclinations, he is for the same reason equally afraid to leave her behind.[9] So as he blocks her desires, he blocks his own and makes himself as much a prisoner as she is in his apartment.

> If I had never seen Venice, I had dreamed of it incessantly since those Easter holidays which, when still a boy, I had been going to spend there. . . . The Fortuny gown which Albertine was wearing that evening seemed to me the tempting phantom of that invisible Venice. It was covered with Arab ornamentation, like the Venetian palaces hidden like sultan's wives behind a screen of pierced stone, like the bindings in the Ambrosian Library, like the columns from which the oriental birds that symbolised alternatively life and death were repeated in the shimmering fabric, of an intense blue which, as my eyes drew nearer, turned into a malleable gold by those same transmutations which, before an advancing gondola, change into gleaming metal the azure of the Grand Canal. [RTP 3:401][10]

Embracing her in the dress arouses his desire to go to Venice, as though he could reach the materiality of the city through her, just as earlier at Balbec he seemed able embrace the beach: "I kissed her . . . pressing to my heart the shimmering golden azure of the Grand Canal and the mating birds, symbols of death and resurrection" (RTP 3:406).[11] The birds are associated several times with the Fortuny dresses worn by Albertine. Clothes forgotten for centuries are reborn, as Elstir predicts in *Within a Budding Grove*, in the sumptuous dresses created by Fortuny. And the reason is the law of return written in Saint Mark's.[12] A little further on the memory of old desire, recently "reawakened by the Fortuny gown in blue and gold," evokes the name of Venice and its luxuriant springtime: "a decanted springtime, which is reduced to its own essences" translating a "blue and virginal water" (RTP 3:419).[13]

It is after this passage that the narrator calls for a guidebook of Venice and a timetable, and Françoise announces that Albertine has gone from his apartment for good. After the departure and then the death of Albertine, Marcel no longer desires to go to Venice. Only later is he able to measure his own indifference to her when he finds himself in Venice with his mother, during the episode mapped out in the sequence of letters cited above. It is then that Venice and the Combray of his childhood come to be superimposed (RTP 3:629), as the three women—Albertine, his mother, and his grandmother—become associated in blue.[14]

Marcel recounts going upstairs in his hotel in Venice to get notebooks for his project on Ruskin and being struck by the feeling of sea air coming in his window. The warmth of the sun and the coolness of the shade bring recollections of Combray as he descends the marble staircase to go out with his mother. They would set out for Saint Mark's by gondola: "The church represented for me not simply a monument but the terminus of a voyage on these vernal, maritime waters, with which, I felt, St Mark's formed an indivisible and living whole" (RTP 3:660).[15]

He and his mother enter the baptistery, "treading underfoot the marble and glass mosaics of the paving" in front of them. The wide arcades' curved pink surfaces "slightly warped by time" gave the church "the appearance of having been built of a soft and malleable substance like the wax in a giant honeycomb, and, where time ha[d] shrivelled and hardened the material and artists ha[d] embellished it with gold tracery, of being the precious binding, in the finest Cordoba leather, of the colossal Gospel of Venice" (RTP 3:661).[16] Seeing that Marcel needed to stand for a long time gazing at these mosaics representing the Baptism of Christ (a symbol of resurrection),[17] and "feeling the icy coolness that pervaded the baptistery," his mother threw a shawl over his shoulders.[18] The same gesture of cloaking is repeated by Albertine, Fortuny, and the narrator. Shawls and coats are taken to be interchangeable in cloaking, though their provenance is critical, as we shall see.[19]

At this moment in his description, the narrator changes subjects brusquely as something Albertine said at Balbec comes back to him, and here begins the key to Proust's theory of ekphrasis. She had, so he thought, revealed "one of those *insub-*

stantial illusions which clutter the minds of so many people who do not *think clearly* when she used to speak of the pleasure—to [his] mind baseless—that she would derive from seeing works of art with [Marcel]" (RTP 3:661). To this notion, he gave no credence at the time. "I felt [pleasure] myself in front of beautiful things only if I was alone or pretended to be alone and did not speak" (RTP 2:1027).[20] But today he is sure that the pleasure does exist less in seeing than in having seen something beautiful with a "particular" person. Far from being the property of any "particular" person, however, this process of interpretation is later generalized to a tradition and hermeneutic history: "Certain people, whose minds are prone to mystery, like to believe that objects retain something of the eyes which have looked at them, that old buildings and pictures appear to us not as they originally were but beneath a perceptible veil woven for them over the centuries by the love and contemplation of millions of admirers" (RTP 3:920).[21] This visual hermeneutics is one in which relinquishing the hope of finding any original object is compensated for by the objectification of meaning in time. "This fantasy, if you transpose it into the domain of what is for each one of us the sole reality, the domain of his own sensibility, becomes the truth" (RTP 3:920).[22]

It is the passage from private to public, particular to general, that provides objectification; the objectification in this case can become meaningful only because at its inception there was symbiosis between the narrator and his mother.[23] The time has now come when "remembering the baptistery of St Mark's—contemplating the waters of the Jordan in which St John immerses Christ" while the gondola awaits him and his mother at the landing of the Piazzetta—is no longer a matter of indifference to him: "Beside me in that cool penumbra, there should have been a woman draped in her mourning with the respectful and enthusiastic fervour of the old woman in Carpaccio's *St Ursula* in the Accademia, and that that woman, with her red cheeks and sad eyes and in her black veils, whom nothing can ever remove from that softly lit sanctuary of St Mark's where I am always sure to find her because she has her place reserved there as immutably as a mosaic, should be my mother" (RTP 3:661).²⁴ It is this passage that fixes the mother in mosaic and becomes the point of reference for involuntary memory.²⁵ What is evoked in the purity of the memory later on is complete recall, knowledge as a vision, an epiphany, not a vision of particulars, in the restoration of Venice.

The sequence from mosaic to mother to memory differs from the passage that follows, in which Carpaccio provides the connection to Albertine. The narrator begins: "Carpaccio, *as it happens*, who was the painter we visited most readily when I was not working in St Mark's, almost succeeded one day in reviving my love for Albertine." That day, he was seeing for the first time the painting that he calls *The Patriarch of Grado Exorcising a Demoniac*, now titled *The Legend of the True Cross: The Healing of the Demoniac* (1495).

> "I looked at the marvellous rose-pink and violet sky and the tall encrusted chimneys silhouetted against it, their flared stacks, blossoming like red tulips, reminiscent of so many Whistlers of Venice. Then my eyes travelled from the old wooden Rialto to that fifteenth-century Ponte Vecchio with its marble palaces decorated with gilded capitals, and returned to the canal on which the boats are manoeuvered by adolescents in pink jackets and plumed toques, the spitting image of those avowedly [*vraiment*] inspired by Carpaccio in that dazzling *Legend of St. Joseph* by Sert, Strauss and Kessler." [RTP 3:661–62]

Proust's evocation of Richard Strauss's ballet *The Legend of Joseph* brings together a network of important associations. The 1914 performance of the ballet situated this biblical story (Genesis 39) in the context of Renaissance Venice.²⁶ Proust saw the evocation of this music as a counter to the narrator's painful forgetting of Albertine. The juxtaposition of Albertine and the Joseph of the biblical story had already occurred in *Within a Budding Grove:* a discussion between the hero and Elstir of the façade of the church in Balbec, described as a "vast theological poem," immediately precedes a view of Albertine from the painter's studio. It provides an oblique displacement from the image of the church to that of the coat via the relation to woman (Albertine, his grandmother, and his mother) in the depths of an internalized Venice.[27] And it prepares the dramatic moment in the description of the painting by Carpaccio in what follows:

"Finally, before leaving the picture, my eyes came back to the shore, swarming with the everyday Venetian life of the period. I looked at the barber wiping his razor, at the negro humping his barrel, at the Muslims conversing, at the noblemen in wide-sleeved brocade and damask robes and hats of cerise velvet, and *suddenly I felt a slight gnawing at my heart*. On the back of one of the *Compagni della Calza*[28] identifiable from the emblem, embroidered in gold and pearls on their sleeves or their collars, of the merry confraternity to which they were affiliated, I had just recognized the *cloak which Albertine had put on to come with me to Versailles* in an open carriage on the evening when I so little suspected that scarcely fifteen hours separated me from the moment of her departure from my house. Always ready for anything, when I had asked her to come out with me on that melancholy evening which she was to describe in her last letter as 'doubly crepuscular in that dusk was falling and we were about to part,' she had flung over her shoulders a Fortuny cloak which she had taken away with her next day and which I had never thought of since. It was from this Carpaccio picture that that inspired son of Venice had taken it, it was from the shoulders of this *Compagno della Calza* that he had removed it in order to drape it over the shoulders of so many Parisian women who were certainly unaware, as I had been until then, that the model for it existed in a group of noblemen in the foreground of the *Patriarch of Grado* in a room in the Accademia in Venice. I had recognized it down to the last detail, and, that cloak having restored to me as I looked at it the eyes and the heart of him who had set out that evening with Albertine for Versailles, I was overcome for a few moments by a vague feeling of desire and melancholy." [RTP 3:662][29]

Proust's description here follows a pattern developed throughout, in which what Ruskin called "the accidental connections of ideas and memories with material things,"—in this case a coat seen in a painting by Carpaccio—bring forth the pain or pleasure associated with them.[30] What is at stake here is not just the loss and destruction of the narrator's love for Albertine, the process of forgetting, of which the coat or dress appears to be a fragmentary emblem; it is the way in which the artist resurrects the fragmentary past through memory—of people and places in their relationship to art—in the attempt to create a new whole.

Proust explicitly attempts to discover something that addresses itself to his imagination, some general element common to several aspects and yet truer than their sum in the link of Fortuny's coats and dress to the painting by Carpaccio. Proust superimposes two movements in the work, two visions of the totality, that reproduce the dominant thinking patterns of the nineteenth and twentieth centuries and are reflected in three images: the cathedral, the dress and the stew. The only real unity, Proust writes in a sketch, is a "harmonious diversity" that comes from the "differential quality in a discordant identity."[31]

Although the cathedral as a monument—albeit often unfinished[32]—inscribes history in stones of grandeur and helps the narrator fix his mother in memory, the passage discussed above provides an image for the organization of the book and reflects the displacement of models for the book to be announced only a few pages later when the narrator writes: *"Pinning here and there an extra page, I should construct my book, I dare not say ambitiously like a cathedral, but quite simply like a dress"* (RTP 3:1090; emphasis added).[33] The displacement of images had been prepared by the reference to Strauss through the associative network mentioned above. Its effect is to weaken the unitary vision of the novel, granting to it an open-ended construction in multiple images: "So that this book, I was building it like a gown (enumeration of other images) and gathering it like a jelly (add this image)."[34]

As the temporal incarnation of the transcendent truth, the cathedral is a monument in time (in the structure and layers of architecture that attest to different periods) which endures and pays tribute to a higher order. It is identified through the heterogeneity of time with the logos as totality. The abandonment of this image does not mean that art replaces religion. Rather, the metamorphosis of the image that the narrator announces here serves as a diagnosis for a recognized ill: the disuse of the religious monument as the sole emblem for art.[35] His constant allusions to the way in which churches and cathedrals enter into everyday perception parallel in many ways the shading of light in Monet's series of cathedrals, which never appear the same.

Early on in the novel, it appeared that associative thought could not threaten the disintegration of the image of the cathedral. In Bergotte's work, for example, the invocation of a cathedral became the occasion for a creative outpouring: "In [Bergotte's] later books, if he had hit upon some great truth, or upon the name of an historic cathedral, he would break off his narrative, and in an invocation, an apostrophe, a long prayer, would give free rein to those exhalations which, in the earlier volumes, had been immanent in his prose" (RTP 1:102).[36] In a lighter and somewhat more equivocal vein, the image returns when during the performance of Vinteuil's septet, this model of a *grand plan d'ensemble*, Madame Verdurin histrionically buries her face in her hands: "Did the Mistress wish to indicate by this meditative attitude that she considered herself as though in church, and regarded this music as no different from the most sublime of prayers? Did she wish, as some people do in church, to hide from prying eyes, out of modesty or shame, their presumed fervour or their culpable inattention or an irresistible urge to sleep?" (RTP 3:253).[37] The supposition regarding an "urge to sleep" arises because a rhythmic, nonmusical noise is detected—coming not from Mme Verdurin but from her dog. Even Charlus is somewhat comic in the "religious silence" he imposes on others with his presence. So the question modulates from "What literature could take the place or fulfill the function of the Bible?" to "How can one transfer to other images the force of this one?"

From the inception of the project, the mention of cathedrals evokes the image of a book to be understood. Speaking of the porch of a Gothic cathedral—and here he thinks of Amiens—Proust means the Bible.[38] In a letter to Jean de Saigueron in 1919 he says that he had never told anyone else, but he had wanted to take the names for his work from the different parts of the cathedral: porch, stained glass windows of the apse. He gave up these architectural titles because they seemed, he said, too pretentious.[39]

Proust writes notes on the two images: "Literature there must be something in the things that one means suggesting that it has been shelled like peas as well as built, let's not say pretentiously a cathedral but a dress (for the composition) clearing the roads and laying a bridge (less good)."[40] It will be recalled that in his early plan for the book sketched in *Contre Saint-Beuve*, he had thought to "build" one of two articles, a term that in French (*bâtir*) brings together architecture and sewing.[41]

Now the image of the dress, with its seams and patches, has been diversely interpreted. Gilles Deleuze argues that time cannot be conceived as a whole because it is time that prevents the very perception of wholeness: "The world has no significant contents according to which we could systematize it, nor ideal significations according to which we could regulate and hierarchize it. Nor has the subject an associative chain which could surround the world or stand for its unity."[42] Jean-Pierre Richard's analysis of dresses is consonant with his general position that Proust's work always moves from fragmentation to unity. He suggests that the description of dress is a gesture of unification that gives an enveloping form to the discontinuity of things. The whims of fashion in general may be seen in the same way. The early figures of fashion—specifically in Odette's ways of dressing—are dominated by unbridled heterogeneity, cutting up the notion of a line and dislocating the possibility of a personally defined style.[43] Odette appears as a kind of free-floating collage: she has "the appearance of being composed of several

disparate pieces which there was no individuality to bind together" (RTP 1:665).[44] Even in moving from a fragmented to a more
simple and unified style, Odette still retains vestiges of "de-
throned fashions." Her style of dressing sums up a whole historical period: "She need only 'hold out' like this for a little longer
and young men attempting to understand her *theory of dress*
would say: 'Madame Swann is quite a period in herself, isn't
she?' " (RTP 1:666).[45] Comparing her way of dressing to a fine
literary style that "superimposes different forms" and yet is
"strengthened by a tradition that lies concealed behind them,"
the narrator remarks that "half-tinted memories" of past fashion
"kept alive beneath the concrete form the unfinished likeness of
other, older forms which one would not have been able to find
effectively reproduced by the milliner or the dressmaker, but
about which one's thoughts incessantly hovered" (RTP 1:666).[46]
As in a style composed through the association of memories,
one does not see the palimpsest; one associates from it through
almost imperceptible reminiscences from the past, so that this
or that detail may evoke another from its earlier existence. But
Odette does not dress simply for the "comfort or adornment of
her body," the narrator remarks. She is "surrounded by her gar-
ments as by the delicate and spiritualized machinery of a whole
civilization" (RTP 1:667). This attempt at what Richard calls a
"formalizing federation," where unity and variety coexist, is the
mark of Odette's being. Not only does she sum up an entire
period; she is several periods at once.[47] But what is the status of
Odette as a model for the unity of being? As important neither
as the hero nor even as Swann, she is the object of Swann's love,
a secondary other whose very unity might be questioned as
being of any value at all. Her truth, like Swann's, takes on meaning by analogy.

On numerous occasions the narrator compares flowers to
dresses,[48] and in one instance, the flower, the dress, and association all come together in Odette: "Suddenly, on the gravelled
path, unhurrying, cool, luxuriant, Mme Swann would appear,
blossoming out in a costume which was never twice the same
but which I remember as being typically mauve; then she would

hoist and unfurl at the end of its long stalk, just at the moment when her radiance was at its zenith, the silken banner of a wide parasol of a shade that matched the showering petals of her dress" (RTP 1:683).[49] Her dress became "like an organized and living form."[50] The image of the stem or stalk returns (see Chapter 1) at a turningpoint where the theory of the dress superimposes styles and forms.

Despite their importance, or perhaps because of it, the flower and the dress seem incapable of setting the scene for involuntary memory.[51] They serve as mere mnemonic devices for recalling the past. Yet the narrator compares the book bindings collected from a certain period to the function of the dress: "Like the dress which a woman was wearing when we saw her for the first time, they would help me to rediscover the love that I then had, the beauty on which I have since superimposed so many . . . images" (RTP 3:923).[52] But the more reasoned the image, the narrator concludes, the less it is loved.

If we understand the construction of the book and the images that reflect it as an attempt to constitute the subject, then the coat or dress in its relation to the essence of being recalls the analogy put forth by Socrates in the *Phaedo* concerning the status of the soul after death: when an old weaver dies, the coat he has woven remains, whole and undecayed. The question is whether the man or the coat endures longer. While the weaver survives many coats, he is outlived by only one: his last. In like manner, the soul wears out many bodies, which simply means that if the body decays, the soul weaves another garment and repairs the waste. This argument precedes Socrates' death by only a few pages, and it is following this discussion that Socrates reminds his friends that all knowledge is recollection. To learn, in short, is to remember. It is a process of reminiscence that works by association and becomes, through argumentation, analogy.

The move toward a humble form of art in the image of the dress suggests once again that the essence of art may arise not out of universals but out of an individuating process: the ability of the artist to find links and new combinations of affect through associations with art and the past. Like Madame Swann's dress, a beautiful style is meant to superimpose different forms, which at once fortify a hidden tradition and exhibit what is new.[53] The loss of universal or objective meaning is transformed into a sense of affective gain in the description of particulars that are often not intelligible upon the moment. As in those Byzantine churches that Proust describes in his essay on Ruskin, where the "biblical texts are accompanied by lettering forming a quotation from the Gospel or the prophecies," the dress figures Delphic wisdom in its materiality, through the search for knowledge of the self.[54] Appearing as a mere emblem of fashion, the dress suggests, in its link to Venice and his mother, the right both to the wholeness of being, as the essence of art, and to the imperative of singularity in the power of associative thinking. It translates the "soul" of the artist through a fragmentary process of connecting images, which in the end leads to the miracle of analogy in the creation of the work of art. For the generic concept of man in the Platonic tradition is properly his soul. To love the material object is to love the things of the material world over those of the spirit. Commenting on Ruskin's work, Proust speaks of loving the robe of an actress or society lady because a given painter has painted or a given writer described it, but he observes that once the spirit of the person has left the object, it is no more than a sign devoid of signification. To continue to adore the object is idolatry.

The third generalizing image for the work of art is culinary. In a letter to Céline Cottin, Proust comments that he would like his writing to be as good as her stewed beef with carrots: his style as brilliant as her jelly, his ideas as tasty as her carrots and as nourishing and fresh as her meat.[55] The stew makes its appearance in the first volume, when Françoise becomes the "Michael Angelo of our kitchen," and reappears in the final volume when the narrator discusses how the many images from life (women, churches, sonatas) go into making one image in the work of art.[56] Proust serves up Françoise's stew: just as the jelly shouldn't stick and the beef takes on the perfume of the carrots, so every element in the work of art is changed by every other element and contributes to the whole without ever losing its own properties.[57] In one description of the blossoming girls the group is likened to a trembling and glittering jelly, [58] and in another the narrator compares a menu to the four leaves that were sculpted in the thirteenth century on the porch of the cathedrals: they reflected the rhythm of the seasons and the episodes of life.[59]

Like Ruskin, Proust maintains that what endures in every particular element of a work of art, however beautiful, is the part of infinite beauty it incarnates.[60] It is not because the artist places a beautiful object in a painting that the painting is beautiful, or because the aesthetic object is intrinsically "interesting," but rather because the object is linked in the artist's thought to a past from which it cannot escape. If Proust did not consider the subject in art to be of great importance, he warned that the artist must nevertheless shun the sophism of freedom, the notion that he creates his art personally without influence. Rather, Proust suggests, it is when the artist believes he or she is *not* creating an independent work, *not* arbitrarily choosing an object, that a creative force emerges. The novelist's subjects, the poet's vision, the truth of the philosopher all come from necessity, something outside rational thought. In the realization of that vision the artist approaches truth and becomes him- or herself.

The laws of ekphrasis presented here are those of a heuristics of creation and repeat the structure of love for Proust: from indifference to hope and desire and back to indifference. The constitution of the self comes through the affect rendered intelligible. And this self, the only one capable of involuntary memory and creating art, goes beyond and yet depends upon rational thought. That is why love—of mother, lover, and art—as the force of desire to create defines the artist's will. Realism in description becomes a foil, permitting the fabric of an inner vision to emerge.

The paragraphs following the "discovery" of Albertine's coat bear out this movement. When Marcel's mother decides they should leave Venice, "the old desire to rebel against an imaginary plot woven against [him] by [his] parents" (RTP 3:666) causes a defiant spirit to surge within him, and he stays behind. As the hour of his mother's train approaches, he finds himself alone on the terrace overlooking the canal at sunset, listening to a musician sing a sentimental ditty, "O Sole Mio." The entire picture is desolate. As he realizes that his mother will soon be gone, the town before him, now unremarkable and strange, ceases to be Venice: "Its personality, its name, seemed to me to be mendacious fictions which I no longer had the will to impress upon its stones." Everything is reduced to vulgar material elements; he can no "longer tell it anything about [himself] . . . leave nothing of [himself] imprinted upon it" (RTP 3:667).[61] The strains of the song rise like a dirge bearing witness to his misery; unable to rise to go to catch up with his mother, he knows that these familiar strains cannot give him the "resolution" that he needs. Each note, uttered with force and ostentation, stabs him to the heart, for just as the song is ending, the singer begins relentlessly each time anew.

With his mother gone, the now insubstantial palaces are reduced to dust and ashes; the ruin of Venice is complete. Yet once again from the "defensive power of inveterate habit" (RTP 3:670),[62] he is able to rise from "these dark caverns"; his will to action rushes back, and he dashes off to join his mother. As he leaves behind the fading light of the sun beyond San Giorgio Maggiore, a mosaic remains in his memory of the city mingled with his own throb of emotion and the "bronze voice of the singer in an equivocal, unalterable and poignant alloy" (RTP 3:669). Where once Fortuny and Carpaccio were fused and confused with desire for Albertine, now, as Marcel leaves, the soul of Venice and his mother merge. Death through separation and forgetting can be overcome only by their survival in reminiscence and the creation of true art. That is why Venice will now return in involuntary memory only and his mother in the writing of the book. It is she who restores the force of thought through her function as muse, as he turns from external models of the work of art toward creation. The subject that commands him to write imposes itself from without in the form of aesthetic imperatives that constitute the foundation of his being: the knowledge of self in the juxtaposition of present contingencies with past givens, of art with life. It is a process of de-forming and re-forming experience through association in ekphrasis; it is the subject of his art.

The editors of the 1987–89 Gallimard edition follow the images from the cathedral to the dress and *boeuf mode* to describe the problems involved with establishing the text.[63] In Chapter 4, I discussed the important addition to the Montjouvain scene in the Grasset edition. The process of excision concerns me here (a reduction from 267 pages in the Pléiade edition of 1954 to 159 pages in the Grasset edition), since the centerpiece for this chapter has been eliminated from the Grasset version of *Albertine disparue*. Proust's streamlining, while giving this version aesthetic concision, deleted the description leading up to and within the section analyzed above.

Proust jotted in a *nota bene*, "From 648 to 898, nothing[,] I took everything out."[64] The passages that he cut include those concerning Albertine's innocence (RTP 3:614–22); the article in the *Figaro* with the "Clochers de Martinville" (RTP 2:347); and the encounter with Gilberte, who has become Mme Forcheville (RTP 3:559–95). Most important for the arguments here, he excised the visit with his mother to the baptistery, the passages about Albertine in "A Venise" which reignite his feelings for her, and the ekphrasis of the painting by Carpaccio.

Proust had already made a series of substitutions for this scene. One version has the hero going to Venice with Mme Putbus's maid and staying there with her. This would account in the final version for his initial refusal to leave with his mother and would motivate the scene with "O Sole Mio."[65] A long development concerning Mme Putbus was then modified to include her in Venice in order to reevoke the memory of Albertine. This resurrection was to replace the resurrection of the memory of the hero's grandmother, now situated in Balbec; then the painting by Carpaccio took over this function from Mme Putbus.[66] This part would have constituted the final stage in the mourning for Albertine, a stage designed to elaborate further the "general law of forgetting" at work both in death and in absence.[67] If the major contribution of the Grasset edition were to confer a sense of unity through the simultaneous disappearance of Albertine and Venice, it would represent only a minor editorial thorn.[68] But Proust tightened up this version, making it more dramatic and coherent by putting a stop to both the jealousy and the mourning with the reintroduction of Combray, and thus created both technical and interpretive problems.

What makes this little book unmanageable, impossible to incorporate into the "complete" editions of the larger novel, is that so much important material was cut: if this version precedes the final volume, *Time Regained* no longer coheres. To bridge these gaps would require a volume that does not exist (*Sodome et Gomorrhe 4*, according to one hypothesis).[69] Even if the Grasset edition is considered to be no more than one variant among many, with the excision of the passage in the baptistery and Albertine, suppression has nevertheless become a means to clarity, displacing the sense of loss into positive statements. In the Grasset edition the narrator no longer confuses who it is who mourns, and his mother has begun to recover from the death of his grandmother. The important superimposition of Combray on Venice is reduced to the description of a hotel window that reminds him of Aunt Léonie's house and in which his mother is framed. This window, the form of whose "ribs" had since been preserved in casting museums and illustrated books of home architecture from the Middle Ages, retains the past and now speaks to him positively: "I remember your mother very well."[70] The allusion to Giotto brings an echo of Combray through the *Vice and Virtues of Padua*, and the reference to the *Thousand and One Nights* makes a connection to the "precious stones" of the septet, although the references to Ruskin are gone.[71] The "insignificant" and "vulgar" song "O Sole Mio," this antithesis in music of the model for art, now provides the cadence to this text in the Grasset edition:

> We guess as we read, we create; everything starts from an
> initial error; those that follow (and this applies not only to
> the reading of letters and telegrams, not only to all read-
> ing), extraordinary as they may appear to *a person who has*

not begun at the same starting-point, are all quite natural. A large part of what we believe to be true (and this applies even to our final conclusions) with an obstinacy equalled only by our good faith, springs from an original mistake in our premises. [RTP 3:671; emphasis added][72]

Here ends the Grasset edition of *Albertine disparue*, whereas the Gallimard edition continues. Taken as a final statement, this sentence reads as though a corrective act had taken place and the Albertine affair with its attendant cognitive problems were closed. Albertine appears, and she disappears. Taken as a final statement, this sentence offers a cliffhanger, however, with respect to the question of truth. The narrator had understood that the material of his art would need to be different from memories if he wanted to "paint" such scenes as those of the restaurant at Rivebelle. "This would be a new and distinct material, of a transparency and a sonority that were special, compact, cool after warmth, rose-pink" (RTP 3:904).[73] The passage from life to art could be accomplished only on the assumption that like the different reference systems portrayed in the restaurant, one was separate from the other. Love was not art, reminiscence not metaphor.

But one must ask why Proust renders so benign and banal a passage such as this one concerning error, which is so important to the question of art as truth. To suppose that he did so because of the particularly painful quality of the recognition and memory of lost love does not suffice. Too much else has been probed; the question of why Proust eliminated the centerpiece of the *The Fugitive* remains still unanswered. What is the sense of it? Several hypotheses come to mind. First, the one offered by the Gallimard editors: Proust removed this part for publication of "le séjour à Venise" in *Les Feuillets d'art*. The removal of all allusions to Albertine and the death of his grandmother, as well as the reference to his mother at Saint Mark's, demonstrates the importance of the passage. Beyond this, the scene prepares the involuntary memory in the final volume, at the reception of the Princess of Guermantes, which leads to the discovery of the vocation of writing. No other moment of involuntary memory is prepared in the same way within the work: giving the context, the feelings, and the characters with whom pleasure can be associated later, even miming syntactically how this image of Venice emerges in memory.[74] Did Proust want these pages there? The answer in one volume is yes, in another no. The Gallimard edition has restored this text in the name of the coherence of the whole; it is a reconstruction in collage.[75] One can speculate that perhaps to prepare such a crucial scene risked reducing involuntary memory to a merely intellectual function. With the indication of a place and a moment in which to situate the temporal "cause" of involuntary memory, making this obscure and miraculous memory literarily explainable, the event loses its force. Involuntary memory becomes an association like any other, even if stronger and more intense.

In addition, the key characters in the love constellation of *Albertine disparue* are on the verge of disappearance: mother, grandmother, and Albertine. As inextricable as they are from the conception of this work of art, as distinct from *the* work of art, they must appear to be only ancillary or even invisible. For the work to be authentic, it must theoretically emerge from nowhere, though in Chapter 2 we saw that Proust had turned to precedents for his description. Thus, within this variant—if we assume it to be one—Proust may have rescued the "hysteria of his own genius" through the control of intellect, a quality he attributed to Racine.[76] In piecing out these passages, Proust breaks the direct link between the pain of love and the book— with the result that Venice disintegrates into a kind of vacant lot where nothing very special happens, where in principle he establishes the limits of mourning within which no residue, no flair-ups of past selves and loves may irrupt. The cuts may have made manageable an excessive text dealing with the excessive compulsion to knowledge: of Albertine. But with respect to totality and the total work, the one the hero intends to write, nothing has been achieved.

If there is one thing to be learned from the variants and the critical apparatus of the editions appearing in the 1980s, it is that a complete, definitive work—even technically—is difficult to achieve, despite the masterful editions that now exist. The story of Albertine's disappearance is finally one in a sequence of variants. Both the addition discussed in Chapter 5 and the deletions discussed here demonstrate a strong impulse to put an end to the infinite interpretations to which love and jealousy give rise, even though they are the stuff of the work. Given the paradoxes of *The Fugitive* and *Albertine disparue*, one might almost fantasize that Proust put this manuscript away so that someday it might be found and come to modify the rest of the work. It is almost as if Proust wrote his seemingly unending changes right into the posthumous history of the book. The death and resurrection of foundations for the book, his and ours, continue.

L ike many a great cathedral, *Remembrance of Things Past* remains unfinished. Like a great cathedral, the material structure inscribes transcendental traces. But Proust built obsolescence into his project. He designed it, on the one hand, to mediate rational thought in the search for a total work and a theory of the artistic subject and, on the other, to be the operator of affective movements which, without being classifiable as simply irrational, escape the logic of rationality. The writer translates the association of memories to ensure the survival and growth of the self as the subject of his art. The associations of memory emerge as the basic organization for thought and writing.

In organizing this book I have followed a tripartite strategy revealed in Proust's conception of association. The first is that of involuntary memory, giving access to essence as the absolute singularity of being. The "peduncle of reminiscences" evoked to "imitate involuntary memory" translates the *feeling of form* and the *joy of certainty* arising from it which sustain belief in the work of art. This association prepares the writer's passage to art through ideal metaphor. But if truth for the artist comes from affect, it must nevertheless be rendered by the intellect. Proust moderated his attack on the intellect as he moved away from the *Contre Sainte-Beuve*, because neither intelligence nor sensibility alone would suffice. From the singular experience, intelligence moves toward the generalization of knowledge: in "objective subjectivism" the narrator reveals truth of the self, whereas in "subjective objectivism" the artist finds the general model from which she or he may draw. General laws can appear only in a humble, particular form.[1] Singular thoughts, feelings, and events thus reveal a determined system, bearing witness to the way in which contingency in the present becomes a past given. Association dislocates thought, reorganizing it temporally and spatially. This dislocation occurs through "delayed significa-tion" in a structure of deferral that seems always to promise meaning and finality. It occurs also because of textual disper-sion—the addition of sketches, letters, and variants—where work in progress and a sense of the absolute collide.

The second level of association includes opinion and the gen-eralities of thought in which no essential truth can ever be reached. The question of ethics for the artist raised by the Drey-fus affair is the case in point. The writer must articulate the re-lationship between necessity and contingency, between atavism and opinion, in order to argue for freedom in art. In allowing for diversity, great art may entertain many points of view but must never be reduced to the kind of parodic inconsistencies exhibited by some of Proust's characters. At stake here are prob-lems that still remain unresolved in the late twentieth century: what is the role of art (here, writing) in society? How can an ethical position be elaborated in the absence of absolutes? If Proust offers no solutions at the ethicopolitical level to the prob-lems he raises, he does take an important stand for art and the artist when it comes to the question of freedom. In relation to ethical choices, the focus on freedom in aesthetic values makes clear the need for a structure grounded in a truth that demands to be worked out in the world.

The third level is that in which substitutions occur at the level of the signifier (from Forcheville to d'Eporcheville, for example) through error and subsequent misinterpretation. But the errors to which such slippages give rise do not constitute the truth of thought. Because of a fundamental difference in premises, only the chosen few may understand involuntary memory. This rare sense constitutes the pedicel of the book in which memory goes deep within like the stalk of the water lilies around the Vivonne. But just as some plants must cut their stems and float at large to fecundate, so the narrator plumbs the depths of association in order to shift reference schemes and bring to fruition what is "real" and "passionate." The sections of the novel dealing with love and jealousy compel the pulverization of meanings in association through the search for knowledge. They present the problem of interpretation as more than a hermeneutic question: how to complete meaning in understanding (who is Albertine?). By relativizing perception as a counterforce to memory, they present the incommensurability of otherness. Associations may either confer value through belief or lead to indeterminacy in the anguished tracking of knowledge.

The order of the foregoing chapters neither attempts to reverse the phenomenological logic that leads from the heterogeneity of the world to the unity of the mind nor operates according to a teleology where all paths lead to a semiological structure. The order leads from the project to the text by deviation and displacement. The genesic structure of the novel is plural, imposing a linear order—whether from heterogeneity to unity or from project to digression—upon a circular composition: the narrator ends his monumental search at the very moment that he is to undertake writing the book, a plan inscribed from the beginning of the project.

I have followed questions of structure to involuntary memory, then to ethics, and to the interminable search for knowledge in love, moving from the initial project to the seemingly endless proliferations of the text. We can now chart the changes, the additions and cuts, because of the remarkable editions from the 1980s and the accessibility of the correspondence. Proust moves beyond the two sharply elucidated sides of thought—the one affective, the other intellectual—intertwining them in the conceptual metaphors for the project: the book, the cathedral, the stew, the dress. The dress becomes the privileged image along with the septet, as the "*scarlet-clad Mantegna archangel sounding a trumpet* from a grave" (RTP 3: 262; emphasis added)[2] provides art's triumphant counterpart to the joy of a certainty in involuntary memory. But the exemplary moment, when the narrator puts Fortuny and Carpaccio together and finds an element common to both and deeper than either in the memory of Albertine, narrativizes the ideal of metaphor. That Proust should choose to cut this scene from *Albertine disparue* suggests that the force of writing, like the force of reading, emerges in the gaps. It is when diversion becomes the principle of operation that "true" meaning arises from a sequence of images in collage, this *suite coupée de lacunes* composed of connections and misconnections. At the most general level, reading in the gaps may be like interpreting a text. But Proust refines his notion of reading, grounds the essence of being in singularity rather than universality, and in so doing moves away from the rationalist tradition of thought. This indeed makes of association the unanalyzed domain of thought and the premise upon which Proust's sense of literature is built. It is thus that Proust's art, like much great art, remains work in progress, a textual fabric of self-revision.

NOTES

INTRODUCTION

1. "Nous sommes là . . . essayant de chasser toute autre pensée, tâchant de comprendre le sens de chaque couleur, chacune appelant dans notre mémoire des impressions passées, qui s'associent en aussi aérienne et multicolore architecture que les couleurs sur la toile et édifient dans notre imagination un paysage." (CSB 1954: 397–98). (All translations from the French of Proust and others which are not otherwise attributed in the text or notes are my own.) Monet painted his *Water Lilies* between 1905 and 1908, removing the sense of any framing of the subject, and forcing the eye from detail to detail.

2. Gilles Deleuze (*Proust and Signs*, 55) pointed out that "the formal importance of an associationist psychology in Proust has often been noted. But it would be a mistake to reproach him for this: associationism is less outmoded than the critique of associationism. We must therefore ask from what viewpoint the cases of reminiscence effectively transcend the mechanisms of association; but also from what viewpoint they effectively refer to such mechanisms."

3. Ferdinand de Saussure, the founder of modern semiology, put forth no theory of association yet made it the basis of his thought in *Cours de linguistique générale*, developed during the year 1906 in Geneva. The fundamental principle of semiology is that the linguistic sign cannot be tied to both a name and a thing, as the Judeo-Christian and Platonic tradition taught, but rather that the sign brings together arbitrarily a concept and acoustic image. What links the two parts of the sign is an association between two abstract realities, the signifier and the signified, both of which are psychic. "Les termes impliqués dans le signe linguistique [signifiant et signifié] sont tous deux psychiques et sont unis dans notre cerveau par le lien de l'association. Insistons sur ce point" (*Cours*, 98). This association cannot operate at the level of utterance (*parole*) alone. Even though it manifests itself in particular speech acts, the sign can be understood only in its generality, as a system, where every element depends on all others. It is the coherence of the system that ensures the intelligibility of the sign, and therefore the association, for Saussure. It follows that the notion of the arbitrariness of the sign, as the pivotal concept for modern linguistics, requires the reconstruction of a system as its only motivation. The arbitrariness of the sign, however systematic its study, retains within it the potential for the infinite generation of unbounded meaning. Proust sensed the power of language to carry the subject away from any possible guarantee of self-identity.

4. Associationism was borrowed and circulated largely throughout academia in the nineteenth century through Brentano, Herbart, Lipps, Wundt, and the *Akt Psychology* school, and it no longer referred to early thought. See David Rapaport, *The History of the Concept of Association*, 27.

5. Psychoanalytic studies of Proust include Malcolm Bowie, *Freud, Proust, and Lacan: Theory as Fiction;* Jean-Louis Baudry, *Proust, Freud et l'autre;* Serge Doubrovsky, *La Place de la madeleine;* Jeffrey Mehlman, *A Structural Study of Autobiography: Proust, Sartre, Leiris, Lévi-Strauss;* Randolph Splitter, *Proust's 'Recherche': A Psychoanalytic Interpretation.*

6. François Roustang, *Elle ne le lâche pas*, points out that the technique of free association is an invention imported into psychoanalysis from literature.

7. See Antoine Compagnon's excellent book, *Proust entre deux siècles,* which shows historically how Proust's work lies between the two centuries in its themes and textual strategies.

8. Leopold Bellak, "Free Association: Conceptual and Clinical Aspects," 18.

9. "Derrière l'enchaînement des associations libres (contenus manifestes) l'analyste recherche l'attitude affective qui régit cet enchaînement et qui est pour ainsi dire sa loi d'intelligibilité"(Nicolas Abraham, *L'Ecorce et le noyau,* 21).

10. Sigmund Freud. "Psychotherapy of Hysteria," 302–3.

11. In this regard, see the consequential reading by Ginette Michaud, "Monsieur Songe sans y penser dit que . . . ," 108, of *The Psychopathology of Everyday Life* in relation to Freud's theories of free association.

12. In *La Droite révolutionnaire: Les Origines françaises du fascisme, 1885–1914,* Zeev Sternhell points out that at the end of the nineteenth century a major event took place: the discovery of the unconscious. Gustave Le Bon (who wrote *Les Lois psychologiques de l'évolution des peuples,* 1894, and *Psychologie des foules,* 1895) had an important part to play in the development of the idea because he adhered to an anti-individualist notion of race which arose out of organic naturalism, the critique of individualism, democracy, and its institutions. It was a fundamentally irrational vision determined by historical and biological constraints. Sternhell, (*La Droite,* 148) suggests that Le Bon has perhaps been forgotten because of the praise his ideas received from Hitler and Mussolini.

13. Bowie (*Freud,* 70) points out that "At . . . [certain] moments Proust's narrator is an associationist psychologist of an entirely traditional stamp."

14. John Locke, *An Essay on Human Understanding*, xxv.

15. The English School of Sensualism, those who followed the philosophical or psychological questions related to association, included—in addition to Locke and Hume—Hobbes, Berkeley, James, Mill, Thomas Brown, Hartley, Bain, and Spencer. For a history of the association of ideas, see Rapaport, *History,* and Howard Warren, *A History of the Association Psychology.* For a recent formulation of the problem in eighteenth- and twentieth-century thought, as well as a bibliography on the subject, see Christie McDonald and Ginette Michaud, eds. *Ça*

me fait penser. See also Patrick Mahony, "The Boundaries of Free Association," in his *Psychoanalysis and Discourse,* 16–56.

16. Arthur Schopenhauer, *The World as Will and Representation,* 2:135.

17. "Les associations d'idées ont la force de croyances, d'erreurs" (RTP Gall. 1, *Esquisse* 62:861).

18. A term coined by Leo Bersani in *Marcel Proust: The Fictions of Life and Art.*

19. "On raisonne, c'est-à-dire on vagabonde, chaque fois qu'on n'a pas la force de s'astreindre à faire passer une impression par tous les états successifs qui aboutiront à sa fixation, à l'expression" (RTP Gall. 4:461). Proust referred to these *états successifs* as *états chimiques* in *La Matinée chez la Princesse de Guermantes,* 381

20. "L'impression est pour l'écrivain ce qu'est l'expérimentation pour le savant, avec cette différence que chez le savant le travail de l'intelligence précède et chez l'écrivain vient après" (RTP Gall. 4:459).

21. "Des impressions obscures avaient quelquefois . . . sollicité ma pensée, à la façon de ces réminiscences, mais qui cachaient non une sensation d'autrefois mais une vérité nouvelle" (RTP Gall. 4:456).

22. Already in 1966, Gérard Genette (*Figures of Literary Discourse,* 223–24) had sensed how marvelous and yet dizzying it would be if there were a new edition of the Proust volumes: "All these transformations, these substitutions, these unpredictable splittings and fusions, not to mention what still lies hidden in the unpublished notebooks, add to the Proustian palimpsest almost unfathomable depths. One dreams of a monstrous edition in which, around the *Recherche du temps perdu,* would be gathered all the preparations and successive modifications which—as work in progress—culminated in that final state, which as we know was the result not of an act of completion, but of a sudden interruption, outside the profound law of this work, which was to go on growing ceaselessly and never to reach its end. Similarly no page of the *Recherche* can be regarded as truly definitive, none of its variants can be absolutely rejected. Starting from *Les Plaisirs et les jours,* Proust's work exists and did not cease to move until November 18, 1922."

23. See "*Introduction générale,*" RTP Gall. 1:ix–cvii. The publication dates of the volumes of the *Recherche,* and their English titles, are *Du côté de chez Swann,* or *Swann's Way,* 1913; *A l'ombre des jeunes filles en fleurs* or *Within a Budding Grove,* 1919; *Le Côté de Guermantes,* or *The*

Guermantes Way, 1920, 1921; *Sodome et Gomorrhe*, or *Cities of the Plain*, 1921, 1922; *La Prisonnière*, or *The Captive*, 1923 (posthumous); *La Fugitive/Albertine disparue*, or *The Fugitive*, 1925 (posthumous); *Le Temps retrouvé*, or *Time Regained*, 1927 (posthumous).

24. "Le livre n'a jamais été fait, il a été récolté" (Maurice Blanchot, *Le Livre à venir*, 33).

25. They belong to the French government and may be consulted, although the rights to previously unpublished material belong to Gallimard.

26. The information concerning the editions has been culled both from their introductions and from an article announcing their publication: Catherine Sauvat, "Du côté des recherches," *Magazine littéraire* 246 (October 1987): 22–25. See also *Lire* 145 (October 1987): 43–50.

27. Nathalie Mauriac, granddaughter on her paternal side of François Mauriac and on her maternal side of Mme Mante-Proust (who was Proust's niece and heir), discovered the unknown text in a trunk in 1986. It was a typescript of the *La Fugitive* (here titled *Albertine disparue*) that Proust had corrected in his own hand, and his correspondence with Gaston Gallimard. Proust gave up the title *La Fugitive* because it had already been used by Rabindranath Tagore. The Pléiade edition of 1954 restored it, though Jean Milly's pocketbook edition opted for *Albertine disparue*. See "Notice," RTP Gall. 4:993–1043; and Genette, *Seuils*, 506.

28. Judith Schlanger, *Les Métamorphoses de l'organisme*, has suggested that a history of the ideas and inventions not retained might be very revealing, though little such information is available.

29. See Jean-Jacques Nattiez, *Proust musicien*.

30. "Il est indubitable que l'on peut reconnaître dans le roman de Marcel Proust deux formes aussi distinctes l'une de l'autre que si l'on avait devant soi un texte dû à deux écrivains qui collaborent" (Albert Feuillerat, *Comment Marcel Proust a composé son roman*, 7).

31. "Proust mondain, Proust écrivain. Deux figures d'un même homme que l'hagiographie critique se plaît à distinguer, opposer, hiérarchiser. Une vie à deux temps. D'abord les plaisirs des salons, ensuite l'ascèse de l'écritoire. La société, la solitude. Les sorties, l'enfermement. L'agitation, le recueillement. La vie, le souvenir. L'illusion du moment, la vérité du roman. Le superficiel, l'essentiel. L'éphémère, l'éternel. C'est

oublier que le mondain pratiquait déjà l'écriture et publiait régulière-ment, que l'écrivain cloîtré ne renoncera jamais complètement au monde, entretenant sa situation et cultivant ses relations fût-ce à dis-tance" (Alain Buisine, *Proust et ses lettres*, 9).

32. Georges Poulet, in *Proustian Space*, shows the importance of time and memory. See also Jean-Pierre Richard, *Proust et le monde sensible*, for a hermeneutics of the object.

33. See Genette, *Figures* and *Figures 3*, to cite only two of many. (Se-lections from *Figures*, *Figures 2*, and *Figures 3* are available in English translation in Genette, *Figures of Literary Discourse*.)

34. See *Essais de critique génétique*.

35. Raymonde Debray-Genette (*Métamorphoses du récit*, 33) suggests that genetic studies reveal the openness of the unfinished text, its in-decision, uncertainty, and undecidability. See Paul de Man's decon-structive analysis of the inability of the text to constitute stable meaning: "Reading Proust," in *Allegories of Reading: Figural Language in Rousseau, Nietzsche, Rilke, and Proust*.

36. Deleuze, *Proust and Signs*, 89–90.

37. Paul Ricoeur, *Temps et récit 2: La Configuration dans le récit de fiction*, 195.

38. Compagnon, *Proust*.

39. See Vincent Descombes, *Proust: Philosophie du roman*, 1–19. In *Théories pour une esthétique*, Anne Henry looks into the philosophical background of Proust's thinking: showing his debt to and the trans-formation of his thought from readings of Schopenhauer, Schelling, and Tarde, to name a few thinkers passed in review. Henry asserts that Proust was not content to put into motion in novelistic form principles of a philosophy of art. Rather, he channeled into an imaginative or-dering what otherwise would have had a dogmatic one: an aesthetic treatise, for example. His genius, she contends, is to have succeeded in making a rigorously coherent novelistic situation out of an aesthetic system, to have transformed each demonstration scrupulously into a dramatic structure. While her analysis is intriguing, and convincing with respect to the theoretical matrix out of which Proust's thought comes, it is too mechanical in the way it assumes a one-to-one relation between the demonstration of ideas and the dramatic structure. See also Henry, *Proust romancier: Le tombeau egyptien*.

40. See Richard Rorty, *Contingency, Irony, and Solidarity*.

41. Leo Bersani, " 'The Culture of Redemption': Marcel Proust and Melanie Klein,"416, 417.

42. "Ce qu'il y a de plus beau dans Giotto ce ne sont nullement des idées mais *certain un sentiment de la forme*" (letter 4 to André Maurel, January 1906, *Corr.* 5:25).

CHAPTER ONE

1. "Au fond, toute ma philosophie revient comme toute philosophie vraie à justifier, à reconstruire ce qui est" (cited in Henry, *Théories*, 260).

2. "La paresse ou le doute ou l'impuissance se réfugiant dans l'incertitude sur la forme d'art. Faut-il faire un roman, une étude philosophique, suis-je romancier?" (Proust, *Le Carnet de 1908*, 61). See also Anthony R. Pugh, *The Birth of "A la recherche du temps perdu,"* 32.

3. "Le redressement de l'oblique discours intérieur" (RTP Gall. 4:458).

4. "Qui va s'éloignant de plus en plus de l'impression première et centrale" (RTP Gall. 4:458).

5. Letter to Louis de Robert, *Letters of Marcel Proust*, 218 (emphasis added). "J'ai travaillé vous le saurez peut-être depuis que je suis si malade à un long ouvrage que j'appelle roman . . . je serais incapable d'en dire le genre" (letter 133, October 28, 1912, *Corr.* 11:251).

6. A term coined by Gérard Genette in *Seuils*.

7. Letter to René Blum, February 24, 1913, *Letters*, 218. "Il y a un monsieur qui raconte et qui dit: Je." (letter 30, February 23, 1913, *Corr.* 12:92).

8. "L'ouvrage est un roman; si la liberté de ton l'apparente semble-t-il à des Mémoires, en réalité une composition très stricte (mais à ordre trop complexe pour être d'abord perceptible) le différencie extrêmement des mémoires: il n'y a dedans de contingent que ce qui est nécessaire pour exprimer la part du contingent dans la vie. Et par conséquent dans le livre, ce n'est plus contingent" (letter 127 to Antoine Bibesco, October 1912, *Corr.* 11:235).

9. "Enfin je trouve un lecteur qui *devine* que mon livre est un ouvrage dogmatique et une construction" (letter 43 to Jacques Rivière, February 6, 1914, *Corr.* 13:98. A few days later, he wrote: "Mon livre (essentiellement dogmatique d'ailleurs et dont la composition n'apparaîtra

qu'à la fin du troisième volume)" (letter to Henry Bordeaux, February 14, 1914, *Corr.* 13:103).

10. Proust, *On Reading Ruskin*, 146 (emphasis added). "Il passe d'une idée à l'autre sans aucun ordre apparent. Mais en réalité la fantaisie qui le mène suit ses affinités profondes qui lui imposent malgré lui une logique supérieure. Si bien qu'à la fin il se trouve avoir obéi à une sorte de plan secret qui, dévoilé à la fin, impose rétrospectivement à l'ensemble une sorte d'ordre et le fait apercevoir magnifiquement étagé jusqu'à cette apothéose finale" (Proust, *Sésame et les lys*, 104). Between 1904 and 1906 Proust published translations of two Ruskin works: *The Bible of Amiens* and *Sesame and Lilies*. For prefaces to and selections from these works, see the sources cited above and Proust, *La Bible d'Amiens*.

11. *Modern Painters* (in *The Works of John Ruskin*), 71–72, cited in David Ellison, *The Readings of Proust*, 53.

12. Proust, *On Reading Ruskin*, 144 (emphasis added). "Dès le début Ruskin expose ainsi ... thèmes et à la fin ... il les mêlera inextricablement dans la dernière phrase où sera rappelée dans l'accord final la tonalité du début" (*Sésame*, 102).

13. "J'ai tâché de faire tenir toute ma philosophie de résonner toute ma 'musique'" (letter 135 to Eugène Fasquelle, October 28, 1912, *Corr.* 11:256).

14. "La vérité, même littéraire, n'est pas le fruit du hasard, et on pourrait s'asseoir devant son piano pendant cinquante ans et essayer toutes combinaisons de notes, sans trouver telle divine phrase de tel grand musicien. Je crois que la vérité (littéraire) se découvre à chaque fois, comme une *loi* physique. On la trouve ou on ne la trouve pas" (letter 23 to Léon Daudet, early March 1917, *Corr.* 16:65).

15. Preface to *La Bible d'Amiens*, in Proust, *On Reading Ruskin*, 60 (emphasis added). "Le sujet du romancier, la vision du poète, la vérité du philosophe s'imposent à eux d'une façon presque nécessaire, extérieure pour ainsi dire à leur pensée. Et c'est en soumettant son esprit à rendre cette vision, à approcher de cette vérité que l'artiste devient vraiment lui-même" (*La Bible*, 94).

16. Proust, *On Reading Ruskin*, 146. "Si le désordre est le même dans tous ses livres, le même geste de rassembler à la fin ses rênes et de

feindre d'avoir contenu et guidé ses coursiers n'existe pas dans tous. Aussi bien ne faudrait-il pas voir là plus qu'un jeu" (*Sésame*, 104).

17. "Quant à ce livre-ci, c'est au contraire un tout très composé, quoique d'une composition si complexe que je crains que personne ne le perçoive et qu'il apparaisse comme une suite de digressions. C'est tout le contraire" (letter 26 to René Blum, February 20, 1913, *Corr.* 12:82).

18. "Il y a beaucoup de personnages; ils sont 'préparés' dès ce premier volume. . . . La composition . . . est si complexe qu'elle n'apparaît que très tardivement quand tous les 'Thèmes' ont commencé à se combiner" (letter 30 to René Blum, February 23, 1913, *Corr.* 12:92).

19. See RTP Gall. 4:65–66. See also Nattiez, *Proust as Musician*, for Proust's view of Wagner's composition and conception of the total work; and Compagnon, *Proust*, 38–42, for a discussion of Proust's fear that his work would be considered fragmented or dispersed, which for him meant being considered a *fin de siècle* decadent.

20. "Je viens de commencer—et de finir—tout un long livre. . . . Si tout est écrit, beaucoup de choses sont à remanier" (letter 81 to Madame Straus, c. August 16, 1909, *Corr.* 9:163).

21. "C'est un livre d'événements, de reflets d'événements les uns sur les autres à des années d'intervalle et cela ne peut paraître que par grandes tranches" (letter 78 to Alfred Vallette, mid-August 1909, *Corr.* 9:15).

22. I agree with Compagnon's comparison (*Proust*, 43) between Diderot's *scène composée* and Proust's defense of his work as *tout composé*: a work whose unity depends on the interworking of many complex elements.

23. For more information on the manuscripts of the *Contre Sainte-Beuve*, see Claudine Quémar, "Autour de trois 'avant-textes' de l'ouverture' de *la Recherche*: Nouvelles Approches des problèmes du *Contre Sainte-Beuve*," *Bulletin d'Informations Proustiennes* 3 (Spring 1976): 7–29. See also Pugh, *The Birth*, 48.

24. I am indebted to Bernard Brun's discussion of the problem raised by the early versions of the *Contre Sainte-Beuve* in "L'Edition d'un brouillon et son interprétation: Le Problème du *Contre Sainte-Beuve*," 153–92. Jean-Yves Tadié (*Proust*, 139) also points out in what ways both editions are incorrect and incomplete: while Fallois understood Proust's intention to mix aesthetics and criticism, and put together

various texts without any attempt at a comprehensive description of the whole, Clarac presents only the texts of literary criticism.

25. "[Cette errance] apparaît surtout comme la marque d'une impossibilité à penser le projet proustien ailleurs que dans les limites d'un cadre rigide . . . autrement qu'à travers des catégories de la critique qui oblitèrent le travail de l'écrivain" (Brun, "L'Edition d'un brouillon," 163).

26. Emphasis added. "Je vais écrire quelque chose sur Sainte-Beuve. J'ai en quelque sorte deux articles bâtis dans ma pensée. . . . L'un est un article de forme classique. . . . L'autre débuterait par le récit d'une matinée, Maman viendrait près de mon lit et je lui raconterais un article que je veux faire sur Sainte-Beuve. Et je le lui développerais. Qu'est-ce que vous trouvez le mieux?" (letter 170 to Georges de Lauris, mid-December 1908, *Corr.* 8:320).

27. "Quand on aura fini le livre, on verra (je le voudrais) que tout le roman n'est que la mise en oeuvre des principes d'art émis dans cette dernière partie, sorte de préface si vous voulez mise à la fin" (letter 78 to Alfred Vallette, mid-August 1909, *Corr.* 9:156).

28. In his preface to *Du côté de chez Swann*, xxv, Antoine Compagnon points out that although Proust wrote the passage in 1909, he did not place it in *Time Regained* until 1911; he had thus written the last page—without knowing it—from the very first.

29. "Quand [la sonnette] avait tinté j'existais déjà, et depuis pour que j'entendisse encore ce tintement, il fallait qu'il n'y eût pas eu discontinuité, . . . puisque cet instant ancien tenait encore à moi, que je pouvais encore le retrouver, retourner jusqu'à lui, rien qu'en descendant plus profondément en moi" (RTP Gall. 4:624).

30. An expression coined by Compagnon (*Proust*, 149) from a passage concerning the grandmother in the novel and Proust's displacement of narrative from his mother to his grandmother: "Dans cette chambre de Milan où j'avais pour la première fois perdu—et retrouvé—ma grand'mère" (RTP Gall. 3:1038).

31. "Au moment où je venais de commettre une faute telle que je m'attendais à être obligé de quitter la maison, mes parents m'accordaient plus que je n'eusse jamais obtenu d'eux comme récompense d'une belle action" (RTP Gall. 1:37).

32. "La maison où cela se passait n'existe plus. Et l'image qu'il y en a dans mon souvenir est peut-être la seule 'épreuve' qui en reste encore et qui sera bientôt détruite. La possibilité de telles heures est à jamais anéantie. Depuis bien des années déjà, mon père et ma mère ne peuvent plus rien pour moi que par l'influence qui continue au-delà du tombeau" (RTP Gall. 1, *Esquisse* 10:675). See also RTP Gall. 1, *Esquisse* 34:808–9.

33. "Quand je lisais, je rêvassais souvent, pendant des pages entières, à tout autre chose. Et aux lacunes que cette distraction laissait dans le récit, s'ajoutait, quand c'était maman qui me lisait à haute voix, qu'elle passait toutes les scènes d'amour" (RTP Gall. 1:41).

34. RTP Gall. 1:41. Proust changed the book from *La Mare au diable* to *François le Champi*; see RTP Gall. 4, *Esquisse* 10:676.

35. "Je suis si fatigué que je ne sais pas si tu peux sentir à travers ces lignes incohérentes la joie que j'ai de te sentir plus près de moi et de penser que bientôt nous ne ferons plus qu'une personne comme nous ne faisons qu'un coeur" (letter 131 to Mme Proust, August 15, 1904, *Correspondance avec sa mère*, 245).

36. "Voici que mille riens de Combray . . . sautaient légèrement d'eux-mêmes et venaient à la queue leu leu se suspendre au bec aimanté, en une chaîne interminable et tremblante de souvenirs" (RTP Gall. 4:463).

37. "Tandis que dans la chambre mortuaire les employés des pompes funèbres se préparent à descendre la bière, le fils d'un homme qui a rendu des services à la patrie serre la main aux derniers amis qui défilent, si tout à coup retentit sous les fenêtres une fanfare, il se révolte, croyant à quelque moquerie dont on insulte son chagrin. Mais lui, qui est resté maître de soi jusque-là, ne peut plus retenir ses larmes; car il vient de comprendre que ce qu'il entend c'est la musique d'un régiment qui s'associe à son deuil et rend honneur à la dépouille de son père" (RTP Gall. 4:461–62).

38. "En réalité ils n'ont jamais cessé" (RTP Gall. 1:36–37).

39. See "Sentiments filiaux d'un parricide" (written in 1907), CSB 1971, 150–59. See also Proust and Gide, *Autour de la Recherche*, xxi.

40. "Rêve . . . Illusion absolue de la vie. Donc tu vois que mort on est presque en vie. Peut-être se tromperait-il dans les réponses mais enfin simulacre de la vie. Peut-être n'est-il pas mort" (RTP Gall. 3, *Esquisse* 12:1031).

41. "Je pense tant à Papa que je lui écrirai directement pour épancher mes sentiments.... Du moins ma tête lui écrit" (letter 74, September 25, 1889, *Correspondance avec sa mère*, 149).

42. "Cet étranger, c'était moi-même, c'était l'enfant que j'étais alors, que le livre venait de susciter en moi, car de moi ne connaissant que cet enfant, c'est cet enfant que le livre avait appelé tout de suite, ne voulant être regardé que par ses yeux, aimé que par son coeur, et ne parler qu'à lui" (RTP Gall. 4:463). See also RTP Gall. 4, *Esquisse* 24:812.

43. In Cahier 57, fol. 32v, Proust writes: "L'élan profond qui est comme le battement, l'acte même de la vie, n'est pas intellectuel, il faut qu'en nous la sensibilité l'imite, nous le joue, le répète, se fasse élan de vie. Mais l'intelligence peut servir. Elle sait que cet élan si particulier qu'il soit est comparable à d'autres, à quelque chose de général, peut être défini. Cela la sensibilité ne pourrait le faire car si l'intelligence n'est pas capable de la vie, la sensibilité ne connaît pas le général" (cited in Edward J. Hughes, *Marcel Proust: A Study in the Quality of Awareness*).

44. Proust, *By Way of Sainte-Beuve*, 21; emphasis added. "On s'étonnera peut-être que, faisant peu de cas de l'intelligence, j'aie donné pour sujet aux quelques pages qui vont suivre justement quelques-unes de ces remarques que notre intelligence nous suggère, en contradiction avec les banalités que nous entendons dire ou que nous lisons. A une heure où mes heures sont peut-être comptées (d'ailleurs tous les hommes n'en sont-il pas là?) c'est peut-être être bien frivole que de faire oeuvre intellectuelle. Mais d'une part les vérités de l'intelligence, si elles sont moins précieuses que ces secrets du sentiment dont je parlais tout à l'heure, ont aussi leur intérêt. Un écrivain n'est pas qu'un poète. Même les plus grands de notre siècle, dans notre monde imparfait où les chefs-d'oeuvre de l'art ne sont que les épaves naufragées de grandes intelligences, ont relié d'une trame d'intelligence les joyaux de sentiment où ils n'apparaissent que ça et là. Et si on croit que sur ce point important on entend les meilleurs de son temps se tromper, il vient un moment où on secoue sà paresse et où on éprouve le besoin de le dire. La méthode de Sainte-Beuve n'est peut-être pas au premier abord un objet si important. Mais peut-être sera-t-on amené, au cours de ces pages, à voir qu'elle touche à de très importants problèmes intellectuels, peut-être au plus grand de tous pour un artiste, à cette

infériorité de l'intelligence dont je parlais au commencement. Et cette infériorité de l'intelligence, c'est tout de même à l'intelligence qu'il faut demander de l'établir. Car si l'intelligence ne mérite pas la couronne suprême, c'est elle seule qui est capable de la décerner. Et si elle n'a dans la hiérarchie des vertus que la seconde place, il n'y a qu'elle qui soit capable de proclamer que l'instinct doit occuper la première" (CSB 1954, 58–59).

45. A number of attempts are crossed out; then follows this version: *"Ce n'est pas en elle que nous pouvons trouver//cette réalité*, . . . *Elle ne retient rien de la réalité* Cette réalité qui est la matière.

"Ce n'est qu'en cachette d'elle, *hors des confins/hors des bor[nes]*/hors des limites de sa lumière* hors de *sa* sa zone de lumière, que l'artiste peut *aper[cevoir]/retrouver* trouver la réalité perdue et la recréer. *Vu/Pour l'intelligence le passé est perdu* Si nous nous en tenons à l'intelligence, *le passé*, *matière de not[r]e* notre passé, matière de l'art, semble perdu. En fait il ne l'est pas, mais chaque *jour* heure *passée* morte est allée s'incarner *dans un objet matériel,/dans une* dans un objet *dans une sensation toute [matérielle]* matériel et y restera *inconnue* inconnue jusqu'à ce que" (cited in Brun, "L'Edition d'un brouillon," 176–77). Words crossed out by Proust are shown in italics; successive erasures are marked by a slash (/); an asterisk is placed after a word whose meaning is conjectural; restorations are enclosed in brackets; a double slash (//) indicates the passage from one folio to another.

46. *"Pour l'intelligence, le passé est vraiment le passé* Pour l'intelligence, les heures que nous vivons meurent les unes après les autres, elle est impui[ssante]" (cited in Brun, "L'Edition d'un brouillon," 177).

47. "Bien que chaque jour j'attache moins de prix à la critique et même, s'il faut le dire, à l'intelligence, car de plus en plus je la crois impuissante à cette recréation de la réalité qui est tout l'art, c'est à l'intelligence que je me fie aujourd'hui pour écrire un essai tout critique" (CSB 1971, 216).

48. "L'intelligence n'est pas l'instrument le plus subtil, le plus puissant, le plus approprié pour saisir le vrai, ce n'est qu'une raison de plus pour commencer par l'intelligence et non par un intuitivisme de l'inconscient, par une foi aux pressentiments toute faite" (RTP Gall. 4:7). "Par une de ces malchances où il y a peut-être de grands déclenchements

de l'inconscient" (letter to Lucien Daudet, mid-November 1915, *Corr.* 14:293).

49. "Je ne crois même pas l'intelligence *première* en nous . . . je pose avant elle l'inconscient qu'elle est destinée à clarifier—mais qui fait la réalité, l'originalité d'une oeuvre. Et, sans doute, qu'elle puisse la clarifier, en donner des équivalents, signifie qu'ils ne sont pas choses irréductibles" (letter 29 to Jacques Rivière, September 1919, Proust and Rivière, *Correspondance*, 64). In RTP Gall. 1, *Esquisse* 62:862, Proust again refers to the *inconscient* whose meaning the intelligence must take over.

50. In Letter 80 to Jacques Copeau, May 22, 1913 (*Corr.* 12:180), Proust writes the following about a sentence in *Crime and Punishment:* "Encore quelque chose d'extrêmement contingent et accidentel relativement à 'mon' souvenir, où tous les éléments matériels constitutifs de l'impression antérieure se trouvant modifiés le souvenir prend au point de vue de l'inconscient la même généralité, la même force de réalité supérieure que la *loi* en physique, par la variation des circonstances."

51. "Une oeuvre où il y a des théories est comme un objet sur lequel on laisse la marque du prix" (RTP Gall. 4:461). This sentence was a late addition; see RTP Gall. 4:1173, and RTP Gall. 4, *Esquisse* 24:821. "En un de ces endroits en elles-même déjà je n'aimais pas ces théories parce qu'elles étaient tranchantes, orgueilleuses parce qu'elles étaient des théories; leur contenu logique pouvait m'imposer, mais je sentais que leur existence était déjà une preuve d'infériorité, comme un enfant vraiment sincère bon et bien élevé, s'il va jouer chez des amis dont les parents lui disent: 'Pourquoi ne dites-vous pas votre pensée, nous avant tout nous sommes francs' sent que tout cela dénote une qualité morale inférieure à la bonne action pure et simple qui ne dit rien" (Proust, *Matinée*, 317).

52. "Mais cette évolution d'une pensée, je n'ai pas voulu l'analyser abstraitement mais la recréer, la faire vivre" (letter to Jacques Rivière, February 6, 1914, *Corr.* 13:98).

53. "Notre âme n'est jamais une" (RTP Gall. 1, *Esquisse* 31:753).

54. He wrote: "Il est regrettable infiniment qu'on ne puisse répandre partout ce livre comme un modèle de *forme, la plus savante* que je

sache, comme un modèle d'analyse sans égal" (letter 3 to Henri Ghéon, quoting letter from Jammes of January 2, 1914, *Corr.* 13:26).

55. "Mes théories littéraires, je trouve les images nées d'une impression supérieure à celles qui servent seulement à illustrer un raisonnement" (letter to Jacques-Emile Blanche, May 1915, *Corr.* 14:121).

56. See CSB 1954, 53–59; in this edition it is the preface to the work. See also CSB 1971, 211–18. To the text of the preface titled "Contre Sainte-Beuve," Clarac adds two preparatory sketches from other pages that are in direct relation to the preface. One concerns the incarnation of souls in objects; the other, a conversation with Proust's mother, intended to be the final pages of the larger work.

57. "L'organisation de ma mémoire, de mes préoccupations, était liée à mon oeuvre, peut-être parce que . . . l'idée de mon oeuvre était dans ma tête, toujours la même, en perpétuel devenir" (RTP Gall. 4:619). It was, as Luc Fraisse puts it, an immense variation on a fundamental fragment (*Le procesus de la création chez Marcel Proust: le fragment expérimental,* 384), though what the term *variation* means in this context depends upon the status accorded to the fragment.

58. "Le dernier chapitre du dernier volume a été écrit tout de suite après le premier chapitre du premier volume. Tout'l'entre-deux' a été écrit ensuite" (letter to Paul Souday, *Corr. gén.* 3:72).

59. Compagnon questions Proust's affirmation in a letter to Benjamin Crémieux that "on ne pourra le nier quand la dernière page du *Temps retrouvé* (écrite avant le reste du livre) se refermera exactement sur la première de *Swann*" (Crémieux, *Du côté de Marcel Proust,* 159; cited in Compagnon, Preface, xxv). Compagnon analyzes a process of substitutions to which I return later; what is important here is Proust's insistence on a rigorous construction to the book.

60. "C'est un livre extrêmement réel mais supporté en quelque sorte, pour imiter la mémoire involontaire . . . par une grâce, un pédoncule de réminiscences. Ainsi une partie du livre est une partie de ma vie que j'avais oubliée et que tout d'un coup je retrouve en mangeant un peu de madeleine. . . .Une autre partie du livre renaît des sensations du réveil, quand on ne sait où on est et qu'on se croit deux ans avant dans un autre pays. Mais tout cela n'est que la tige du livre. Et ce qu'elle supporte est réel, passionné" (letter 134 à René Blum, early November 1913, *Corr.* 12:295). See also RTP Gall. 1, *Esquisse* 14:700–

701, in which the tea cake and uneven paving stones are evoked at a two-page interval. The word peduncle occurs only three times in the novel: RTP Gall. 1:166, in a transposition from Monet's paintings of water lilies.; RTP Gall. 1:625, in a description of Mme Swann's dress; and RTP Gall. 3:915, in relation to Swann.

61. In Gérard Genette's divisions, the sketches would probably fit into the category of a declaration of intention, with the emergence of newness as its object. See *Seuils* (esp. 182–219), in which Genette classifies all kinds of paratexts, from prefaces to epigrams, titles, notes, etc.

62. CSB 1954, 53–55.

CHAPTER TWO

1. "Le devoir et la tâche d'un écrivain sont ceux d'un traducteur" (RTP Gall. 4:469).

2. "Des impressions obscures . . . cachaient non une sensation d'autrefois mais une vérité nouvelle" (RTP Gall. 4:456).

3. See Julia Kristeva's discussion of Western man's conviction that he can translate his mother and thereby bridge separation from her through naming (*Soleil noir: Dépression et Mélancolie*, 78).

4. "En réalité, chaque lecteur est quand il lit le propre lecteur de soi-même. L'ouvrage de l'écrivain n'est qu'une espèce d'instrument optique qu'il offre au lecteur afin de lui permettre de discerner ce que sans ce livre il n'eût peut-être pas vu en soi-même. La reconnaissance en soi-même, par le lecteur, de ce que dit le livre, est la preuve de la vérité de celui-ci, et vice versa, au moins dans une certaine mesure, la différence entre les deux textes pouvant être souvent imputée non à l'auteur mais au lecteur" (RTP Gall. 4:489–90).

5. To Marie Nordlinger, Proust writes: "J'ai clos à jamais l'ère des traductions, que Maman favorisait" (letter 179, December 7, 1906, *Corr.* 6:308).

6. In a sketch Proust writes, "Rêve de Maman, sa respiration, se retourne, gémit—. 'Toi qui m'aimes ne me laisse pas réopérer, car je crois que je vais mourir, et ce n'est pas la peine de me prolonger' " (RTP Gall. 3, *Esquisse* 12:1031).

7. "Ce livre essentiel, le seul livre vrai, un grand écrivain n'a pas, dans le sens courant, à l'inventer puisqu'il existe déjà en chacun de nous, mais à le traduire" (RTP Gall. 4:469).

8. "Comme si nos plus belles idées étaient comme des airs de musique qui nous reviendraient sans que nous les eussions jamais entendus, et que nous nous efforcerions d'écouter, de transcrire" (RTP Gall. 4:456–57; see *Esquisse* 24:817).

9. See "Lectures" in Jacques Derrida, *Les Fins de l'homme*, 270–81; and "Roundtable on Translation," in Derrida, *The Ear of the Other*, 93–163.

10. Clément Rosset (*L'Objet singulier*, 20) writes of the fundamental problem of allowing singularity to emerge: "La pensée de l'identité rassemble et confond les deux idées contraires du même et de l'autre: désignant à la fois et contradictoirement ce qui est *sans égal* et ce qui est *égal à quelque autre chose.*"

11. "À moi qui considérais un livre nouveau non comme une chose ayant beaucoup de sembables, mais comme une personne unique, n'ayant de raison d'exister qu'en soi" (RTP Gall. 1:41).

12. Emphasis added. "Je n'avais pas su comprendre que l'insignifiance dans un sujet insignifiant est la marque de l'originalité vraie" (letter 32 to Robert Dreyfus, March 21 or 22, 1909, *Corr.* 9:68).

13. "Quant au livre intérieur de signes inconnus . . . pour la lecture desquels personne ne pouvait m'aider d'aucune règle, cette lecture consistait en un acte de création où nul ne peut nous suppléer ni même collaborer avec nous" (RTP Gall. 4:458).

14. "Seule l'impression, si chétive qu'en semble la matière, si insaississable la trace, est un critérium de vérité" (RTP Gall. 4:458).

15. "De quelque idée laissée en nous par la vie qu'il s'agisse, sa figure matérielle, trace de l'impression qu'elle nous a faite, est encore le gage de sa vérité nécessaire" (RTP Gall. 4:458).

16. See Descombes, *Proust*, 244.

17. "Nous sentons dans un monde, nous pensons, nous nommons dans un autre, nous pouvons entre les deux établir une concordance mais non combler l'intervalle" (RTP Gall. 2:349).

18. Descombes, *Proust*, 242.

19. Ibid., 239–40. Descombes sees the entire phenomenological project of Edmund Husserl and Maurice Merleau-Ponty here: beginning with

an attempt to give a pure description of what is given within to consciousness.

20. "Ce livre, le plus pénible de tous à déchiffrer, est aussi le seul que nous ait dicté la réalité, le seul dont 'l'impression' ait été faite en nous par la réalité même" (RTP Gall. 4:458).

21. "Noter ne signifie rien, ce qu'il faut c'est traduire. Il est probable que si une traduction complète de l'univers pouvait être donnée, nous serions devenus éternels et que tous les problèmes qui se posent actuellement dans les nations seraient résolus et c'est sans doute impossible. Mais du moins le devoir de traduction est-il le plus haut de ceux qui peuvent incomber aux hommes qui ont reçu le pouvoir d'être des traducteurs" (Proust, *Matinée*, 384).

22. "You must understand next that the poet being for Ruskin, as for Carlyle, a sort of scribe writing down at nature's dictation a more or less important part of her secret, the artist's first duty is to add nothing of his own pressing to this message from God" (ASB 166). "Vous comprendrez ensuite que, le poète étant pour Ruskin, comme pour Carlyle, une sorte de scribe écrivant sous la dictée de la nature une partie plus ou moins importante de son secret, le premier devoir de l'artiste est de ne rien ajouter de son propre cru à ce message divin" (CSB 1971, 111).

23. "Tel nom lu dans un livre autrefois, contient entre ses syllabes le vent rapide et le soleil brillant qu'il faisait quand nous le lisions" (RTP Gall. 4:463).

24. Walter Benjamin, "The Task of the Translator," in *Illuminations*. Benjamin had a project to translate Proust's *Sodome and Gomorrhe* into German and wrote in 1925–26 that he had thought for a long time of titling an article "On Translating Proust." It was to have consisted of a series of his observations in aphoristic form; it was to have been about Proust, not an abstract treatise (Benjamin, *Correspondance*, 1:394). Abandoning both his translation and the article, he wrote "The Task of the Translator" instead. See Peter Szondi, *On Textual Understanding and Other Essays*, 145–61.

25. Benjamin, "The Task of the Translator," 75 (emphasis added).

26. " 'Zut, zut, zut, zut' " (RTP Gall. 1:153).

27. "La plupart des prétendues traductions de ce que nous avons ressenti ne font ainsi que nous en débarrasser en le faisant sortir de nous

sous une forme indistincte qui ne nous apprend pas à le connaître" (RTP Gall. 1:153).

28. For a variant, see RTP Gall. 1:836.

29. Descombes points out (*Proust*, 237) that the "myth of interiority" should be understood in a sense attributed to Wittgenstein: "Le mythe de l'intériorité démasqué par Wittgenstein apparaît dans la théorie de la signification que donnent généralement les philosophes depuis l'époque de Descartes et de Locke. Il y a mythe en ce sens qu'il est fait appel à des entités au statut impossible au moment de rendre compte de la façon dont les signes du langage signifient. Ces entités d'ordre mythique sont les 'idées'. Selon la théorie de ces philosophes, un signe communique une signification en ce qu'il est une entité physique (son, marque) à laquelle est associée par convention une entité mentale dans la tête du locuteur: selon les uns, une 'idée représentative' (par exemple, une image); selon d'autres une 'intention' de la conscience (autrement dit, que la pensée soit tournée vers tel ou tel objet)."

30. "Mais les livres sont des rêves plus clairs, qu'on se rappelle plus longtemps" (RTP Gall. 1:753).

31. "D'un rêve plus clair que ceux que nous avons en dormant" (RTP Gall. 1:84). In the last volume the narrator states that dreams confirm the mental character of reality for him and the usefulness of dreams for the composition of his book. "Le rêve était encore un de ces faits de ma vie, qui m'avait toujours le plus frappé, qui avait dû le plus servir à me convaincre du caractère purement mental de la réalité, et dont je ne dédaignerais pas l'aide dans la composition de mon oeuvre" (RTP Gall. 4:493). Michel Grimaud ("La Rhétorique du rêve: Swann et la psychanalyse," 90–91) suggests that the entire Proustian text functions like a dream; that is, the coherence of *Remembrance* rests on paradigmatic associations linked to the unconscious and its mechanisms. See Pierre V. Zima, *L'Ambivalence romanesque: Proust, Kafka, Musil*, 252.

32. This is the starting point of a convincing argument by Grimaud in "La Rhétorique du rêve," 90–91.

33. Referring to his walks, the narrator muses: "Sometimes the fragment of landscape . . . transported into the present will detach itself in such isolation from all associations that it floats uncertainly in [his] mind like a flowering Delos," and he is "unable to say from what place, from what time—perhaps, quite simply, from what dream—it comes"

(RTP 1:201). "Parfois ce morceau de paysage amené ainsi jusqu'à aujourd'hui se détache si isolé de tout, qu'il flotte incertain dans ma pensée comme une Délos fleurie, sans que je puisse dire de quel pays, de quel temps—peut-être tout simplement de quel rêve—il vient" (RTP Gall. 1:182). A distinct attraction is their potency, the ability to accomplish "intravenous injections of love" ("piqûres intraveineuses d'amour": RTP Gall. 4:490) which rush back "with the speed of light" (RTP 3:950).

34. "Ce qu'il y avait d'abord en moi, de plus intime, la poignée sans cesse en mouvement qui gouvernait le reste, c'était ma croyance en la richesse philosophique, en la beauté du livre que je lisais, et mon désir de me les approprier, quel que fût ce livre" (RTP Gall. 1:83).

35. "C'est toujours cette invisible croyance qui soutient l'édifice de notre monde sensitif, et c'est privé d'elle qu'il chancelle" (RTP Gall. 4:29).

36. "On cherche à retrouver dans les choses, devenues par là précieuses, le reflet que notre âme a projeté sur elles, on est déçu en constatant qu'elles semblent dépourvues dans la nature, du charme qu'elles devaient, dans notre pensée, au voisinage de certaines idées" (RTP Gall. 1:186).

37. In "A propos du 'style de Flaubert,' " first published in *Nouvelle Revue Française*, January 1920, Proust responded to issues raised by Albert Thibaudet in "Une Querelle littéraire sur le style de Flaubert" (*Nouvelle Revue Française*, November 1919): "In *Du côté de chez Swann*, certain people, highly literate ones even, not recognizing its rigorous though veiled structure (the harder to discern perhaps for the compass-legs having been opened so wide and for the passages symmetrical with an earlier passage, the cause and the effect, being at a considerable distance one from the other), thought that my novel was a sort of collection of memories, their sequence determined by the fortuitous laws of the association of ideas. In support of which counter-truth, they cited passages in which a few crumbs of 'madeleine', dipped in an infusion, recall to me (or at least recall to the narrator who says 'I' but who is not always myself) a whole period of my life forgotten in the early part of the work. But, not to speak at this moment of the value I find in these unconscious remembrances on which, in the final volume—and not as yet published—of my work, I base my whole theory

of art, and to confine myself to the standpoint of the composition, in order to move from one plane on to another plane, I simply made use not of a fact, but of what I had found to be purer and more precious as a junction, a phenomenon of memory" (ASB, 272–73). "Dans *Du côté de chez Swann*, certaines personnes, mêmes très lettrées, méconnaissant la composition rigoureuse bien que voilée (et peut-être plus difficilement discernable parce qu'elle était à large ouverture de compas et que le morceau symétrique d'un premier morceau, la cause et l'effet, se trouvaient à un grand intervalle l'un de l'autre) crurent que mon roman était une sorte de recueil de souvenirs, s'enchaînant selon les lois fortuites de l'association des idées. Elles citèrent à l'appui de cette contre-vérité, des pages où quelques miettes de 'madeleine', trempées dans une infusion, me rappellent (ou du moins rappellent au narrateur qui dit 'je' et qui n'est pas toujours moi) tout un temps de ma vie, oublié dans la première partie de l'ouvrage. Or, sans parler en ce moment de la valeur que je trouve à ces ressouvenirs inconscients sur lesquels j'asseois, dans le dernier volume—non encore publié—de mon oeuvre, toute ma théorie de l'art, et pour m'en tenir au point de vue de la composition, j'avais simplement pour passer d'un plan à un autre plan, usé non d'un fait, mais de ce que j'avais trouvé plus pur, plus précieux comme jointure, un phénomène de mémoire" (CSB 1971, 598–99). The dissociation from a mechanical sense of association is firm in the novel: "As habit gives to the mere association of ideas between two phenomena, according to a certain school of philosophy, the illusory force and necessity of a law of causation" (RTP 3:514). "Comme l'habitude donne à la simple association d'idées entre deux phénomènes, à ce que prétend une certaine école philosophique, la force, la nécessité illusoires d'une loi de causalité" (RTP Gall. 4:85).

38. "Un plaisir délicieux m'avait envahi, isolé, sans la notion de sa cause" (RTP Gall. 1:44).

39. "Ou plutôt cette essence n'était pas en moi, elle était moi" (RTP Gall. 1:44).

40. "D'où venait-elle? Que signifiait-elle? Où l'appréhender?" (RTP Gall. 1:44).

41. "[L'esprit] . . . est en face de quelque chose qui n'est pas encore et que seul il peut réaliser, puis faire entrer dans sa lumière" (RTP Gall. 1:45).

42. "Certes, ce qui palpite ainsi au fond de moi, ce doit être l'image, le souvenir visuel, qui, lié à cette saveur, tente de la suivre jusqu'à moi. Mais il se débat trop loin, trop confusément; à peine si je perçois le reflet neutre où se confond l'insaisissable tourbillon des couleurs remuées; mais je ne peux distinguer la forme, lui demander, comme au seul interprète possible, de me traduire le témoignage de sa contemporaine, de son inséparable compagne, la saveur, lui demander de m'apprendre de quelle circonstance particulière, de quelle époque du passé il s'agit" (RTP Gall. 1:45–46).

43. RTP Gall. 1:47; RTP Gall. 1, *Esquisse* 14:697.

44. Sigmund Freud, *Totem and Taboo*, 93–94.

45. "Cet être-là n'était jamais venu à moi, ne s'était jamais manifesté, qu'en dehors de l'action, de la jouissance immédiate, chaque fois que le miracle d'une analogie m'avait fait échapper au présent. Seul, il avait le pouvoir de me faire retrouver les jours anciens, le temps perdu, devant quoi les efforts de ma mémoire et de mon intelligence échouaient toujours" (RTP Gall. 4:450).

46. "Toujours le lieu actuel avait été vainqueur; toujours c'était le vaincu [le passé] qui m'avait paru le plus beau" (RTP Gall. 4:453).

47. Poulet, *Proustian Space*, 105.

48. On several occasions Proust protested that he did not at all intend to write a novel that would work out Bergsonian philosophic problems. The *Mercure de France* announced on December 16, 1913: "DU COTE DE CHEZ SWANN: Sous ce titre plein de mystère, M. Marcel Proust publie l'épisode initial d'un roman qui n'intéressera pas moins le philosophe que le lettré. Une telle oeuvre est l'illustration littéraire la plus émouvante des théories fameuses de M. Bergson et de la philosophie nouvelle." Proust wrote to Henri Ghéon: "Jamais je n'ai eue une idée pareille! Et comme je vois une annonce du livre (probablement envoyée et rédigée par mon éditeur) où ce même noble dessein m'est prêté, je vous demande de croire, si vous l'avez lue aussi que jamais je n'eus intention aussi saugrenue. J'ai assez à faire avec ce que j'ai senti, et à tâcher de le convertir—dans la mesure où la lumière et les forces m'ont été données—en idées claires, sans chercher à mettre en roman la philosophie de M. Bergson!" (letter 18, n. 18, January 6, 1914, *Corr.* 13:41). And again: "Je n'ai prononcé qu'une seule fois le nom de Bergson . . . ce fut pour dire que rien n'était moins 'bergsonien' qu'un

tel livre. Mais depuis ce moment-là, je suis tour à tour félicité et blâmé d'être l'auteur d'un roman 'bergsonien' " (letter 13 to Gaston de Pawlowski, January 11, 1914, *Corr.* 13:54).

49. "Au moment où j'entrais dans la chambre, le ciel violet, semblant stigmatisé par la figure raide, géométrique, passagère et fulgurante du soleil . . . s'inclinait vers la mer sur la charnière de l'horizon comme un tableau religieux au-dessus du maître-autel, tandis que les parties différentes du couchant, exposées dans les glaces des bibliothèques basses en acajou qui couraient le long des murs et que je rapportais par la pensée à la merveilleuse peinture dont elles étaient détachées, semblaient comme ces scènes différentes que quelque maître ancien exécuta jadis pour une confrérie sur une châsse et dont on exhibe à côté les uns des autres dans une salle de musée les volets séparés que l'imagination seule du visiteur remet à leur place sur les prédelles du retable" (RTP Gall. 2:160).

50. "L'oeuvre proustienne est faite, et reste faite, d'épisodes distincts. Cependant ces épisodes se mettent en rapport, ils échangent leurs informations, se confèrent une sorte d'intelligibilité réciproque. Tout se passe comme si, au lieu de se succéder les uns aux autres, ils se contentaient de s'ajouter simplement au total en cours, à la façon d'une suite de tableaux dont un amateur grossirait constamment sa collection" (Georges Poulet, *L'Espace proustien*, 133).

51. "Ainsi un amateur d'art à qui on montre le volet d'un retable se rappelle dans quelle église, dans quels musées, dans quelle collection particulière les autres sont dispersés . . . il peut reconstituer dans sa tête la prédelle, l'autel tout entier" (RTP Gall. 4:551).

52. "Rien qu'un moment du passé? Beaucoup plus, peut-être; quelque chose qui, commun à la fois au passé et au présent, est beaucoup plus essentiel qu'eux deux" (RTP Gall. 4:450).

53. "Une joie pareille à une certitude" (RTP Gall. 4:446).

54. See Leo Bersani, "Deguisements du moi en art fragmentaire," 20. Bersani adds that the impossibility of knowing truth transforms life into a novel of infinite development.

55. "Le souvenir . . . nous fait tout à coup respirer un air nouveau, précisément parce que c'est un air qu'on a respiré autrefois, cet air plus pur que les poètes ont vainement essayé de faire régner dans le paradis et qui ne pourrait donner cette sensation profonde de renouvellement

que s'il avait été respiré déjà, car les vrais paradis sont les paradis qu'on a perdus" (RTP Gall. 4:449).

56. "Je me suis élevé à la raison du plaisir . . . que sa 'reconnaissance', sa notion claire n'a pas suivi. Cette raison c'est qu'en nous il y a un être qui ne peut vivre que de l'essence des choses, laquelle ne peut être saisie qu'en dehors du temps" (RTP Gall. I, *Esquisse* 14: 700–701).

57. See Claudia Brodsky, "Remembering Swann," 1014–43.

58. Doubrovsky, *La Place*, 31.

59. Freud considered that all screen memories could be accounted for as translations ("Screen Memories," 321). See Patrick Mahony, *Freud as a Writer*, 7.

60. See "A propos du 'style de Flaubert,'" ASB, 273; CSB 1971, 598–99. See also the letter to Maria de Madrazo cited in Chapter 6, note 3.

61. Pugh, *The Birth*, 85.

62. Ibid.

63. The illumination occurs in 1910; it is the moment when Proust, out walking, substitutes the name Garmantes (not Guermantes) for Villebon to identify a path and associates it with the sight of a woman: "'C'est la comtesse de Garmantes', nous dit un paysan. He explains: 'la comtesse du château de Garmantes.' And a few lines lower down: 'Tel était le côté de Garmantes.' Claudine Quémar ["Sur deux versions anciennes des 'côtés' de Combray," 252] calls this 'une illumination décisive.' . . . Here, then, is the 'illumination' for which we have been seeking. It came when Proust was already giving shape to his fiction. Through a name, Guermantes/Garmantes, Sainte-Beuve is absorbed into fiction, and the reveries of the present are absorbed into a more authentic fictional identity, whose experience is rooted in the events of a childhood. . . . [Quémar (240–67) showed how] the two ways served as a perpetual stimulus to find more and more elements which could enrich these pages; and, as these elements were added a deep structure developed. Once this deep structure was found, the text did not have to be so manifestly symmetrical. This occurs principally in Cahier 12°, but the corner was turned with Cahier 4°. It is the two walks, as they take shape in Cahier 4°, that mark the creating of significant form in Proust's enterprise" (Pugh, *The Birth*, 66–67).

64. Descombes, *Proust*, 241.

65. "Un des chefs-d'œuvre de la littérature française, *Sylvie*, de Gérard de Nerval, a, tout comme le livre des *Mémoires d'Outre-Tombe* relatif à Combourg, une sensation du même genre que le goût de la madeleine et 'le gazouillement de la grive'. Chez Baudelaire enfin, ces réminiscences, plus nombreuses encore, sont évidemment moins fortuites et par conséquent, à mon avis, décisives. C'est le poète lui-même qui, avec plus de choix et de paresse, recherche volontairement, dans l'odeur d'une femme par exemple, de sa chevelure et de son sein, les analogies inspiratrices qui lui évoqueront 'l'azur du ciel immense et rond' et 'un port rempli de flammes et de mâts'. J'allais chercher à me rappeler les pièces de Baudelaire à la base desquelles se trouve ainsi une sensation transposée, pour achever de me replacer dans une filiation aussi noble, et me donner par là l'assurance que l'oeuvre que je n'avais plus aucune hésitation à entreprendre méritait l'effort que j'allais lui consacrer, quand . . ." (RTP Gall. 4:498). And the editors of the Pléiade edition mention a text by Ernest Renan from 1906 which presents a structure of reminiscence almost identical to what later became Proust's: "Singulier fait psychologique—j'entends une charrette passer dans la rue avec une cloche suspendue au-dessus, et tintant pour avertir. . . . Cela me rappelle par une association d'idées très vive tous mes souvenirs de Bretagne, où ces charrettes de campagne ont aussi une cloche. Ajoutez que le tintement était le même. Tout à coup je me rappelle par une conception *se rapportant aux yeux* que j'ai vu quelquefois cette charrette dans la rue, et qu'elle n'a rien d'analogue pour la vue avec la Bretagne. Je cherche de nouveau à réexciter l'association d'idées d'après l'*ouïe*, et, chose singulière, je ne puis, le souvenir de la vue est plus fort, et ce n'est que quand ce souvenir est oblitéré que j'ai retrouvé mon association d'idées par les oreilles" (Renan, *Cahiers de jeunesse,* septième cahier, 60; cited in RTP Gall. 1:1123–24).

66. A text first published in *Le Figaro* in 1907 under the title "Impressions de route en automobile." See Compagnon, Preface, x.

67. "Sans me dire que ce qui était caché derrière les clochers de Martinville devait être quelque chose d'analogue à une jolie phrase, puisque c'était sous la forme de mots qui me faisaient plaisir, que cela m'était apparu . . . je composai malgré les cahots de la voiture, pour soulager ma conscience et obéir à mon enthousiasme, le petit morceau suivant" (RTP Gall. 1:179).

68. "For what had happened was that, while I recognised in this passage the same taste for uncommon phrases, the same musical outpouring, the same idealist philosophy which had been present in the earlier passages without my having recognised them as being the source of my pleasure, I now had the impression of being confronted not by a particular passage in one of Bergotte's works, tracing a purely bi-dimensional figure upon the surface of my mind, but rather by the 'ideal passage' of Bergotte, common to every one of his books, to which all the earlier, similar passages, now becoming merged in it, had added a kind of density and volume by which my own understanding seemed to be enlarged" (RTP 1:101–2). "C'est que, reconnaissant alors ce même goût pour les expressions rares, cette même effusion musicale, cette même philosophie idéaliste qui avait déjà été les autres fois, sans que je m'en rendisse compte, la cause de mon plaisir, je n'eus plus l'impression d'être en présence d'un morceau particulier d'un certain livre de Bergotte, traçant à la surface de ma pensée une figure purement linéaire, mais plutôt du 'morceau idéal' de Bergotte, commun à tous ses livres et auquel tous les passage analogues qui venaient se confondre avec lui, auraient donné une sorte d'épaisseur, de volume, dont mon esprit semblait agrandi" (RTP Gall. 1:93). See Antoine Compagnon, *La Troisième République des Lettres*, 250.

69. See Richard, *Proust*.

70. See RTP Gall. 2:691 and 4:478.

71. Proust, *On Reading Ruskin*, xiv.

72. " 'In what tempting and magnificent forms falsehood may have insinuated itself into the very heart of his intellectual sincerity . . . ' This is what I meant to say: there is a sort of idolatry which no one has defined better than Ruskin himself, in a passage from the *Lectures on Art*: 'Such I conceive generally, though indeed with good arising out of it, for every great evil brings some good in its backward eddies—such I conceive to have been the deadly function of art in its ministry to what, whether in heathen or Christian lands, and whether in the pageantry of words, or colours, or fair forms, is truly, and in the deep sense, to be called idolatry—the serving with the best of our hearts and minds, some dear or sad fantasy which we have made for ourselves, while we disobey the present call of the Master, who is not dead, and who is not now fainting under His cross, but requiring us to take up

ours' " (ASB, 182–83). " 'Sous quelles formes magnifiques et tentatrices le mensonge a pu se glisser jusqu'au sein de sa sincérité intellectuelle.' Voici ce que je voulais dire: il y a une sorte d'idolâtrie que personne n'a mieux définie que Ruskin dans une page de *Lectures on Art*: 'Ça été, je crois, non sans mélange de bien, sans doute, car les plus grands maux apportent quelques biens dans leur reflux, ça été, je crois, le rôle vraiment néfaste de l'art, d'aider à ce qui, chez les païens comme chez les chrétiens—qu'il s'agisse du mirage des mots, des couleurs ou des belles formes,—doit vraiment, dans le sens profond du mot, s'appeler idolâtrie, c'est-à-dire le fait de servir avec le meilleur de nos coeurs et de nos esprits quelque chère ou triste image que nous nous sommes créée, pendant que nous désobéissons à l'appel présent du Maître, qui n'est pas mort, qui ne défaille pas en ce moment sous sa croix, mais nous ordonne de porter la nôtre.' " (CSB 1971, 129).

73. ASB, 184; CSB 1971, 130.

74. "Il n'y a pas de meilleure manière d'arriver à prendre conscience de ce qu'on sent soi-même que d'essayer de recréer en soi ce qu'a senti un maître. Dans cet effort profond c'est notre pensée elle-même que nous mettons, avec la sienne, au jour" (CSB 1971, 140).

75. "La transcription d'un univers qui était à redessiner tout entier" (RTP Gall. 1:623).

76. "Elstir ne pouvant regarder une fleur qu'en la transplantant d'abord dans ce jardin intérieur où nous sommes forcés de rester toujours. Il avait montré dans cette aquarelle l'apparition des roses qu'il avait vues et que sans lui on n'eût connues jamais; de sorte qu'on peut dire que c'était une variété nouvelle dont ce peintre, comme un ingénieux horticulteur, avait enrichi la famille des roses" (RTP Gall. 3:334).

77. "Mais j'y pouvais discerner que le charme de chacune consistait en une sorte de métamorphose des choses représentées, analogue à celle qu'en poésie on nomme métaphore" (RTP Gall. 2:191).

78. "La vérité ne commencera qu'au moment où l'écrivain prendra deux objets différents, posera leur rapport, analogue dans le monde de l'art à celui qu'est le rapport unique de la loi causale dans le monde de la science, et les enfermera dans les anneaux nécessaires d'un beau style. Même, ainsi que la vie, quand, en rapprochant une qualité commune à deux sensations, il dégagera leur essence commune en les réunissant l'une et l'autre pour les soustraire aux contingences du temps,

dans une métaphore" (RTP Gall. 4:468). In letter 95 to Maurice Duplay, June 1907, Proust writes: "Non l'image doit avoir sa raison d'être en elle-même, sa brusque naissance toute divine" *(Corr.* 7:167).

79. "Qu'il s'agît d'impressions comme celle que m'avait donnée la vue des clochers de Martinville, ou de reminiscences comme celle de l'inégalité des deux marches ou le goût de la madeleine, il fallait tâcher d'interpréter les sensations comme les signes d'autant de lois et d'idées, en essayant de penser, c'est-à-dire de faire sortir de la pénombre ce que j'avais senti, de le convertir en un équivalent spirituel. Or, ce moyen qui me paraissait le seul, qu'était-ce autre chose que faire une oeuvre d'art?" (RTP Gall. 4:457).

80. "Si Dieu le Père avait créé les choses en les nommant, c'est en leur ôtant leur nom, ou en leur en donnant un autre qu'Elstir les recréait. Les noms qui désignent les choses répondent toujours à une notion de l'intelligence, étrangère à nos impressions véritables, et qui nous force à éliminer d'elles tout ce qui ne se rapporte pas à cette notion" (RTP Gall. 2:191).

81. Proust, "Preface to Morand," ASB, 275. "Mon cher maître Anatole France . . . vient d'écrire dans *La revue de Paris*, un article où il déclare que toute singularité dans le style doit être rejetée. Or il est certain que le style de Paul Morand est singulier. Si j'avais la joie de revoir M France dont les bontés pour moi sont encore vivantes sous mes yeux, je lui demanderais comment il peut croire à l'unité du style, puisque les sensibilités sont singulières. Même la beauté du style est le signe infaillible que la pensée s'élève, qu'elle a découvert et noué les rapports nécessaires entre des objets que leur contingence laissait séparés" (Proust, Preface to *Tendres Stocks*, 12).

82. Proust, "Preface to Morand," ASB, 281. " 'Quel est votre canon?' nous demande . . . [M. France]. Nous refusons le principe même du 'canon', qui signifierait l'indépendance d'un style unique à l'égard d'une pensée multiforme" (Proust, Preface to *Tendres Stocks*, 23).

83. See ASB, 261; CSB 1971, 586. Walter Benjamin wrote to Hugo von Hofmannsthal that he admired Proust's way of doing what poets had probably always done: taking his metaphors from anything at hand, mired even in the most banal of situations, to bring forth a magnificent image with depth and density (letter 149, December 28, 1925, *Cor-*

respondance, 1:371). See Marcel Muller, "Proust et Flaubert: Une Dimension intertextuelle de *A la recherche du temps perdu*," 57–71.

84. "Le rafraîchissement . . . de confronter, comme la cathédrale, à la fleur sculptée, la fleur vivante, est attendrissant mais superflu" (letter 109 to Jean Cocteau, December 1910, *Corr.* 10:232).

85. In the history of rhetoric, thinkers such as Gérard Genette, Roman Jakobson, and Jacques Lacan have regarded metaphor and metonymy as the two main tropes. Genette shows how the terms metaphor and metonymy are already metaphorized through a spatialized perceptive model according to which metonymy is used for contiguity or proximity or juxtaposition, synecdoche for intersection, metaphor for resemblance (*Figures* 3, 28–34, 41–66). For Jakobson, all poetic thought is organized according to the distinction of metonymy as a combinatory move within language based on contiguity, and metaphor as a selective move based on similarity. Lacan relates metaphor to condensation and metonymy to displacement. See Roman Jakobson, *Fundamentals of Language*, 55–82; and Jacques Lacan, "L'instance de la lettre dans l'inconscient," in *Ecrits: A Selection*, 146–78. See also Jonathan Culler, *The Pursuit of Signs*, 188–209; Mahony, *Freud*, 134–35; Naomi Schor, *Reading in Detail: Aesthetics and the Feminine*, 71; Philippe Lejeune, "Les carafes de la Vivonne," 285–305.

86. "Il y avait eu en moi, irradiant une petite zone autour de moi une sensation" (RTP Gall. 4:452).

87. Genette, *Figures* 3, 58. "Cette obscure fraîcheur de ma chambre offrait à mon imagination le spectacle total de l'été" (RTP Gall. 1:82).

88. "Il semble bien que Proust ait voulu, et dès le début, ce rythme de plus en plus heurté, d'une massivité et d'une brutalité beethoveniennes, qui contraste si vivement avec la fluidité presque insaisissable des premières parties, comme pour opposer la texture temporelle des événements les plus anciens et celle des plus récents: comme si la mémoire du narrateur, à mesure que les faits se rapprochent, devenait à la fois plus sélective et plus monstrueusement grossissante" (Genette, *Figures* 3, 128).

89. As Ellison (*Readings of Proust*, 108) points out, narratology cannot provide the answer to the problem of discontinuity.

90. Zima, *L'Ambivalence*, 260, 153, 169, 230. See also Ellison, *Readings*

of *Proust*, 102–16; and Maria Paganini, *A la peche au poisson-loup: Cho-régraphie de l'écriture proustienne*.

91. Zima, *L'Ambivalence*, 235. Zima singles out three points. (1) Construction is not logico-causal; systematic syntagmatic representation is considered false. (2) Semantic affinities and spontaneity of the associative process engender paradigms in the unconscious realm. (3) The idea of a vital unity, discovered a posteriori, in which the parts rejoin spontaneously to compose a whole, saves the notion of the particular.

92. "Le contraire de l'art mufle étant celui des architectes des cathé-drales qui faisaient des sculptures aussi raffinées *derrière* une statue, à une hauteur où personne ne les verrait, impression accrue pour nous de tout le symbolisme dépensé que nous ne connaissons pas, sauf les érudits" (letter 93 to Robert Dreyfus, Cabourg, September 1 or 2, 1909, *Corr.* 9:183).

93. See Nattiez, *Proust as Musician,* for an analysis of how music functions within Proust's novel. Nattiez and I differ on the status and concept of totality in its working out within the *The Captive* and *The Fugitive*.

94. "Quand la vision de l'univers se modifie, s'épure, devient plus adéquate au souvenir de la patrie intérieure, il est bien naturel que cela se traduise par une altération générale des sonorités chez le musicien comme de la couleur chez le peintre" (RTP Gall. 3:761).

95. "Dans le vestiaire de sa mémoire" (RTP Gall. 1:345).

96. "Comme une déesse protectrice et confidente de son amour . . . avait revêtu le déguisement de cette apparence sonore" (RTP Gall. 1:342).

97. "Les refrains oubliés du bonheur" (RTP Gall. 1:339).

98. "Il regrettait presque qu'elle eût une signification, une beauté intrinsèque et fixe . . . comme . . . en des lettres écrites par une femme aimée, nous en voulons . . . aux mots du langage, de ne pas être faits uniquement de l'essence d'une liaison passagère et d'un être particulier" (RTP Gall. 1:215–16). Note 1 (RTP Gall. 1:216) suggests that this passage was inspired by a passage about lying in JS, 760–63.

99. "C'est dans un rose d'aurore que, pour se construire progressivement devant moi, cet univers inconnu était tiré du silence et de la nuit" (RTP Gall. 3:754).

100. "La timide interrogation à laquelle répondait la petite phrase, de

la supplication haletante pour trouver l'accomplissement de l'étrange promesse, qui avait retenti" (RTP Gall. 3:759). See RTP Gall. 1:757.

101. RTP Gall. 1:759. "La musique de Vinteuil étendait, notes par notes, touches par touches, les colorations inconnues, inestimables, d'un univers insoupçonné, fragmenté par les lacunes que laissaient entre elles les auditions de son oeuvre" (RTP Gall. 3:759). See RTP Gall. 3, *Esquisse* 13:1148: "Comme il y avait une certaine unité aux fragments dispersés çà et là, d'une certaine coloration, qui était l'unité d'Elstir, de même, la musique de Vinteuil, note par note, touche par touche, étendait une coloration spéciale qu'on n'avait jamais vue ailleurs."

102. "Une véritable différence, celle qu'il y avait entre la pensée de tel musicien et les éternelles investigations de Vinteuil, la question qu'il se posa sous tant de formes, son habituelle spéculation, mais aussi débarrassée des formes analytiques du raisonnement que si elle s'était exercée dans le monde des anges, de sorte que nous pouvons en mesurer la profondeur, mais pas . . . la traduire en langage humain" (RTP Gall. 3:760).

103. "Chaque artiste semble ainsi comme le citoyen d'une patrie inconnue, oubliée de lui-même" (RTP Gall. 3:761).

104. "Patrie intérieure" (RTP Gall. 3:761).

105. "Transposition, dans l'ordre sonore, de la profondeur" (RTP Gall. 3:761) .

106. "Enfin le motif joyeux resta triomphant, ce n'était plus un appel presque inquiet lancé derrière un ciel vide, c'était une joie ineffable qui semblait venir du Paradis; une joie aussi différente de celle de la Sonate que, d'un ange doux et grave de Bellini, jouant du théorbe, pourrait être, vêtu d'une robe d'écarlate, quelque archange de Mantegna sonnant dans un buccin" (RTP Gall. 3:764–65).

107. "Mais serait-elle jamais réalisable pour moi?" (RTP Gall. 3:765).

108. "Ces impressions qu'à des intervalles éloignés je retrouvais dans ma vie comme les points de repère, les amorces, pour la construction d'une vie véritable: l'impression éprouvée devant les clochers de Martinville, devant une rangée d'arbres près de Balbec" (RTP Gall. 3:765).

109. "De papiers plus illisibles que des papyrus ponctués d'écriture cunéiforme, la formule éternellement vraie, à jamais féconde, de cette joie inconnue, l'espérance mystique de l'ange écarlate du matin" (RTP Gall. 3:766–67).

110. "C'était grâce à elle ... qu'avait pu venir jusqu'à moi l'étrange appel que je ne cesserais plus jamais d'entendre comme la promesse qu'il existait autre chose, réalisable par l'art" (RTP Gall. 3:767).

CHAPTER THREE

1. A reformulation of the question posed by Barbara Freeman for "The Ethics of Ethics: Literature," a session of the Modern Language Association meeting (New Orleans, 1988) at which a shortened version of this chapter was presented: "If there were no absolutes, what ethical bond could function in place of universal moral law in the postmodern world?"

2. See Descombes, *Proust,* 17.

3. "Quand les systèmes philosophiques qui contiennent le plus de vérité sont dictés à leurs auteurs, en dernière analyse, par une raison de sentiment, comment supposer que, dans une simple affaire politique comme l'affaire Dreyfus, des raisons de ce genre ne puissent, à l'insu du raisonneur, gouverner sa raison? Bloch croyait avoir logiquement choisi son dreyfusisme, et savait pourtant que son nez, sa peau et ses cheveux lui avaient été imposés par sa race. Sans doute la raison est plus libre; elle obéit pourtant à certaines lois qu'elle ne s'est pas données" (RTP Gall. 2:593).

4. "We must make some initial place for what is still the predominant form of literary and cultural criticism today [ethical criticism], in spite of its repudiation by every successive generation of literary theorists (each for a different reason)" (Fredric Jameson, *The Political Unconscious,* 59). Wayne Booth (*The Company We Keep,* 15) discusses the "ethical value of the stories we tell each other as 'imitations of life,' whether or not they depict actual events."

5. Miller, *The Ethics of Reading,* 2.

6. See Paul Smith, *Discerning the Subject* .

7. "Aucune action extérieure à soi n'a d'importance" (Proust, *Carnet de 1908,* 101).

8. JS, Hopkins, 351. " 'Je jure que ce ne peut être de l'écriture de Dreyfus.' Ces paroles sont émouvantes à entendre, car on sent qu'elles

sont simplement la conclusion d'un raisonnement fait d'après des rè-
gles scientifiques et en dehors de toute opinion sur cette affaire" (JS,
650).

9. JS, Hopkins, 351–52. "La vérité est quelque chose qui existe réelle-
ment en soi, en dehors de toute opinion, . . . la vérité à laquelle le
savant s'attache est déterminée par une série de conditions qui ne se
trouvent nullement dans les convenances humaines même les plus
hautes, mais dans la nature des choses. . . . Et plus . . . [l]'opinion [des
hommes] est différente de ce qu'on aurait dû présumer, plus on sent
avec plaisir que la Science est quelque de tout autre que toutes les
choses humaines et politiques" (JS, 650).

10. Julian Benda, *La Jeunesse d'un clerc*, 204 (emphasis added), cited
in Susan Suleiman, "The Literary Significance of the Dreyfus Affair,"
117. Benda argued in favor of rational thought tied to freedom, against
intuition and emotion (in particular he denounced Bergson). In *La
Trahison des clercs,* he attacked the intellectuals as traitors in the defense
of justice and truth. Suleiman argues that one of the important and
unique aspects of the Dreyfus case was the impact of writers upon
politicians who changed their positions.

11. JS, Hopkins, 352–53. "Nous n'osons pas nous fier à notre opinion
et nous nous rangeons à l'opinion qui nous est le moins favorable. Et,
juif, nous comprenons l'antisémitisme, et, partisan de Dreyfus, nous
comprenons le jury d'avoir condamné Zola" (JS, 651).

12. On November 27 or 28, 1898, Proust declared: "I know that my
name will add nothing to the list. But the fact of figuring on the list
will add to my name: one doesn't miss an occasion to inscribe one's
name on a pedestal" (letter to "Monsieur le Directeur," assumed to
be the managing editor of either *Le Siècle* or *L'Aurore*, the Republican,
socialist paper that published Zola's "J'accuse"), addressed in the English translation (*Selected Letters*) to Ernest Vaughan.

13. "Ne me croyez surtout pas devenu anti-dreyfusard. J'écris sous la
dictée de mes personnages et il se trouve que beaucoup de ce volume-
ci, le sont" (*Corr. gén*. 6:236; cited in RTP Gall. 2:450n).

14. Emphasis added. "Est-ce que vous avez été dreyfusard jadis? je l'ai
été passionnément. Or, comme dans mon livre je suis absolument ob-
jectif, il se trouve que *Le Côté de Guermantes* a l'air anti-dreyfusard.

Mais *Sodome et Gomorrhe* 2 sera entièrement dreyfusard et rectificatif" (*Corr. gén.* 3:19; cited in RTP Gall. 2:450n).

15. Hannah Arendt describes the relation between truth and *doxa* in much the same terms. The following discussion is indebted to her text as excerpted from the unpublished manuscript of a lecture presented in 1954 (Library of Congress, Washington) and cited in her "Philosophie et politique."

16. JS Hopkins, 337. "Un philosophe dont la pensée . . . cherchait sans cesse à éclaircir les notions qui se présentaient à elle" (JS, 637).

17. JS Hopkins, 342. "C'est ce sentiment qu'on pouvait éprouver en entendant le colonel Picquart et qui nous émeut tant dans le Phédon, quand en suivant le raisonnement de Socrate nous avons tout d'un coup le sentiment extraordinaire d'entendre un raisonnement dont aucune espèce de désir personnel n'est venue altérer la pureté" (JS, 641).

18. As Henri Atlan (*A tort ou à raison*, 313) has put it: "Le transcendantal du vécu est celui de l'absence de tout sens possible par rapport à notre expérience du sens, après qu'on a réalisé que tout sens est dans le monde parce que tout sens est interprétation, construction, autocréation."

19. Bernard Brun ("Brouillons et brouillages," 110–28) has analyzed the changes within the early versions of certain passages concerning Judaism.

20. "[M. Swann] était, quoique beaucoup plus jeune, le meilleur ami de mon grand-père qui pourtant n'aimait pas les juifs. C'était chez lui une de ces petites faiblesses, de ces préjugés absurdes comme il y en a *quelquefois* précisément chez les natures les plus droites, les plus fermes pour le bien. Par exemple le préjugé artistocratique chez un St Simon, le préjugé contre les dentistes chez certains médecins, contre les comédiens chez certains bourgeois" (cited in Brun, "Brouillons et brouillages," 115–16).

21. "Voilà, il est dreyfusard, il n'y a plus l'ombre d'un doute"; "Non décidément il est antidreyfusard, c'est couru" (RTP Gall. 2:537).

22. "L'élasticité, la mobilité qu'exige un changement de milieu . . . cette souplesse de l'organisme" (cited in Brun, "Brouillons et brouillages, 123).

23. "Cet ensemble inchangeable et réglé semblait, comme l'univers nécessaire de Kant, suspendu à un acte suprême de liberté" (RTP Gall. 1:497). He refers here to the moral law described by Kant which allows discovery of freedom only in relation to phenomena in space and time, and not with respect to those concepts called noumena, which cannot be experienced.

24. "Les gens du monde en furent stupéfaits et, sans se soucier d'imiter la duchesse, éprouvèrent pourtant de son action l'espèce de soulagement qu'on a dans Kant quand, après la démonstration la plus rigoureuse du déterminisme, on découvre qu'au-dessus du monde de la nécessité il y a celui de la liberté" (RTP Gall. 2:768).

25. "[La duchesse de Guermantes] fût antidreyfusarde (tout en croyant à l'innocence de Dreyfus, de même qu'elle passait sa vie dans le monde tout en ne croyant qu'aux idées)" (RTP Gall. 2:767).

26. "J'avais vu dans l'affaire Dreyfus . . . croire que la vérité est un certain fait, que les ministres, le médecin, possèdent un oui ou non qui n'a pas besoin d'interprétation, qui fait . . . que les gens du pouvoir *savaient* si Dreyfus était coupable" (RTP Gall. 4:493).

27. Proust, *Letters*, 153 (in this Curtiss edition, the letter is dated July, 13, 1906). "Pour eux [Dreyfus et Picquart] les peines reposaient sur des erreurs. Bienheureux ceux qui sont victimes d'erreurs judiciaires ou autres! Ce sont les seuls humains pour qui il y ait des revanches et des réparations. D'ailleurs je ne sais pas qui dans cette réparation est le metteur en scène des derniers 'tableaux'. Mais [Dreyfus] est incomparable et même émouvant. Et il est impossible de lire le 'dernier tableau' de ce matin: 'Dans la cour de l'école militaire, avec cinq cents figurants' sans avoir les larmes aux yeux" (letter 91 to Mme Straus, July 21, 1906, *Corr.* 6:159).

28. Aleksander Wat describes reading Proust while in prison: "I realized that my entire value system had not been destroyed but had simply been left outside the prison walls. . . . *Swann's Way* did not emerge diminished from that reading. . . . And what was of more importance to me was that in its experience of time past, the book was, first and foremost, a state of constant agony in which nothing had yet died but everything was dying" (*New York Review of Books,* December 8, 1988, 29).

29. RTP Gall. 1:508. Such, for example, was the effect of reversing the social hierarchy with the Dreyfus affair: Jews went to the bottom of the social ladder, and obscure nationals rose to take their place.

30. "Le dreyfusisme avait rendu Swann d'une naïveté extraordinaire. Au moment même où, si lucide, il lui était donné, grâce aux données héritées de son ascendance, de voir une vérité encore cachée aux gens du monde, se montrait pourtant d'un aveuglement comique. Il remettait toutes ses admirations et tous ses dédains à l'épreuve d'un critérium nouveau, le dreyfusisme" (RTP Gall. 2:869–70).

31. Le Siècle, a newspaper published from 1836 to 1917, supported revision of the Dreyfus trial. L'Aurore, a daily newspaper founded in 1897, published Zola's famous letter "J'accuse" on January 13, 1898.

32. "Il s'appelle? La princesse de Guermantes" (RTP Gall. 3:109).

33. "C'est un soulagement pour moi de ne plus avoir à me tenir loin de vous et surtout que vous sentiez bien que si j'avais pu être dans d'autres sentiments, c'est que je n'avais pas un doute sur le bien-fondé du jugement rendu. Dès que j'en eus un, je ne pouvais plus désirer qu'une chose, la réparation de l'erreur" (RTP Gall. 3:110).

34. In a variant, the narrator sees tears come to Swann's eyes (RTP Gall. 3:110a).

35. "Monseigneur, je ne suis plus qu'une princesse française, et je pense comme tous mes compatriotes" (RTP Gall. 3:104).

36. "En entendant M. de Charlus dire . . . : 'Tiens, il aime le sexe fort', avec la même certitude que celle qui permet de condamner, pour un juge un criminel qui n'a pas avoué, pour un médecin un paralytique général qui ne sait peut-être pas lui-même son mal mais qui a fait telles fautes de prononciation d'où on peut déduire qu'il sera mort dans trois ans" (RTP Gall. 3:356).

37. "Comme les Juifs encore . . . se fuyant les uns les autres . . . ; mais aussi rassemblés à leurs pareils par l'ostracisme qui les frappe, l'opprobre où ils sont tombés, ayant fini par prendre, par une persécution semblable à celle d'Israël, les caractères physiques et moraux d'une race . . . si bien que, tout en niant qu'ils soient une race . . . , ils les démasquent volontiers . . . , et allant chercher, comme un médecin l'appendicite, l'inversion jusque dans l'histoire, ayant plaisir à rappeler que Socrate était l'un d'eux, comme les Israélites disent que Jésus était juif, sans songer qu'il n'y avait pas d'anormaux quand l'homosexualité était la

norme, pas d'antichrétiens avant le Christ, que l'opprobre seul fait le crime, parce qu'il n'a laissé subsister que ceux qui étaient réfractaires à toute prédication, à tout exemple, à tout châtiment, en vertu d'une disposition innée tellement spéciale qu'elle répugne plus aux autres hommes . . . que de certains vices qui y contredisent comme le vol, la cruauté, la mauvaise foi, mieux compris, donc plus excusés du commun des hommes" (RTP Gall. 3:18).

38. "Les femmes n'entendent rien à la politique" (RTP Gall. 3:551).

39. "C'était le moment où des suites de l'affaire Dreyfus était né un mouvement antisémite parallèle à un mouvement de pénétration plus abondant du monde par les Israélites. Les politiciens n'avaient pas eu tort en pensant que la découverte de l'erreur judiciaire porterait un coup à l'antisémitisme. Mais, provisoirement au moins, un antisémitisme mondain s'en trouvait au contraire accru et exaspéré" (RTP Gall. 4:155).

40. "Il est difficile, quand on est troublé par les idées de Kant et la nostalgie de Baudelaire, d'écrire le français exquis d'Henri IV, de sorte que la pureté même du langage de la duchesse était un signe de limitation, et qu'en elle l'intelligence et la sensibilité étaient restées fermées à toutes les nouveautés" (RTP Gall. 2:792).

41. "Dès qu'on parlait de l'affaire Dreyfus, 'bel et bien' surgissait: 'Affaire Dreyfus, affaire Dreyfus, c'est bientôt dit et le terme est impropre; ce n'est pas une affaire de religion, mais *bel et bien* une affaire politique' " (RTP Gall. 3:549).

42. Norpois exclaims, for example, "M. Picquart . . . fit bel et bien fiasco" (RTP Gall. 2:537). The English here does not render the expression: "M. Picquart might move heaven and earth at the subsequent hearings, but he came completely to grief" (RTP 2:248).

43. "Car ce crime affreux n'est pas simplement une cause juive, mais *bel et bien* une immense affaire nationale qui peut amener les plus effroyables conséquences pour la France d'où on devrait expulser tous les Juifs" (RTP Gall. 3:551).

44. "Nous n'avons de l'univers que des visions informes, fragmentées et que nous complétons par des associations d'idées arbitraires, créatrices de dangereuses suggestions" (RTP Gall. 4:154).

45. "En faisant manœuvrer sa langue dans la pointe de sa bouche en

cul de poule: 'A propos de l'affaire Dreyfus' (pourquoi de l'affaire Dreyfus? il s'agissait seulement d'une robe rouge)" (RTP Gall. 3:550).

46. "On ne l'aurait pas cru si facilement traître '*a priori*'" (RTP Gall. 3:551).

47. "Je sentais que cela allait se gâter et je me remis précipitamment à parler robes" (RTP Gall. 3:551).

48. "Quant à se demander ce qu'il valait en soi, personne n'y songeait, pas plus pour l'admettre maintenant qu'autrefois pour le condamner. Il n'était plus *shocking*" (RTP Gall. 4:305).

49. "Quelque chose d'aussi profond . . . qu'une période géologique" (RTP Gall. 4:306).

50. "(A vrai dire, ce changement profond opéré par la guerre était en raison inverse de la valeur des esprits touchés, du moins à partir d'un certain degré. Tout en bas, les purs sots, les purs gens de plaisir, ne s'occupaient pas qu'il y eût la guerre. Mais tout en haut, ceux qui se sont fait une vie intérieure ambiante ont peu égard à l'importance des événements. Ce qui modifie profondément pour eux l'ordre des pensées c'est bien plutôt quelque chose qui semble en soi n'avoir aucune importance et qui renverse pour eux l'ordre du temps en les faisant contemporains d'un autre temps de leur vie. On peut s'en rendre compte pratiquement à la beauté des pages qu'il inspire: un chant d'oiseau dans le parc de Montboissier, ou une brise chargée de l'odeur de réséda, sont évidemment des événements de moindre conséquence que les plus grandes dates de la Révolution et de l'Empire. Ils ont cependant inspiré à Chateaubriand dans les *Mémoires d'outre-tombe* des pages d'une valeur infiniment plus grande)" (RTP Gall. 4:306).

51. " 'Faire sortir l'artiste de sa tour d'ivoire', et à traiter des sujets non frivoles ni sentimentaux, mais peignant de grands mouvements ouvriers, et, à défaut de foules, à tout le moins non plus d'insignifiants oisifs ('j'avoue que la peinture de ces inutiles m'indiffère assez', disait Bloch), mais de nobles intellectuels, ou des héros" (RTP Gall. 4: 460).

52. "L'art véritable n'a que faire de tant de proclamations et s'accomplit dans le silence" (RTP Gall. 4:460).

53. "L'idée d'un art populaire comme d'un art patriotique, si même elle n'avait pas été dangereuse, me semblait ridicule. S'il s'agissait de le rendre accessible au peuple, en sacrifiant les raffinements de la forme, 'bons pour des oisifs', j'avais assez fréquenté de gens du monde pour

savoir que ce sont eux les véritables illettrés, et non les ouvriers électriciens" (RTP Gall. 4:466).

54. "Je déteste tellement les ouvrages idéologiques où le récit n'est tout le temps qu'une faillite des intentions de l'auteur" (letter 43 to Jacques Rivière, February 6, 1914, *Corr.* 13:98). See also Proust, *Matinée,* 117–18.

55. "On cherche à se dépayser en lisant, et les ouvriers sont aussi curieux des princes que les princes des ouvriers. Dès le début de la guerre M. Barrès avait dit que l'artiste (en l'espèce Titien) doit avant tout servir la gloire de sa patrie. Mais il ne peut la servir qu'en étant artiste, c'est-à-dire qu'à condition, au moment où il étudie ces lois, institue ces expériences et fait ces découvertes aussi délicates que celles de la science, de ne pas penser à autre chose—fût-ce à la patrie—qu'à la vérité qui est devant lui. N'imitons pas les révolutionnaires qui par 'civisme' méprisaient, s'ils ne les détruisaient pas, les oeuvres de Watteau et de La Tour, peintres qui honorent davantage la France que tous ceux de la Révolution" (RTP Gall. 4:467).

56. "La fausseté même de l'art prétendu réaliste" (RTP Gall. 4:460).

57. Quoted in Booth, *Company,* 12. See also Richard Ellmann, *Oscar Wilde,* 300–359, esp. 302–5.

58. ASB, 12. "Un livre est le produit d'un autre moi que celui que nous manifestons dans nos habitudes, dans la société, dans nos vices" (CSB 1971, 221).

59. "Notre personnalité sociale est une création de la pensée des autres" (RTP Gall. 1:19).

60. "Quant au livre intérieur de signes inconnus. . . . Aussi combien se détournent de l'écrire! Que de tâches n'assume-t-on pour éviter celle-là! Chaque événement, que ce fût l'affaire Dreyfus, que ce fût la guerre, avait fourni d'autres excuses aux écrivains pour ne pas déchiffrer, ce livre-là; ils voulaient assurer le triomphe du droit, refaire l'unité morale de la nation, n'avaient pas le temps de penser à la littérature. Mais ce n'était que des excuses, parce qu'ils n'avaient pas, ou plus, de génie, c'est-à-dire d'instinct" (RTP Gall. 4:458).

61. "L'affaire Dreyfus . . . avait changé pour eux la valeur des êtres et classé autrement les partis, lesquels s'étaient depuis encore défaits et refaits" (RTP Gall. 4:570).

62. So great is the power of forgetting that at the end of the novel Mme de Guermantes would swear—such is the irony of the novel—that Bloch was born into and raised in her world; see RTP Gall. 4:550.

63. "La diversité des points de ma vie par où avait passé le fil de celle de chacun de ces personnages avait fini par mêler ceux qui semblaient le plus éloignés, comme si la vie ne possédait qu'un nombre limité de fils pour exécuter les dessins les plus différents" (RTP Gall. 4:550).

64. "Car il y a entre nous et les êtres un liséré de contingences" (RTP Gall. 4:553).

65. "Il est difficile de parler de choses qui n'ont point de précédent et des répercussions sur l'organisme d'une opération qu'on tente pour la première fois. Généralement, il est vrai, les nouveautés dont on s'alarme se passent fort bien" (RTP Gall. 4:376).

66. "Quand on s'appelle le marquis de Saint-Loup, on n'est pas dreyfusard, que voulez-vous que je vous dise!" (RTP Gall. 2:532).

67. "Je n'ai pas besoin qu'on me dise pourquoi Dreyfus a trahi. En psychologie, il me suffit de savoir qu'il est capable de trahir et il me suffit de savoir qu'il a trahi. L'intervalle est rempli. Que Dreyfus est capable de trahir, je le conclus de sa race. Qu'il a trahi, je le sais parce que j'ai lu les pages de Mercier et de Roger qui sont de magnifiques travaux" (Maurice Barrès, *Scènes et doctrines du nationalisme* [Paris: Plon, 1925], 165, cited in Sternhell, *La Droite,* 163).

68. See Zeev Sternhell's coinage of this term and elaboration of anti-Semitism in *fin de siècle* France, (*La Droite,* 163).

69. " 'Mais oui! le milieu n'a pas d'importance.' . . . 'La vraie influence, c'est celle du milieu intellectuel! On est l'homme de son idée!' " (RTP Gall. 4:417).

70. "Je savais que, aussi profond, aussi inéluctable que le patriotisme juif ou l'atavisme chrétien chez ceux qui se croient le plus libérés de leur race, habitait sous la rose inflorescence d'Albertine, de Rosemonde, d'Andrée, inconnu à elles-mêmes, tenu en réserve pour les circonstances, un gros nez, une bouche proéminente, un embonpoint qui étonnerait mais était en réalité dans la coulisse, prêt à entrer en scène, imprévu, fatal, tout comme tel dreyfusisme, tel cléricalisme, tel héroïsme national et féodal, soudainement issus, à l'appel des circonstances, d'une nature à l'individu lui-même, par laquelle il pense, vit,

évolue, se fortifie ou meurt, sans qu'il puisse la distinguer des mobiles particuliers qu'il prend pour elle" (RTP Gall. 2: 245–46).

CHAPTER FOUR

1. "L'accident vient du côté auquel on ne songeait pas, du dedans, du coeur" (RTP Gall. 1:619).

2. RTP 1:149–50; RTP Gall. 1:135–37.

3. "Tout à coup, je m'arrêtai, je ne pus plus bouger, comme il arrive quand une vision ne s'adresse pas seulement à nos regards, mais requiert des perceptions plus profondes et dispose de notre être tout entier. Une fillette d'un blond roux qui avait l'air de rentrer de promenade et tenait à la main une bêche de jardinage, nous regardait, levant son visage semé de taches roses. Ses yeux noirs brillaient et comme je ne savais pas alors, ni ne l'ai appris depuis, réduire en ses éléments objectifs une impression forte, comme je n'avais pas, ainsi qu'on dit, assez 'd'esprit d'observation' pour dégager la notion de leur couleur, pendant longtemps, chaque fois que je repensai à elle, le souvenir de leur éclat se présentait aussitôt à moi comme celui d'un vif azur, puisqu'elle était blonde: de sorte que, peut-être si elle n'avait pas eu des yeux aussi noirs—ce qui frappait tant la première fois qu'on la voyait—je n'aurais pas été, comme je le fus, plus particulièrement amoureux, en elle, de ses yeux bleus" (RTP Gall. 1:139).

4. In a notebook from 1909, Proust writes of the lines of his mother's Jewish face, a face marked by Christian softness and Jansenist courage; to this sentence he adds her black eyes, a detail which he then suppresses. See Etienne Brunet, *Le Vocabulaire de Proust*, 111–12. Proust had read Thomas Hardy's *A Pair of Blue Eyes* (*1873*) in the French translation of 1910 in the *Journal des Débats*–the story of a tragic heroine, Elfride Swancourt, with blue eyes. See RTP Gall. 3:1640.

5. RTP Gall. 4:124.

6. In *The Well-Beloved*, another Hardy novel that Proust knew well, a man searches for women who exhibit some fragment of ideal love (a smile, a gesture), and his love extends through three generations of women in one family; the title page reads, "One Shape of Many Names." It is the parallelism in Hardy's novels that so interests the

narrator: "The parallel between *The Well-Beloved,* where the man loves three women, and *A Pair of Blue Eyes,* where the woman loves three men, and in short all those novels which can be superimposed on one another like the houses piled up vertically on the rocky soil of the island" (RTP 3:383). "Le parallélisme entre *La Bien-Aimé* où l'homme aime trois femmes, *Les Yeux bleus* où la femme aime trois hommes, etc. et enfin tous ces romans superposables les uns aux autres, comme les maisons verticalement entassées en hauteur sur le sol pierreux de l'île?" (RTP Gall. 3:879).

7. See RTP Gall. 4:558.

8. The full passage involves an analogy with medical diagnosis: "Like those symptoms which the doctor hears his patient describe to him and with the help of which he works back to a deeper cause of which the patient is unaware, similarly our impressions, our ideas, have only a symptomatic value" (RTP 3:572). "Comme ces malaises que le médecin écoute son malade lui raconter et à l'aide desquels il remonte à une cause plus profonde, ignorée du patient, de même nos impressions, nos idées, n'ont qu'une valeur de symptômes" (RTP Gall. 4:141).

9. "Une fois de plus comme quand j'avais cessé de voir Gilberte l'amour de la femme s'élevait de moi, débarrassé de toute association exclusive avec une certaine femme déjà aimée, et flottait comme ces essences qu'ont libérées des destructions antérieures et qui errent en suspens dans l'air printanier, ne demandant qu'à s'unir à une nouvelle créature" (RTP Gall. 4:141). A variant missing from the English edition reads, "I saw her [Gilberte] last year but without recognizing her." "Je l'avais revue il y a un an mais sans la reconnaître" (RTP Gall. 4:142e).

10. "La blonde avait un air un peu plus délicat, presque souffrant, qui me plaisait moins. Ce fut pourtant elle qui fut cause que je ne me contentai pas de les considérer un instant, ayant pris racine, avec ces regards qui, par leur fixité impossible à distraire, leur application comme à un problème, semblent avoir conscience qu'il s'agit d'aller bien au-delà de ce qu'on voit. Je les aurais sans doute laissées disparaître comme tant d'autres mais au moment où elles passèrent devant moi la blonde . . . me lança furtivement un premier regard, puis m'ayant dépassé . . . un second qui acheva de m'enflammer. Mon ardeur eût sans doute fini par tomber, si elle n'avait été centuplée par le fait suivant" (RTP Gall. 4:142–43)

11. "Au service du roman que je venais d'ébaucher" (RTP Gall. 4:146).

12. "Certains philosophes disent que le monde extérieur n'existe pas et que c'est en nous-mêmes que nous développons notre vie. Quoi qu'il en soit, l'amour, même en ses plus humbles commencements, est un exemple frappant du peu qu'est la réalité pour nous" (RTP Gall. 4:146).

13. " 'De l'Orgeville, *de* particule, *orge* la graminée, comme du seigle, *ville* comme une ville, petite, brune, boulotte, est en ce moment en Suisse.' Ce n'était pas elle" (RTP Gall. 4:146–47).

14. "Ma pensée . . . continua un instant encore à raisonner comme si elle n'avait pas compris que c'était mon article, comme les vieillards qui sont obligés de terminer jusqu'au bout un mouvement commencé, même s'il est devenu inutile, même si un obstacle imprévu devant lequel il faudrait se retirer immédiatement le rend dangereux" (RTP Gall. 4:148).

15. "En elle-même ma double erreur de nom, m'être rappelé de L'Orgeville comme étant d'Éporcheville et avoir reconstitué en Éporcheville ce qui était en réalité Forcheville n'avait rien d'extraordinaire. Notre tort est de croire que les choses se présentent habituellement telles qu'elles sont en réalité, les noms tels qu'ils sont écrits, les gens tels que la photographie et la psychologie donnent d'eux une notion immobile. Mais en fait ce n'est pas du tout cela que nous percevons d'habitude. Nous voyons, nous entendons, nous concevons le monde tout de travers" (RTP Gall. 4:153).

16. "Nous répétons un nom tel que nous l'avons entendu jusqu'à ce que l'expérience ait rectifié notre erreur, ce qui n'arrive pas toujours. . . . Cette perpétuelle erreur qui est précisément la vie, ne donne pas ses milles formes seulement à l'univers visible et à l'univers audible, mais à l'univers social, à l'univers sentimental, à l'univers historique, etc. . . . Nous n'avons de l'univers que des visions informes, fragmentées et que nous complétons par des associations d'idées arbitraires, créatrices de dangereuses suggestions. Je n'aurais donc pas eu lieu d'être très étonné en entendant le nom de Forcheville . . . si la jeune fille blonde ne m'avait dit aussitôt, désireuse sans doute de prévenir avec tact des questions qui lui eussent été désagréables: 'Vous ne vous souvenez pas que vous m'avez beaucoup connue autrefois, vous veniez à la maison, votre amie Gilberte. J'ai bien vu que vous ne me reconnaissiez pas. Moi je vous ai bien reconnu tout de suite' " (RTP Gall. 4:153–54).

17. "Le plus souvent maintenant quand je pensais à elle, je la voyais devant le porche d'une cathédrale, m'expliquant la signification des statues, et, avec un sourire qui disait du bien de moi, me présentant comme son ami, à Bergotte. Et toujours le charme de toutes les idées que faisaient naître en moi les cathédrales, le charme des coteaux de l'Ile-de-France et des plaines de la Normandie faisait refluer ses reflets sur l'image que je me formais de Mlle Swann" (RTP Gall. 1:99).

18. See RTP Gall. 4:123, 665, 669 670. "L'armature intellectuelle qui chez moi avait relié ces faits, tous faux, était elle-même la forme si juste, si inflexible de la vérité que quand, trois mois plus tard, ma maîtresse (qui alors songeait à passer toute sa vie avec moi) m'avait quitté, ç'avait été d'une façon absolument identique à celle que j'avais imaginée la première fois" (RTP Gall. 4:10).

19. "I had recognised to be an inner state wherein I drew from myself alone the particular quality, the special character of the person I loved, everything that rendered her indispensable to my happiness" (RTP 1:905) "J'avais reconnu pour un être intérieur où je tirais de moi seul la qualité particulière le caractère spécial de l'être que j'aimais, tout ce qui le rendait indispensable à mon bonheur" (RTP Gall. 2:202).

20. "Tout part d'une erreur initiale. . . . Une bonne partie de ce que nous croyons, et jusque dans les conclusions dernières c'est ainsi, avec un entêtement et une bonne foi égales, vient d'une première méprise sur les prémisses" (RTP Gall. 4:235).

21. RTP Gall. 2:144.

22. "Mes pensées se prolongeaient en elle sans subir de déviation parce qu'elles passaient de mon esprit dans le sien sans changer de milieu, de personne" (RTP Gall. 2:28).

23. "L'extrêmité de la digue où elles faisaient mouvoir une tache singulière, je vis s'avancer cinq ou six fillettes, aussi différentes, par l'aspect et par les façons, de toutes les personnes auxquelles on était accoutumé à Balbec, qu'aurait pu l'être, débarquée on ne sait d'où, une bande de mouettes qui exécute à pas comptés sur la plage—les retardataires rattrapant les autres en voletant—une promenade dont le but semble aussi obscur aux baigneurs qu'elles ne paraissent pas voir, que clairement déterminé pour leur esprit d'oiseaux" (RTP Gall. 2:146).

24. See Bardèche, *Marcel Proust*, 2:37.

25. "Le beau cortège de jeunes filles" (RTP Gall. 2:180).

26. "C'était pour moi les ondulations montueuses et bleues de la mer, le profil d'un défilé devant la mer" (RTP Gall. 2:189).

27. "Sorte de blanche et vague constellation . . . la nébuleuse indistincte et lactée" (RTP Gall. 2:180).

28. "Propageait à travers leur groupe un flottement harmonieux, la translation continue d'une beauté fluide, collective, mobile" (RTP Gall. 2:148).

29. "Je me demande si ce que nous aimons dans la vie, ce qui nous fait plaisir tant de soirs, ce qui nous fait quitter nos parents, torturer une maîtresse, ce n'est pas quelque chose de tout autre que nous ne croyons, quelque chose qui ne nous cause tant de désirs et de troubles que dénaturé, qui ayant subi bien des alliages, mais quelque chose pourtant qui dans les désirs et ses troubles étend, part principale d'eux tous, ses hauteurs brumeuses ou son étendue bleue, quelque chose qui n'est pas un être et qui prête momentanément aux êtres sa valeur, une cathédrale, une vallée, dans le cas actuel, au bord des montagnes bleues de la mer, au soleil, une plage" (RTP Gall. 2:189c).

30. "Comme ces organismes primitifs où l'individu n'existe guère par lui-même, est plutôt constitué par le polypier que par chacun des polypes qui le composent, elles restaient pressées les unes contre les autres" (RTP Gall. 2:180). Schlanger, in *Métamorphoses*, demonstrates the importance of the polyp as a metaphor for conceptual thought in the nineteenth century.

31. "Toutes les transformations possibles pendant la jeunesse et la distance parcourue en peu de temps par les caractères physiques de chacune de ces jeunes filles faisant d'eux un critérium fort vague" (RTP Gall. 2:180–81).

32. "Il avait fallu hier l'indécision et le tremblé de ma perception première pour confondre indistinctement, comme l'avaient fait l'hilarité ancienne et la vieille photographie, les sporades aujourd'hui individualisées et désunies du pâle madrépore" (RTP Gall. 2:181). See Samuel Weber, "Le Madrépore."

33. "Cet ensemble, merveilleux parce qu'y voisinaient les aspects les plus différents, que toutes les gammes de couleurs y étaient rapprochées, mais qui était confus comme une musique où je n'aurais pas su isoler et reconnaître au moment de leur passage les phrases, distinguées mais oubliées aussitôt après" (RTP Gall. 2:148).

34. Johann Gottlieb Fichte, *Addresses to the German Nation*.

35. "La supposition que je pourrais un jour être l'ami de telle ou telle de ces jeunes filles, que ces yeux dont les regards inconnus me frappaient parfois en jouant sur moi sans le savoir comme un effet de soleil sur un mur, pourraient jamais par une alchimie miraculeuse laisser transpénétrer entre leurs parcelles ineffables l'idée de mon existence, quelque amitié pour ma personne, que moi-même je pourrais un jour prendre place entre elles, dans la théorie qu'elles déroulaient le long de la mer,—cette supposition me paraissait enfermer en elle une contradiction aussi insoluble, que si devant quelque frise antique ou quelque fresque figurant un cortège, j'avais cru possible, moi spectateur, de prendre place, aimé d'elles, entre les divines processionnaires" (RTP Gall. 2:153). The English translation is of no help in this instance, as it eliminates the word "theory."

36. RTP Gall. 2:156.

37. "La pensée que je pourrais un jour être l'ami de telle ou telle ou d'entre elles ou de toutes, . . . m'aurait autant étonné que si pendant que je regarde une adorable et étrange frise de Benozzo Gozzoli, on me disait que cette jeune fille à tunique rose, aux yeux verts, au regard mystérieux connaît mon nom, sait que je connais sa chambre et ses parents et que c'est précisément mon image qui est en ce moment devant son regard mystérieux" (RTP Gall. 2, *Esquisse* 45:933). Proust earlier evokes another fresco by Gozzoli (see RTP Gall. 1:525. n.4).

38. Deleuze (*Proust and Signs*, 102) points out that "an associative, incongruous chain is unified only by a creative viewpoint which itself takes the role of an incongruous part within the whole."

39. "Je ne peux pas lui conférer rétrospectivement une identité qu'elle n'avait pas pour moi au moment où elle a frappé mes yeux" (RTP Gall. 2:202).

40. "Si elle était devenue une nouvelle personne, une personne de face, à visage régulier, à robe montante, sévère et beau, la fillette de profil, à nez irrégulier, à visage rieur, à jupe de cycliste était oubliée, il n'y avait pas continuité entre elles, elle n'existait plus—" (RTP Gall. 2, *Esquisse* 43:992).

41. RTP Gall. 2:151.

42. RTP Gall. 2:225.

43. "À chaque fois, une jeune fille ressemble si peu à ce qu'elle était la fois précédente (mettant en pièces dès que nous l'apercevons le souvenir que nous avions gardé et le désir que nous nous proposions) que la stabilité de nature que nous lui prêtons n'est que fictive et pour la commodité du langage. . . . Dans les faces successives qu'après une pulsation de quelques jours nous présente la rose lumière interceptée, il n'est même pas certain qu'un *movimentum* extérieur à ces jeunes filles n'ait pas modifié leur aspect, et cela avait pu arriver pour mes jeunes filles de Balbec. On nous vante la douceur, la pureté d'une vierge. Mais après cela on sent que quelque chose de plus pimenté nous plairait mieux et on lui conseille de se montrer plus hardie. En soi-même était-elle plutôt l'une ou l'autre? Peut-être pas, mais capable d'accéder à tant de possibilités diverses dans le courant vertigineux de la vie" (RTP Gall. 3:573–74).

44. "En elles-mêmes, qu'étaient Albertine et Andrée? Pour le savoir il faudrait vous immobiliser, ne plus vivre dans cette attente perpétuelle de vous où vous passez toujours autres, il faudrait ne plus vous aimer, pour vous fixer ne plus connaître votre interminable et toujours déconcertante arrivée, ô jeunes filles, ô rayon successif dans le tourbillon où nous palpitons de vous voir reparaître en ne vous reconnaissant qu'à peine, dans la vitesse vertigineuse de la lumière. Cette vitesse, nous l'ignorerions peut-être et tout nous semblerait immobile, si un attrait sexuel ne nous faisait courir vers vous, gouttes d'or toujours dissemblables et qui dépassent toujours notre attente" (RTP Gall. 3:573).

45. "Car nous discernons en lui [le hasard] comme un commencement d'organisation, d'effort, pour composer notre vie" (RTP Gall. 2:181).

46. "Et il nous rend facile, inévitable, et quelquefois—après des interruptions qui ont pu faire espérer de cesser de nous souvenir—cruelle, la fidélité à des images à la possession desquelles nous nous croirons plus tard avoir été prédestinés, et que sans lui nous aurions pu, tout au début, oublier, comme tant d'autres, si aisément" (RTP Gall. 2:181).

47. RTP Gall. 2:153. See Richard, *Proust*, 199–201.

48. "D'un plaisir nouveau et [se] trouvant dans cette zone différente où l'exceptionnel nous fait entrer après avoir coupé le fil, patiemment tissée depuis tant de jours, qui nous conduisait vers la sagesse" (RTP Gall. 2:166).

49. "L'incessante révolution des servants innombrables, lesquels parce qu'au lieu d'être assis, comme les dîneurs, . . . étaient debout, évolvaient dans une zone supérieure. Sans doute l'un courait porter des hors-d'oeuvre, changer le vin, ajouter des verres. Mais malgré ces raisons particulières, leur course perpétuelle entre les tables rondes finissait par dégager la loi de sa circulation vertigineuse et réglée" (RTP Gall. 2:168).

50. The comparison between Proust and Einstein was being bandied about in the early 1920s. See the letter from Camille Vettard to Jacques Rivière in *Nouvelle Revue Française*, August 1922 pp. 246–52 and Vettard's article "Proust et le temps," in *La Nouvelle Revue francaise* (special issue: "Hommage à Marcel Proust") 20, no. 112 (January 1, 1923): 204. Proust referred to the new physics in *Contre Sainte-Beuve*: "A new form of literary criticism emerges from *Hérédo* and *Le Monde des images,* those admirable books rich in consequence by M. Léon Daudet, like a new physics, a new medicine, or the philosophy of Descartes. No doubt the profound views of M. Léon Daudet on Molière, Hugo, Baudelaire, etc., are finer still if they are attached by the laws of gravity to those spheres that are Images, but in themselves and detached from his system, they prove the liveliness and profundity of his literary taste" (ASB, 270). "Une nouvelle critique littéraire découle de *l'Hérédo* et du *Monde des images,* ces livres admirables et si grands de conséquence de M. Léon Daudet, comme une nouvelle physique, une nouvelle médecine, de la philosophie cartésienne. Sans doute les vues profondes de M. Léon Daudet sur Molière, sur Hugo, sur Baudelaire, etc., sont plus belles encore si on les rattache par les lois de la gravitation à ces sphères que sont les Images, mais en elles-mêmes et détachées du système elles prouvent la vivacité et la profondeur du goût littéraire" (CSB 1971, 596). Another passage, eliminated from *Swann in Love*, dates from a 1909 notebook: "*Mais* Ces quelques amitiés *où elle fut attirée* brillantes qui l'élevèrent et à *l'appel desquelles* aux signaux appeleurs de qui *les femmes des confrères de son mari/une autre femme de son milieu* . . . <bourgeois> eussent *peut'être* sans doute opposé *une raideur articulaire, un non possumus physiologique si même elles n'eussent pas passé* (aussi bien que s'ils lui avaient été adressé du fond de la planète Mars), une raideur articulaire, un non possumus physiologique, statique, astronomique, *avec des excuses tirées de leur conception spéciale de la gravitation universelle où la force des attractions était en raison inverse du carré des*

distances—si même ils étaient parvenus à pénétrer dans les limites fort resteintes dans leur champ visuel, pour mieux dire de percer l'épaisseur de leur cécité mentale, tiré de leur soumission aux lois de la gravitation qui ne leur permettait de ressentir les attractions qu'en raison inverse du carré des distances et à condition qu'elles parvinssent dans leur 'monde', <ces amitiés brillantes>. Madame Swann qui n'avait aucune vanité, les dissimula naïvement grâce au jeu innocent <et naturel> de sa distinction [500 r°] et de sa délicatesse, à *tous les milieux* tout son entourage de femmes <et notaires et> d'agents" (cited in Brun, "Brouillons et brouillages," 121). Deletions are indicated in italics, additions marked by < >, restorations enclosed in brackets.

51. Einstein published the special theory of relativity in 1905. I am grateful to Jean Le Tourneux for having pointed out to me this passage in Proust. For a general discussion of Einstein and the question of invention with respect to the general theory of relativity, see Jean Le Tourneux, "Pourquoi Einstein créa-t-il une théorie dont personne n'avait besoin?"

52. Albert Einstein, "On the General Theory of Gravitation: An Account of the Newly Published Extension of the General Theory of Relativity against Its Historical and Philosophical Background," *Scientific American* 182, (April 1950).

53. Early on, Proust thought that it was necessary to walk a line between materialist and idealist philosophy. In a letter dated June 4, 1904 to Fernand Gregh, Proust wrote: "Te rappelles-tu de ce qu'on nous disait de la métaphysique d'Aristote? Avant lui, l'erreur des matérialistes croyant par l'analyse la réalité dans la matière, l'erreur des platoniciens la cherchant en dehors de la matière dans des abstractions; Aristote comprenant qu'elle ne peut être dans une abstraction, qu'elle n'est pourtant pas la matière elle-même, mais ce qui en chaque chose individuelle est en quelque sorte derrière la matière elle-même, le sens de sa forme et la loi de son développement" (cited in Juliette Hassine, *Essai sur Proust et Baudelaire,* 100).

54. "Les problèmes insolubles que je me posais à propos de la beauté dénuée de signification de la fille de Minos et de Pasiphaé me fatiguaient davantage et me rendaient plus souffrant" (RTP Gall. 1:92).

55. "Et peut-être n'y a-t-il pas non plus d'acte aussi libre, car il est encore dépourvu de l'habitude, de cette sorte de manie mentale qui

dans l'amour favorise la renaissance exclusive de l'image d'une certaine personne" (RTP Gall. 2:179).

56. "C'est ainsi que les lettres du nom de la femme que j'allais aimer m'avaient été fournies, comme dans ce jeu où on puise dans un alphabet en bois, par la femme que j'avais tant aimée. Une chaîne circule à travers notre vie, reliant ce qui est déjà mort à ce qui est en pleine vie" (Carnet 3, cited by Danièle Gasiglia-Laster, ed., *A l'ombre des jeunes filles en fleurs*, 18, in Jean Milly's 1987 edition of *A la recherche du temps perdu*).

57. See Atlan, *A tort,* 279.

58. They threaten, as Arnold Schönberg's titles for an uncompleted symphony suggest, "Change of Life" and "Death Dance of Principles." Carl Schorske (*Fin-de-siècle Vienna*, 358–59) points out that the symphony was intended to celebrate the death of the Bourgeois God. In this, it differed from Proust's project. Schorske quotes from Schönberg: "A terrible amount of order is in the whole. And just as much disorder. That is, if one asks for sense. All is simultaneously order and disorder" (*Texte* [Vienna; 1926], 23–28).

59. The same world is evoked in Maurice Ravel's *La Valse*; see Schorske, *Fin de siècle Vienna*.

60. "Et ils sont l'enfer le plus impitoyable, le plus dépourvu d'issues pour le malheureux jaloux à qui ils présentent ce plaisir—ce plaisir que la femme aimée goûte avec un autre—comme la seule chose qui existe au monde pour celle qui le remplit tout entier" (RTP Gall. 2:169).

CHAPTER FIVE

1. The 1954 Pléiade edition (2:1173) mentions that certain fragments of *Sodome and Gomorrhe* "avaient, avant la publication des trois volumes, paru dans le no 5 des 'Oeuvres libres' (novembre 1921) sous le titre *Jalousie,* dans la revue *Intentions* d'avril 1922, et dans *Feuilles libres* d'avril-mai 1922." A note follows indicating that "sur la chemise de carton contenant le manuscrit de ce long extrait on avait écrit UNE JALOUSIE: roman inédit par Marcel Proust."

2. "L'œuvre doit être considérée seulement comme un amour malheureux qui en présage fatalement d'autres et qui fera que la vie ressemblera à l'oeuvre, que le poète n'aura presque plus besoin d'écrire,

tant il pourra trouver dans ce qu'il a écrit la figure anticipée de ce qui arrivera" (RTP Gall. 4:483).

3. "Un romancier pourrait au cours de la vie de son héros, peindre presque exactement semblables ses successives amours et donner par là l'impression non de s'imiter lui-même mais de créer, puisqu'il y a moins de force dans une innovation artificielle que dans une répétition destinée à suggérer une vérité neuve" (RTP Gall. 2:248).

4. "Sans quoi je n'aurais pas connu Albertine, mais même les Guermantes . . . , fait la connaissance de Saint-Loup et de M. de Charlus, ce qui m'avait fait connaître la duchesse de Guermantes et par elle sa cousine, de sorte que ma présence même en ce moment chez le prince de Guermantes, où venait de me venir brusquement l'idée de mon oeuvre . . . , me venait aussi de Swann. Pédoncule un peu mince peut-être pour supporter ainsi l'étendue de toute ma vie (le 'côté de Guermantes' s'étant trouvé en ce sens ainsi procéder du 'côté de chez Swann')" (RTP Gall. 4:494).

5. "Je pensais alors à tout ce que j'avais appris de l'amour de Swann pour Odette, de la façon dont Swann avait été joué toute sa vie. Au fond . . . l'hypothèse qui me fit peu à peu construire tout le caractère d'Albertine, et interpréter douleureusement chaque moment d'une vie que je ne pouvais pas contrôler tout entière, ce fut le souvenir, l'idée fixe du caractère de Mme Swann, tel qu'on m'avait raconté qu'il était" (RTP Gall. 3:199).

6. "C'est à cause du récit d'un amour de Swann que Marcel pourra effectivement un jour imaginer une Albertine semblable à Odette . . . et par conséquent s'éprendre d'elle. . . . Si Oedipe peut faire ce que chacun, dit-on, ne fait que désirer, c'est parce qu'un oracle a raconté d'avance qu'il tuerait un jour son père et épouserait sa mère: sans oracle, pas d'exil, donc pas d'incognito, donc pas de parricide et pas d'inceste" (Genette, Figures 3, 251).

7. "Association de souvenirs" (RTP Gall. 1:184).

8. A variant of this passage reads: "J'en avais connu l'histoire avec une précision qui paraîtra peu vraisemblable mais seulement parce qu'on ne s'avise [lecture incertaine] pas du moyen par lequel j'ai pu l'apprendre. Combien d'inventions de la science, de résurrections de l'archéologie, de découvertes par la police, qu'on aurait pu jurer être im-

possibles, tant qu'on ignorait le biais par lequel cette impossibilité a été tournée" (RTP Gall. 1:184n).

9. "Chaque lecteur est, quand il lit, le propre lecteur de soi-même" (RTP Gall. 4:489). See Chapter 1.

10. " 'Moi, je n'ai jamais été curieux, sauf quand j'ai été amoureux et quand j'ai été jaloux.' 'Etes-vous jaloux?' " (RTP Gall. 3:101).

11. "Suffisante pour notre bien est cette vie illusoire que donnent à des rivaux inexistants notre soupçon, notre jalousie" (RTP Gall. 4:484).

12. "Qui veut savoir, souffre pourtant de savoir, et cherche à apprendre davantage" (RTP Gall. 3:566).

13. "Une théorie désire d'être exprimée entièrement" (RTP Gall. 1:553). Elsewhere Proust states: "Ma joie d'avoir possédé un peu de l'intelligence d'Albertine et de son coeur ne venait pas de leur valeur intrinsèque, mais de ce que cette possession était un degré de plus dans la possession totale d'Albertine, possession qui avait été mon but et ma chimère depuis le premier jour où je l'avais vue" (RTP Gall. 4:78).

14. "On n'aime que ce en quoi on poursuit quelque chose d'inaccessible. Mais du même coup on n'aime que ce qu'on ne possède pas" (RTP Gall. 3:885–86).

15. "Il ne naît, il ne subsiste que si une partie reste à conquérir" (RTP Gall. 3:614).

16. "La jalousie nous . . . est une soif de savoir grâce à laquelle, sur des points isolés les uns des autres, nous finissons par avoir successivement toutes les notions possibles sauf celle que nous voudrions" (RTP Gall. 3:593).

17. "Pour peu que la nuit tombe et que la voiture aille vite, à la campagne, dans une ville, il n'y a pas un torse féminin, mutilé comme un marbre antique par la vitesse qui nous entraîne et le crépuscule qui le noie, qui ne tire sur notre coeur, à chaque coin de route, du fond de chaque boutique, les flèches de la Beauté, de la Beauté dont on serait parfois tenté de se demander si elle est en ce monde autre chose que la partie de complément qu'ajoute à une passante fragmentaire et fugitive notre imagination surexcitée par le regret" (RTP Gall. 2:73).

18. "Chaque personne qui nous fait souffrir peut être rattachée par nous à une divinité dont elle n'est qu'un reflet fragmentaire et le dernier degré, divinité (Idée) dont la contemplation nous donne aussitôt de la joie au lieu de la peine que nous avions. Tout l'art de vivre, c'est de

ne nous servir des personnes qui nous font souffrir que comme d'un degré permettant d'accéder à leur forme divine et de peupler ainsi joyeusement notre vie de divinités" (RTP Gall. 4:477). An example of how this pursuit of beauty fails occurs in Paris when, going on an errand with a friend, the narrator sees a stranger and resolves to pursue her. He chases her, losing her at an intersection, finding her again in another street, and finds himself finally breathless face to face with old Madame Verdurin, whom he avoids everywhere and who says to him: "Oh! How nice of you running to say hello to me" (RTP 1:714). "Oh! comme c'est aimable d'avoir couru pour me dire bonjour!" (RTP Gall. 2:73).

19. "C'était la personne invisible qui mettait en mouvement tout cela" (RTP Gall. 2:362).

20. In a completely different context, see the analyses of the relationship between the unusual and the "fundamental melodiousness" of Proust's works in Richard, *Proust*.

21. "Dire que j'ai gâché des années de ma vie, que j'ai voulu mourir, que j'ai eu mon plus grand amour, pour une femme qui ne me plaisait pas, qui n'était pas mon genre!" (RTP Gall. 1:375).

22. "C'est que cette femme n'a fait que susciter par des sortes d'appels magiques mille éléments de tendresse existant en nous à l'état fragmentaire et qu'elle a assemblés, unis, effaçant toute lacune entre eux, c'est nous-même qui en lui donnant ses traits avons fourni toute la matière solide de la personne aimée" (RTP Gall. 4:85).

23. "Il est une portion de notre âme, plus durable que les moi divers qui meurent successivement en nous et qui voudraient égoïstement le retenir, et qui doit . . . se détacher des êtres pour en restituer la généralité et donner cet amour, la compréhension de cet amour, à tous, à l'esprit universel et non à telle puis à telle" (RTP Gall. 4:476). See RTP Gall. 4, *Esquisse* 23:840.

24. "D'ailleurs, pour tous les événements qui dans la vie et ses situations contrastées se rapportent à l'amour, le mieux est de ne pas essayer de comprendre, puisque, dans ce qu'ils ont d'inexorable comme d'inespéré, ils semblent régis par des lois plutôt magiques que rationnelles" (RTP Gall. 1:492).

25. "Et tout se compose bien grâce à la présence suscitée par la jalousie

de la belle fille dont déjà nous ne sommes plus jaloux et que nous n'aimons plus" (RTP Gall. 4:496).

26. "Nous ne songeons pas combien la femme réelle y tient peu de place" (RTP Gall. 2:213). Or again: "Je m'étais mieux rendu compte depuis, qu'en étant amoureux d'une femme nous projetons simplement en elle un état de notre âme; que par conséquent l'important n'est pas la valeur de la femme mais la profondeur de l'état" (RTP Gall. 2:189).

27. "Elle n'était plus animée que de la vie inconsciente des végétaux. . . . Son moi ne s'échappait pas à tous moments . . . par les issues de la pensée inavouée et du regard. Elle avait rappelé à soi tout ce qui d'elle était en dehors, elle s'était réfugiée, enclose, résumée, dans son corps. En la tenant sous mon regard, dans mes mains, j'avais cette impression de la posséder tout entière que je n'avais pas quand elle était réveillée" (RTP Gall. 3:578).

28. "Je n'étais pas un seul homme, mais le défilé d'une armée composite où il y avait selon le moment des passionnés, des indifférents, des jaloux—des jaloux dont pas un n'était jaloux de la même femme" (RTP Gall. 4:71).

29. "Albertine n'avait été pour moi qu'un faisceau de pensées, elle avait survécu à sa mort matérielle tant que ces pensées vivaient en moi; en revanche maintenant que ces pensée étaient mortes, Albertine ne ressuscitait nullement pour moi avec son corps" (RTP Gall. 4:220).

30. "Chaque jour ancien est resté déposé en nous comme dans une bibliothèque immense où il y a des plus vieux livres un exemplaire que sans doute personne n'ira jamais demander" (RTP Gall. 4:125).

31. "L'attrait du plaisir qu'elle éprouverait à être traitée avec douceur par une personne . . . implacable envers un mort sans défense" (RTP Gall. 1:160–61).

32. In a variant to the description of the blossoming girls, the narrator comments that not only were the young girls indistinct one from another but that one would sometimes sit on the knees of another. See RTP Gall. 2:932.

33. "M. Vinteuil, tout absorbé d'abord par les soins de mère et de bonne d'enfant qu'il donnait à sa fille" (RTP Gall. 1:157).

34. "Pauvre M. Vinteuil, disait ma mère, il a vécu et il est mort pour sa fille, sans avoir reçu son salaire" (RTP Gall. 1:158).

35. "On verra plus tard que, pour de tout autres raisons, le souvenir de cette impression devait jouer un rôle important dans ma vie" (RTP Gall. 1:157).

36. "En la supprimant . . . j'aurais fait tomber deux volumes entiers, dont elle est la pierre angulaire, sur la tête du lecteur" (letter, November 10, 1919, *Corr. gén.* 3:69, cited in Maurice Bardèche, *Marcel Proust, romancier*, 2:261. Bardèche writes that (2:215) Proust's "secret" is to be found in *Albertine disparue*. For Bardèche, this scene develops a coherent theme, as clear in its theoretical implications as are those of the madeleine. And letter 43 to Jacques Rivière, February 6, 1914 (*Corr.* 13:99), bears this out: "Dans ce premier volume vous avez vu le plaisir que me cause la sensation de la madeleine trempée dans le thé, je dis que je cesse de me sentir mortel etc. et que je ne comprends pas pourquoi [see RTP Gall. 1:45]. Je ne l'expliquerai qu'à la fin du troisième volume [see RTP Gall. 4:445–58]. Tout est ainsi construit. . . . Vous verrez de même dans le troisième volume la raison profonde de la scène des deux jeunes filles [RTP Gall. 3:766–68, scène du septuor], des manies de ma tante Léonie etc. [see RTP Gall. 3:586–87]."

37. "Albertine n'était, comme une pierre autour de laquelle il a neigé, que le centre générateur d'une immense construction qui passait par le plan de mon coeur" (RTP Gall. 4:22).

38. For Freud, exploring the notion that recreates the origin of the individual, the "primal scene" refers to a child's witnessing his or her parents in the act of making love. And his own position, though it varied on the status of this event as lived experience, was unequivocal: first, in showing that beyond the history of the individual, the event belonged to the collective past of phylogenesis, to mythology; and then, by showing that nevertheless it cannot function solely at the level of transcendental schema.

39. "Ma tendresse pour Albertine, ma jalousie, tenaient . . . à l'irradiation par association d'idées de certains noyaux d'impressions douces ou douloureuses, au souvenir de Mlle Vinteuil à Montjouvain, aux doux baisers du soir qu'Albertine me donnait dans le cou" (RTP Gall. 4:221).

40. "Albertine amie de Mlle Vinteuil et de son amie, pratiquante professionnelle du saphisme . . . c'était une *terra incognita* terrible où je

venais d'atterrir, une phase nouvelle de souffrances insoupçonnées qui s'ouvrait" (RTP Gall. 3:500).

41. "Son rire étrange et profond" (RTP Gall. 3:504).

42. "Elle [Albertine] m'offrait justement—et elle seule pouvait me l'offrir—l'unique remède contre le poison qui me brûlait, homogène à lui d'ailleurs; l'un doux, l'autre cruel, tous deux étaient également dérivés d'Albertine. En ce moment Albertine—mon mal—se relâchant de me causer des souffrances, me laissait-elle, Albertine, remède—attendri comme un convalescent" (RTP Gall. 3:503).

43. "Quand je dis nous voir, je veux dire nous voir lire" (RTP Gall. 1:159).

44. See Jean Laplanche and J.-B. Pontalis, "L'origine des fantasmes, fantasmes originaires," *Temps Modernes* 215 (1964): 18–53.

45. "Quelquefois, comme Eve naquit d'une côte d'Adam, une femme naissait pendant mon sommeil d'une fausse position de ma cuisse. . . . Si, comme il arrivait quelquefois, elle avait les traits d'une femme que j'avais connue dans la vie, j'allais me donner tout entier à ce but: la retrouver, comme ceux qui partent en voyage pour voir de leurs yeux une cité désirée et s'imaginent qu'on peut goûter dans une réalité le charme du songe. Peu à peu son souvenir s'évanouissait, j'avais oublié la fille de mon rêve" (RTP Gall. 1:4–5).

46. "La brume, dès le réveil, avait fait de moi, au lieu de l'être centrifuge qu'on est par les beaux jours, un homme replié, désireux du coin du feu et du lit partagé, Adam frileux en quête d'une Eve sédentaire, dans ce monde différent" (RTP Gall. 2:641).

47. "O grandes attitudes de l'Homme et de la Femme où cherchent à se joindre, dans l'innocence des premiers jours. . . . ce que la Création a séparé, où Eve est étonnée et soumise devant l'Homme au côté de qui elle s'éveille, comme lui-même, encore seul, devant Dieu qui l'a formé" (RTP Gall. 3:587).

48. See Deleuze, *Proust and Signs*.

49. "Les invertis, qui se rattachent volontiers à l'antique Orient ou à l'Age d'or de la Grèce, remonteraient plus haut encore, à ces époques d'essai où n'existaient ni les fleurs dioïques ni les animaux unisexués, à cet hermaphroditisme initial dont quelques rudiments d'organes mâles dans l'anatomie de la femme et d'organes femelles dans l'anatomie de l'homme semblent conserver la trace" (RTP Gall. 3:31).

50. I Corinthians 15:22. "Car comme tous meurent en Adam, tous aussi revivront dans le Christ."

51. See Jean-Pierre Richard, "Proust et l'objet herméneutique."

52. See Daniel Lagache, *La Jalousie amoureuse*, 6.

53. "Si nous n'étions pas pour l'ordre du récit obligé de nous borner à des raisons frivoles, combien de plus sérieuses nous permettraient de montrer la minceur menteuse du début de ce volume où, de mon lit, j'entends le monde s'éveiller. . . . Oui, j'ai été forcé d'amincir la chose et d'être mensonger" (RTP Gall. 3:696).

54. This pattern of growth is paralleled also in the person of Vinteuil: from his timidity and his death such a resurrection occurs in music that he seems to be there, proving the possibility of the transformation, dreamed of by Proust, from social banality to a transcendent ideal in the work of art. This music leaves no doubt about the depth of Vinteuil's audacity; it is immediately recognizable in its difference from that of others.

55. "Si la musique n'était pas l'exemple unique de ce qu'aurait pu être—s'il n'y avait pas eu l'invention du langage, la formation des mots, l'analyse des idées—la communication des âmes. Elle est comme une possibilité qui n'a pas eu de suites, l'humanité s'est engagée dans d'autres voies, celle du langage parlé et écrit" (RTP Gall. 3:762–63).

56. "D'ailleurs, elle n'eût pu lui servir, car cette phrase pouvait bien symboliser un appel, mais non créer des forces et faire de Swann l'écrivain qu'il n'était pas" (RTP Gall. 4:456).

57. "En passant des années à débrouiller le grimoire laissé par Vinteuil, [à établir] la lecture certaine de ces hiéroglyphes inconnus, l'amie de Mlle Vinteuil eut la consolation d'assurer au musicien dont elle avait assombri les dernières années, une gloire immortelle et compensatrice" (RTP Gall. 3:766).

58. "C'était à vrai dire toute l'œuvre de Vinteuil" (RTP Gall. 3:767).

59. "La promesse qu'il existait autre chose, réalisable par l'art" (RTP Gall. 3:767).

60. "Tout s'entre-croise et se superpose dans notre vie intérieure" (RTP Gall. 3:757).

61. "La jalousie est . . . un démon qui ne peut être exorcisé, et reparaît toujours, incarné sous une nouvelle forme" (RTP Gall. 3:611).

62. "L'enveloppe close d'un être qui par l'intérieur accédait à l'infini" (RTP Gall. 3:888).

63. For Swann too, Odette is the promise and deception of a novel: "Odette is in Swann's eyes a difficult woman to conquer, whence he builds up a whole romance [*roman*] which becomes all the more painful when he discovers his error" (RTP 3:585). "Odette est une femme difficile pour Swann, d'où il bâtit tout un roman qui ne devient que plus douleureux quand il comprend son erreur" (RTP Gall. 4:154).

64. "Comme il n'est de connaissance, on peut presque dire qu'il n'est de jalousie que de soi-même" (RTP Gall. 3:887).

65. "Vient d'une première méprise sur les prémisses" (RTP Gall. 4:235).

66. "IMPOSSIBLE VENIR, MENSONGE SUIT" (RTP Gall. 4:281).

67. "Moi qui pendant tant d'années n'avais cherché la vie et la pensée réelles des gens que dans l'énoncé direct qu'ils m'en fournissaient volontairement, par leur faute j'en étais arrivé à ne plus attacher, au contraire, d'importance qu'aux témoignages qui ne sont pas une expression rationnelle et analytique de la vérité; les paroles elles-mêmes ne me renseignaient qu'à la condition d'être interprétées" (RTP Gall. 3:596).

68. "Quand elle mentait, son récit péchait soit par insuffisance, omission, invraisemblance, soit par excès" (RTP Gall. 3:684).

69. "Elle avait, comme il arrive si souvent, atteint la vérité par un autre chemin que celui qu'elle avait voulu prendre" (RTP Gall. 3:839–40).

70. "Ce qui m'avait brusquement rapproché d'elle, bien plus, fondu en elle, ce n'était pas l'attente d'un plaisir . . . c'était l'étreinte d'une douleur" (RTP Gall. 3:840).

71. "C'est . . . une des choses les plus terribles pour l'amoureux que, si les faits particuliers—que seuls l'expérience, l'espionnage, entre tant de réalisations possibles, feraient connaître—sont si difficiles à trouver, la vérité, en revanche, soit si facile à percer ou seulement à pressentir" (RTP Gall. 3:596). But this same confidence in the powers of intuition is directly contradicted in a parenthetical comment: "(C'est étonnant comme la jalousie, qui passe son temps à faire des petites suppositions dans le faux, a peu d'imagination quand il s'agit de découvrir le vrai)" (RTP Gall. 4:18). This passage is not included in the English translation.

72. "Mon pauvre ami, notre petite Albertine n'est plus, pardonnez-moi de vous dire cette chose affreuse, vous qui l'aimiez tant. Elle a été jetée par son chaval contre un arbre pendant une promenade qu'elle

faisait *au bord de la Vivonne*. Tous nos efforts n'ont pu la ranimer. Que ne suis-je morte à sa place!" (*Albertine disparue*, 111; emphasis added).

73. "Cortège insolent et fleuri" (RTP Gall. 3:576).

74. "Tout événement est comme un moule d'une forme particulière, et, quel qu'il soit, il impose à la série des faits qu'il est venu interrompre, et semble en conclure, un dessin que nous croyons le seul possible parce que nous ne connaissons pas celui qui eût pu lui être substitué" (RTP Gall. 4:90).

75. "Quand plus tard avides de découvrir une vérité nous remontons de déduction en déduction, feuilletant notre mémoire comme un recueil de témoignages, quand nous arrivons à cette phrase, à ce geste, impossible de nous rappeler, nous recommençons vingt fois le même trajet, mais inutilement, mais le chemin ne va pas plus loin" (RTP Gall. 4:91).

76. "Les distances ne sont que le rapport de l'espace au temps et varient avec lui. Nous exprimons la difficulté que nous avons à nous rendre à un endroit, dans un sytème de lieues, de kilomètres, qui devient faux dès que cette difficulté diminue. L'art en est aussi modifié, puisqu'un village, qui semblait dans un autre monde que tel autre, devient son voisin dans un paysage dont les dimensions sont changées. En tous cas, apprendre qu'il existe peut-être un univers où 2 et 2 font 5 et où la ligne droite n'est pas le chemin le plus court d'un point à un autre, eût beaucoup moins étonné Albertine que d'entendre le mécanicien lui dire qu'il était facile d'aller dans une même après-midi à Saint-Jean et à la Raspelière" (RTP Gall. 3:385).

77. "Prisonniers aussi hermétiquement enfermés jusque-là dans la cellule de jours distincts que jadis Méséglise et Guermantes" (RTP Gall. 3:385).

CHAPTER SIX

1. "La sensation que j'avais ressentie jadis sur deux dalles inégales du baptistère de Saint-Marc m'avait rendue avec toutes les autres sensations jointes ce jour-là à cette sensation-là, et qui étaient restées dans l'attente, à leur rang, d'où un brusque hasard les avait impérieusement fait sortir, dans la série des jours oubliés" (RTP Gall. 4:446).

2. "J'ai voulu bien des fois vous demander des conseils de toilette féminine, pour aucune maîtresse, mais pour des héroïnes de livre. La même raison m'a rendu fatigant d'écrire. Savez-vous du moins si jamais Fortuny dans des robes de chambre a pris pour motifs de ces oiseaux accouplés, buvant par exemple dans un vase, qui sont si fréquents à Saint-Marc, dans les chapiteaux Byzantins. Et savez-vous aussi s'il y a à Venise des tableaux (je voudrais quelques titres) où il y a des manteaux, des robes, dont Fortuny se serait (ou aurait pu) s'inspirer. Je rechercherais la reproduction du tableau et je verrais s'il peut moi m'inspirer" (letter 16 to Maria de Madrazo, February 6, 1916, *Corr.* 15:49). See Also "Huit lettres inédites à Maria de Madrazo," *Bulletin de la société des amis de Marcel Proust* 3 (1953): 31. With respect to these letters, see Mary Lydon, "Pli selon pli: Proust and Fortuny," *Romanic Review* 82, no. 4 (November 1990):438–54; RTP Gall. 3:1670–75; and also Jean Milly, introduction to *La Prisonnière*, 28–36, 45–53.

3. "Ce désir de la parer [est le même], avec la ressouvenance de ses parures, dans un voyage à Venise, après qu'elle sera morte et où la vue de certains tableaux me fera mal, j'ai construit les choses ainsi. (Mais ne parlez pas de cela) (sauf à Fortuny si vous voulez). Dans le début de mon deuxième volume un grand artiste à nom fictif qui symbolise le grand peintre dans mon ouvrage comme Vinteuil symbolise le grand musicien genre Franck, dit devant Albertine (que je ne sais pas encore être un jour ma fiancée adorée) que à ce qu'on prétend un artiste a découvert le secret des vieilles étoffes vénitiennes etc. C'est Fortuny. Quand Albertine plus tard (troisième volume) est fiancée avec moi, elle me parle des robes de Fortuny (que je nomme à partir de ce moment chaque fois) et je lui fais la surprise de lui en donner. La description très brève, de ces robes, illustre nos scènes d'amour (et c'est pour cela que je préfère des robes de chambre parce qu'elle est dans ma chambre en déshabillé somptueux mais déshabillé) et comme, tant qu'elle est vivante j'ignore à quel point je l'aime, ces robes m'évoquent surtout Venise, le désir d'y aller, ce à quoi elle est un obstacle etc. Le roman suit son cours, elle me quitte, elle meurt. Longtemps après, après de grandes souffrances que suit un oubli relatif je vais à Venise mais dans les tableaux de xxx (disons Carpaccio) je retrouve telle robe que je lui ai donnée. Autrefois cette robe m'évoquait Venise et me donnait envie de quitter Albertine, maintenant le Carpaccio où je la vois m'évoque

Albertine et me rend Venise douloureux" (letter 19 to Madame de Madrazo, February 17, 1916, *Corr.* 15:57).

4. According to Kolb, editor of the complete correspondence (see *Corr.* 15:63 n.2), this book was probably *Vittore Carpaccio: La vie et l'oeuvre du peintre,* by G. Ludwig and P. Molmenti (Paris: Librairie Hachette, 1910), translated by H. L. de Perera, illustrated with 26 photographs and 229 engravings.

5. "Donc quand vous verrez Fortuny vous me ferez grand plaisir en lui demandant la description la plus *plate* de son manteau, comme ce serait dans un catalogue disant étoffe, couleurs, dessin (c'est le personnage qui tourne le dos n'est-ce pas?). Cela me sera infiniment précieux car je vais faire tout un morceau là-dessus" (letter 21 to Madame de Madrazo, March 9, 1916, *Corr.* 15:62–63).

6. "On dit qu'un prompt départ vous éloigne de nous, / Seigneur, *etc.*" (RTP Gall. 4:432).

7. See RTP Gall. 1:386, 432.

8. "Fidèlement antiques mais puissamment originales" (RTP Gall. 3:871).

9. In Cahier 53 (fols. 20–52), the desire to go to Venice corresponds to the desire to end life in Paris with Albertine. See RTP Gall. 3:1673.

10. "Si je n'avais jamais vu Venise, j'en rêvais sans cesse, depuis ces vacances de Pâques, qu'encore enfant, j'avais dû y passer. . . . La robe de Fortuny que portait ce soir-là Albertine me semblait comme l'ombre tentatrice de cette invisible Venise. Elle était envahie d'ornementation arabe comme Venise, comme les palais de Venise dissimulés à la façon des sultanes derrière un voile ajouré de pierre, comme les reliures de la Bibliothèque Ambrosienne, comme les colonnes desquelles les oiseaux orientaux qui signifient alternativement la mort et la vie, se répétaient dans le miroitement de l'étoffe, d'un bleu profond qui au fur et à mesure que mon regard s'y avançait se changeait en or malléable par ces mêmes transmutations qui, devant la gondole qui s'avance, changent en métal flamboyant l'azur du Grand Canal" (RTP Gall. 3:895–96).

11. "Je l'embrassai . . . serrant contre mon coeur l'azur miroitant et doré du Grand Canal et les oiseaux accouplés, symboles de mort et de résurrection" (RTP Gall. 3:900). In his letter of February 6, 1916, to Maria de Madrazo, he had asked: "Savez-vous du moins si jamais For-

tuny dans des robes de chambre a pris pour motifs de ces oiseaux accouplés, buvant par exemple dans un vase, qui sont si fréquents à Saint-Marc, dans les chapiteaux Byzantins" (*Corr.* 15:49). In Cahier 56 (fol. 55v), Proust writes: "A Venise . . . les oiseaux du Palais des Doges me font souffrir en me rappelant le peignoir de Fortuny" (cited in Jo Yoshida, "Proust contre Ruskin: La genèse de deux voyages dans la 'Recherche' d'après des brouillons inédits," 176).

12. "C'était celles dont Elstir, quand il nous parlait des vêtements magnifiques des contemporaines de Carpaccio et de Titien, nous avait annoncé la prochaine apparition, renaissant de leurs cendres somptueuses, car tout doit revenir, comme il est écrit aux voûtes de Saint-Marc, et comme le proclament, buvant aux urnes de marbe et de jaspe des chapiteaux byzantins, les oiseaux qui signifient à la fois la mort et la résurrection" (RTP Gall. 3:871). See Yoshida, "Proust contre Ruskin," 178.

13. "Mais tout à coup le décor changea; ce ne fut plus le souvenir d'anciennes impressions, mais d'un ancien désir, tout récemment réveillé encore par la robe bleu et or de Fortuny, qui étendit devant moi un autre printemps, un printemps plus du tout feuillu mais subitement dépouillé au contraire de ses arbres et de ses fleurs par ce nom que je venais de me dire: 'Venise', un printemps décanté, qui est réduit à son essence, et traduit l'allongement, l'échauffement, l'épanouissement graduel de ses jours par la fermentation progressive, non plus d'une terre impure mais d'une eau vierge et bleue" (RTP Gall. 3:913).

14. See Joan Rosasco, "Le Texte et sa doublure," 93–113.

15. "L'église ne se représentait pas à moi comme un simple monument, mais comme le terme d'un trajet sur l'eau marine et printanière, avec laquelle Saint-Marc faisait pour moi un tout indivisible et vivant" (RTP Gall. 4:224).

16. "Foulant tous deux les mosaïques de marbre et de verre du pavage, ayant devant nous les larges arcades dont le temps a légèrement infléchi les surfaces évasées et roses, ce qui donne à l'église, là où il a respecté la fraîcheur de ce coloris, l'air d'être construite dans une matière douce et malléable comme la cire de géantes alvéoles; là au contraire où il a racorni la matière et où les artistes l'ont ajourée et rehaussée d'or, d'être la précieuse reliure, en quelque cuir de Cordoue, du colossal Évangile de Venise" (RTP Gall. 4:224–25). Peter Collier, in *Proust and Venice*,

shows how Venice demonstrates a *mise-en-abîme* in which memory functions, through cross-referencing, like a work of art.

17. Yoshida, "Proust contre Ruskin," 160.

18. See Rosasco, "Le Texte, " 94, for commentary on the robe in *Jean Santeuil* and the allusion to Vinteuil, who would also put a shawl around Mlle Vinteuil. The analogy between his mother's shawl and Christ receiving a coat from the angels to cover his body chilled from the river Jordan (fol. 62r°) comes from Byzantine iconography. Originally, the angels hid their hands out of respect for Christ; this was misunderstood and changed to show the angels holding Christ's coat (Louis Réau, *Iconographie de l'art chrétien*, 2:298; cited in Yoshida, "Proust contre Ruskin," 161). See also Genette, *Figures*, 3:49.

19. See Mary Ann Caws, "Gestures toward the Self: Representing the Body in Modernism—Cloaking, Re-membering, and the Elliptical Effect," 238–55.

20. "Je ne . . . ressentais [de plaisir] devant les belles choses que si j'étais seul ou feignais de l'être et me taisais" (RTP Gall. 3:384).

21. "Certains esprits qui aiment le mystère veulent croire que les objets conservent quelque chose des yeux qui les regardèrent, que les monuments et les tableaux ne nous apparaissent que sous le voile sensible que leur ont tissé l'amour et la contemplation de tant d'adorateurs, pendant des siècles" (RTP Gall. 4:463).

22. "Cette chimère deviendrait vraie s'ils la transposaient dans le domaine de la seule réalité pour chacun, dans le domaine de sa propre sensibilité" (RTP Gall. 4:463).

23. In response to a letter of condolence from Madame Alphonse Daudet after his mother's death, Proust writes: "J'ai souvent pensé en relisant votre lettre que c'était elle [sa mère] qui la lisait, et chaque délicatesse de sentiment et d'expression, légère, subtile, mystérieuse, poétique, vraiment divine, de vrais 'fils de la Vierge' il me semblait qu'elle me les faisait remarquer" (letter 185, October 26, 1905, *Corr.* 5:355).

24. This woman, in the seventh painting of the St. Ursula cycle is thought to be the donor of the painting, who had died young; here she is portrayed as an old woman. See RTP Gall. 4:225 n.2. One wonders whether Proust finds in her a person mourning not only Ursula but herself as well, as Proust mourns himself when he thinks of his mother

and his past. Yoshida ("Proust contre Ruskin, " 160–61) suggests that the mother is mourning the grandmother, making of Saint Mark's a silent and venerable grave. In *The Stones of Venice*, Ruskin writes about the two parts of Saint Mark's: in one the baptismal fonts are located and in the other the altar; the former signifies the baptism of new life in which carnal desires die so that the life of the spirit may be born.

25. Gérard Genette sees this Carpaccio as a *mise-en-abyme* of Venice in Venice, in which there is an "immobilité hiératique de l'image maternelle" (*Figures* 3, 49). This passage serves as an example for defining *diegesis*, the cinematographic coinage that he invokes to designate the fictive level within narrative. It is also the passage in which he takes all comparisons and metaphors to be *more or less* diegetic, yet he still distinguishes metonymy, which he takes to be largely diegetic, from metaphor, which can go either way. Bowie (*Freud*, 83–94) points to the maternal imagery in this scene, exacting from the narrator's reading of Carpaccio the way in which desire constantly displaces itself, weaving sexual difference into the complex representation of the Carpaccio painting and Venice. For another reading of this passage, see Gérard Macé, *Le Manteau de Fortuny*. See also Collier, *Proust and Venice*. For the question of dress, see Anna Favrichon, *Toilettes et silhouettes féminines*; and Diana Festa-McCormick, *Proustian Optics of Clothes: Mirrors, Masks, Mores*.

26. "The subject, by Hugo von Hofmannsthal and Count Kessler, is founded on the Bible story, but aims at exhibiting the violent conflict resulting from the contact between the sumptuous, shallow, impulsive world of Paganism—in the present case, Pharoah's court—and the mystical purity of Joseph, who represents the Hebraic, monotheistic spirit. . . . Mixing present day with idealism, it is situated not in its historical framework, but in a Venetian context, as the Venetian painters might have interpreted the Bible story. Count Kessler had argued for avoiding historical accuracy in order to leave room for the imagination." (*Musical Times* 55 [May 1, 1924]: 300–301). A review of a performance in Berlin during "fashion week" declared that *Joseph* "expresses exactly the Central Europe of 1919 . . . the Europe whose 'culture' sought its effects in the deliberate contravention of truth. Strauss the German, Hofmannsthal the Austrian, and Bakst the Russian sought to combine the droning splendor of ancient Egypt with the fantastic

opulence of the Italian Renaissance . . . the Israelite Shepherd boy, among the Egyptians, dressed like Venetians of the seicento. . . . Fascinating perversity. The sophistication of innocence" (César Saeringer, "Strauss's 'Legend of Joseph' Feature of Berlin's Fashion Week," *Musical Courier* 82, 17 [1921].

27. "I felt that the Albertine of long ago, invisible to my eyes, was nevertheless enclosed within me as in the 'Piombi' of an inner Venice, the tight lid of which some incident occasionally lifted to give me a glimpse of that past" (RTP 3:654). "Je sentais que l'Albertine d'autrefois, invisible à moi-même, était pourtant enfermée au fond de moi comme aux 'plombs' d'une Venise intérieure, dont parfois un incident faisait glisser le couvercle durci jusqu'à me donner une ouverture sur ce passé" (RTP Gall. 4:218).

28. The Companions of the *Calza* (stocking), so called because it was their distinctive practice to wear stockings of two different colors, were a group of young noblemen of Venice; the function of their club was to organize festivals.

29. "Carpaccio que je viens de nommer et qui était le peintre auquel, quand je ne travaillais pas à Saint-Marc, nous rendions le plus volontiers visite, faillit un jour ranimer mon amour pour Albertine. Je regardais l'admirable ciel incarnat et violet sur lequel se détachent ces hautes cheminées incrustées, dont la forme évasée et le rouge épanouissement de tulipes fait penser à tant de Venises de Whistler. Puis mes yeux allaient du vieux Rialto en bois à ce Ponte Vecchio du XVe siècle aux palais de marbre ornés de chapiteaux dorés, revenaient au Canal où les barques sont menées par des adolescents en vestes roses, en toques surmontées d'aigrettes, semblables à s'y méprendre à tel qui évoquait vraiment Carpaccio dans cette éblouissante *Légende de Joseph* de Sert, Strauss et Kessler. Enfin, avant de quitter les tableaux mes yeux revinrent à la rive où fourmillent les scènes de la vie vénitienne de l'époque. Je regardais le barbier essuyer son rasoir, le nègre portant son tonneau, les conversations des musulmans, des nobles seigneurs vénitiens en larges brocarts, en damas, en toque de velours cerise, quand tout à coup je sentis au coeur comme une légère morsure. Sur le dos d'un des compagnons de la Calza, reconnaissable aux broderies d'or et de perles qui inscrivent sur leur manche ou leur collet l'emblème de la joyeuse confrérie à laquelle ils étaient affiliés, je venais de reconnaître

le manteau qu'Albertine avait pour venir avec moi en voiture découverte à Versailles, le soir où j'étais loin de me douter qu'une quinzaine d'heures me séparaient à peine du moment où elle partirait de chez moi. Toujours prête à tout, quand je lui avais demandé de partir, ce triste jour qu'elle devait appeler dans sa dernière lettre 'deux fois crépusculaire puisque la nuit tombait et que nous allions nous quitter'. Elle avait jeté sur ses épaules un manteau de Fortuny qu'elle avait emporté avec elle le lendemain et que je n'avais jamais revu depuis dans mes souvenirs" (RTP Gall. 4:225–26). Proust pieced together this description from a book called *L'Art religieux du XIIIe siècle en France*; see RTP Gall. 4:1123.

30. Ruskin, *Modern Painters,* 53.

31. RTP Gall. 4, *Esquisse* 35:589.

32. See RTP Gall. 4:10.

33. "Épinglant ici un feuillet supplémentaire, je bâtirais mon livre, je n'ose pas dire ambitieusement comme une cathédrale, mais tout simplement comme une robe" (RTP Gall. 4:610).

34. The full passage reads: "A propos of all the models I had (a church in Caen, etc.) and of constructing a gown etc., I will say that these models (especially the people) were as numerous in having a single residue as the meats which Françoise ordered to compose her *boeuf à la mode*. So that this book, I was building it like a gown (enumeration of other images) and gathering it like a jelly (add this image)." "A propos de tous les modèles que j'ai eus (église de Caen, de Falaise etc.) et de bâtir une robe etc., je dirai que ces modèles (surtout les personnes) étaient aussi nombreuses pour avoir un seul résidu que les viandes que faisait acheter Françoise pour composer son boeuf à la mode. De sorte que ce livre je le bâtissais comme une robe (énumération des autres images) et je le recueillais comme une *gelée*. (Cette image nouvelle à ajouter)" (Proust, *Matinée,* 300). See RTP Gall. 4:611–12; RTP Gall. 4, *Esquisse* 35:857.

35. Proust had written to André Beaunier, in reaction to an article on "les monuments religieux désaffectés" (letter 149, November 10, 1912, *Corr.* 11:371).

36. "Car dans les livres qui suivirent, s'il avait rencontré quelque grande vérité, ou le nom d'une célèbre cathédrale, il interrompait son récit et

dans une invocation, une apostrophe, une longue prière, il donnait un libre cours à ces effluves" (RTP Gall. 1:94).

37. "La Patronne voulait-elle par cette attitude recueillie montrer qu'elle se considérait comme à l'église, et ne trouvait pas cette musique différente de la plus sublime des prières; voulait-elle comme certaines personnes à l'église dérober aux regards indiscrets, soit par pudeur leur ferveur supposée, soit par respect humain leur distraction coupable ou un sommeil invincible?" (RTP Gall. 3:756).

38. "Mais une cathédrale n'est pas seulement une beauté à sentir. Si même ce n'est plus pour vous un enseignement à suivre, c'est du moins encore un livre à comprendre. Le portail d'une cathédrale gothique, et plus particulièrement d'Amiens, la cathédrale gothique par excellence, c'est la Bible" (CSB 1971, 89).

39. Cited in Richard Macksey, introduction to Proust, *On Reading Ruskin,* xxxi.

40. "Littérature il faut qu'il y ait q.q. chose dans les choses qu'on veut dire d'où elle est écossage de pois aussi bien qu'elle est bâtie, ne disons pas pour ne pas être prétentieux une cathédrale mais une robe (ceci pour composition) frayer des routes et jeter des ponts (ceci moins bien)" (Proust, *Matinée,* 299). And again: "Quand je parle du livre à faire: pour qu'il ait plus de force je [le] suralimenterai comme un enfant faible (dans la partie où je dis, le préparerai comme une offensive, je le bâtirai comme une robe, etc.)" (*Matinée,* 316).

41. See Chapter 1. Here Proust relates the structure of a book to other images for the project (a cathedral, a dress, food). For a discussion of the relationship between the metonymic system relating images such as the house to the psychology of a literary character, see Michel Beaujour, *Miroirs d'encre,* 149–50.

42. See Deleuze, *Proust and Signs.*

43. "Chemins accidentés, les rentrants et les sortants factices, les lacis, l'éparpillement composite des modes d'autrefois. . . . Les coussins, les strapontins . . . corsages à basques qui dépassant la jupe et raidis par des baleines" (RTP Gall. 1:607).

44. "L'air d'être composée de pièces disparates qu'aucune individualité ne reliait" (RTP Gall. 1:607).

45. "Madame Swann, n'est-ce pas, c'est toute une époque?" (RTP Gall. 1:608)

46. "Comme dans un beau style qui superpose des formes différentes et que fortifie une tradition cachée, dans la toilette de Mme Swann, ces souvenirs incertains de gilets . . . , faisaient circuler sous la forme concrète la ressemblance inachevée d'autres plus anciennes . . . qu'on n'aurait pu y trouver effectivement réalisé par la couturière ou la modiste, mais auxquelles on pensait sans cesse" (RTP Gall. 1:608).

47. "Elle était entourée de sa toilette comme de l'appareil délicat et spiritualisé d'une civilisation" (RTP Gall. 1:609) See Richard, *Proust*, 199–201.

48. See, e.g., the hawthorns, RTP Gall. 1, *Esquisses,* 862, 864, 869; and the rose, RTP Gall. 1:138.

49. "Tout d'un coup, sur le sable de l'allée, tardive, alentie et luxuriante comme la plus belle fleur et qui ne s'ouvrirait qu'à midi, Mme Swann apparaissait, épanouissant autour d'elle une toilette toujours différente mais que je me rappelle surtout mauve; puis elle hissait et déployait sur un long pédoncule, au moment de sa plus complète irradiation, le pavillon de soie d'une large ombrelle de la même nuance que l'effeuillaison des pétales de sa robe" (RTP Gall. 1:625).

50. "Comme une forme organisée et vivante, du long chaos et de l'enveloppement nébuleux des modes détrônées" (RTP Gall. 1:608).

51. "Dans le lisse éclatant de ses pétales comme une robe de bal intacte . . . je sens comme passer une seconde comme une expression qui est la signification oubliée par moi . . . ; sans que ces obscurs pressentiments de ce qui constitue l'essence de cette fleur se résolvent dans la lumière d'une de ces métaphores sans prix qui sont la formule révélatrice d'une vérité esthétique enfin conquise, et qui font des livres des grands poètes un résumé de découvertes, un trésor de certitudes d'un autre ordre que celui de la science et qui ne peut s'exposer d'une façon rationnelle, mais plus important encore et éclaircissant une réalité plus profonde, plus spirituelle que la réalité physique" (RTP Gall. 1, *Esquisse* 62; 862).

52. "Comme la robe où nous vîmes pour la première fois une femme, elles m'aideraient à retrouver l'amour que j'avais alors, la beauté sur laquelle j'ai superposé trop d'images de moins en moins aimées" (RTP Gall. 4:465–66).

53. See RTP 1:666; RTP Gall. 1:608.

54. ASB, 185. "Dans les églises byzantines le texte biblique, au lieu d'être simplement figuré comme dans la sculpture des églises du Nord

est accompagné, sur les mosaïques, de lettres qui forment une citation de l'évangile ou des prophéties" (CSB 1971, 132).

55. "Je vous envoie vifs compliments et remerciements pour le merveilleux boeuf mode[.] Je voudrais bien réussir aussi bien que vous ce que je vais faire cette nuit, que mon style soit aussi brillant, aussi clair, aussi solide que votre gelée—que mes idées soient aussi savoureuses que vos carottes et aussi nourrissantes et fraîches que votre viande. En attendant d'avoir terminé mon oeuvre, je vous félicite de la vôtre" (letter 71 to Celine Cottin, July 12, 1909, *Corr.* 9:139). He writes to Léon Daudet of his work: "Votre association d'idées entre les preuves de l'existence de Dieu et la meringue est étonnante" (letter 151, mid-November 1912, *Corr.* 11:302).

56. "Le boeuf froid aux carottes fit son apparition, couché par le Michel-Ange de notre cuisine sur d'énormes cristaux de gelée pareils à des blocs de quartz transparent" (RTP Gall. 1:449).

57. "And in yet another way my work would resemble that of Françoise: in a book individual characters, whether human or of some other kind, are made up of numerous impressions derived from many girls, many churches, many sonatas and combined to form a single sonata, a single church, a single girl, so that I should be making my book in the same way that Françoise made that *boeuf à la mode* which M. de Norpois had found so delicious, just because she had enriched its jelly with so many carefully chosen pieces of meat" (RTP 3:1091). "D'ailleurs, comme les individualités (humaines ou non) sont dans un livre faites d'impressions nombreuses qui, prises de bien des jeunes filles, de bien des églises, de bien des sonates, servent à faire une seule sonate, une seule église, une seule jeune fille, ne ferais-je pas mon livre de la façon que Françoise faisait ce boeuf mode, apprécié par M. de Norpois, et dont tant de morceaux de viande ajoutés et choisis enrichissaient la gelée?" (RTP Gall. 4:612). Norpois had commented: "That is a thing you don't get in a chophouse, not even in the best of them: a spiced beef in which the aspic doesn't taste like glue and the beef has caught the flavour of the carrots. It's admirable! (RTP 1:494). "Voilà ce qu'on ne peut obtenir au cabaret, je dis dans les meilleurs: une daube de boeuf où la gelée ne sente pas la colle, et où le boeuf ait pris parfum des carottes, c'est admirable!" (RTP Gall. 1:450).

58. "Confondant ces visages indécis et grimaçant dans la gelée d'une seule grappe scintillatrice et tremblante" (RTP Gall. 2:180).

59. "Si bien que notre menu, comme ces quatre-feuilles qu'on sculptait au XIIIe siècle au portail des cathédrales, reflétait un peu le rythme des saisons et les épisodes de la vie" (RTP Gall. 1:70).

60. "John Ruskin," CSB 1971, 136. For examples of this relationship, and in particular the idolatry of the narrator's mother, see Compagnon, *Troisième République,* 229–32.

61. "Je ne pouvais plus rien lui dire de moi, laisser rien de moi se poser sur lui" (RTP Gall. 4:231).

62. "L'insoupçonnable puissance défensive de l'habitude invétérée" (RTP Gall. 4:233).

63. RTP Gall. 4:1035.

64. "De 648 à 898, rien[,] j'ai tout ôté" (Proust, *Albertine disparue,* 181, 191).

65. See Kazuyoshi Yoshikawa, "Remarques sur les transformations subies par la Recherche autour des années 1913–1914 d'après des cahiers inédits, " 11. See also RTP Gall. 4:13-14.

66. Yoshikawa, "Remarques," 25.

67. "La loi générale de l'oubli" (RTP Gall. 4:223).

68. See Proust, *Albertine disparue,* 191–92, and the notes on pp. 165–203. See also "Notice, " RTP Gall. 4:1019–38.

69. "La mort seule, empêchant que ne soit recomposée pour le tome suivant la matière de ces épisodes, a donné à la suppression opérée par Proust ce caractère catastrophique qui a, indirectement, provoqué la disparition de la dactylographie" (*Albertine disparue,* 182n). The notes to the Pléiade edition concerning the Fortuny passages (see RTP Gall. 3:1670–75) do not and could not take account of such disruptive changes unless they could be considered to be like the other sketches. There is no doubt of the importance of these scenes: "Ainsi, le fil conducteur du motif Fortuny court à travers *La Prisonnière*. Au-delà, et de même que l'ouverture de *La Prisonnière* est un retour à celle de *Du côté de chez Swann*, le motif Fortuny ferme déjà la boucle d'*A la recherche du temps perdu*. Il annonce, comme les morts de Swann et de Bergotte, comme la musique de Vinteuil, la découverte du Temps retrouvé, où l'art donne toute sa réalité à la vie" (RTP Gall. 3:1675).

70. "Je me rappelle très bien votre mère" (*Albertine disparue,* 131).

71. See RTP Gall. 1:81; 1:146–47; 4:226–27. For the relationship between the celebrity and invisibility of the *Thousand and One Nights*, see Georges May, *Les Mille et Une Nuits d'Antoine Galland*.

72. "On devine en lisant, on crée; tout part d'une erreur initiale; celles qui suivent (et ce n'est pas seulement dans la lecture des lettres et des télégrammes, pas seulement dans toute lecture), *si extraordinaires qu'elles puissent paraître à celui qui n'a pas le même point de départ, sont toutes naturelles*. Une bonne partie de ce que nous croyons, et jusque dans les conclusions dernières c'est ainsi, avec un entêtement et une bonne foi égale, vient d'une première méprise sur les prémisses" (*Albertine disparue*, 158–59, RTP Gall. 4:235; emphasis added).

73. "Dans une matière distincte, nouvelle, d'une transparence, d'une sonorité spéciales, compacte, fraîchissante et rose" (RTP Gall. 4:449).

74. Yoshida ("Proust contre Ruskin") has shown how laboriously Proust worked to force writing to follow the birth of these Venitian memories in specific passages (fols. 14r°–15r° and 13v°).

75. See "Notice, " RTP Gall. 4:1034.

76. Proust, preface to *Tendres Stocks*, 26.

AFTERWORD

1. See RTP Gall. 4, *Esquisse* 36:861–65.

2. "Vêtu d'une robe d'écarlate, quelque archange de Mantegna sonnat dans un buccin" (RTP Gall. 3:765).

BIBLIOGRAPHY

WORKS BY PROUST IN FRENCH

A la recherche du temps perdu. Edited by Jean-Yves Tadié. 4 vols. Paris: Gallimard, Bibliothèque de la Pléiade, 1987–89.

A la recherche du temps perdu. Edited by Jean Milly. 10 vols. Paris: Flammarion, 1987.

Albertine disparue. Edited by Nathalie Mauriac and Etienne Wolff. Paris: Grasset, 1987.

Autour de la Recherche: Lettres. With André Gide. Bruxelles: Editions Complexe, 1988

La Bible d'Amiens, translation of *The Bible of Amiens,* by John Ruskin. Edited by Hubert Juin. Paris: Union Générale d'Editions, 1986.

Le Carnet de 1908: Cahiers Marcel Proust 8. Edited by Philip Kolb. Paris: Gallimard, 1976.

Contre Sainte-Beuve. Edited by Bernard de Fallois. Paris: Gallimard, 1954.

Contre Sainte-Beuve. Edited by Pierre Clarac with Yves Sandre. Paris: Gallimard, Bibliothèque de la Pléiade, 1971.

Correspondance. Edited by Philip Kolb. 17 vols. Paris: Plon, 1970– .

Correspondance [1914–22]. With Jacques Rivière. Edited by Philip Kolb. Paris: Gallimard, 1976.

Correspondance avec sa mère [1887–1905]. Edited by Philip Kolb. Paris: Plon, 1953.

Correspondance générale. Edited by Robert Proust and Paul Brach. 6 vols. Paris: Plon, 1919, 1930–36.

Jean Santeuil, précédé de Les Plaisirs et les jours. Edited by Pierre Clarac and Yves Sandre. Paris: Gallimard, 1971.

La Matinée chez la Princesse de Guermantes. Edited by Henri Bonnet with Bernard Brun. Paris: Gallimard, 1982.

Les Plaisirs et les jours. See *Jean Santeuil.*

Sésame et les lys, translation of *Sesame and Lilies*, by John Ruskin. Introduction by Antoine Compagnon. Paris: Editions Complexe, 1987.

Preface to Tendres Stocks, by Paul Morand. Paris: Gallimard, 1921, 1949.

WORKS BY PROUST IN ENGLISH TRANSLATION

Against Sainte-Beuve and Other Essays. Translated by John Sturrock. London: Penguin Books, 1988.

By Way of Sainte-Beuve. Translated by Sylvia Townsend Warner. London: Hogarth Press, 1984.

Jean Santeuil. Translated by Gerard Hopkins. New York: Simon & Schuster, 1956.

Letters of Marcel Proust. Translated and edited by Mina Curtiss. New York: Vintage Books, 1966.

On Reading Ruskin. Translated and edited by Jean Autet, William Burford, and Phillip J. Wolfe. New Haven, Conn.: Yale University Press, 1987.

Remembrance of Things Past. Translated by C. K. Scott-Moncrieff and Terence Kilmartin. New York: Random House, 1981.

Selected Letters [1880–1903]. Edited by Philip Kolb, translated by Ralph Mannheim. New York: Doubleday, 1983.

OTHER SOURCES

Abraham, Nicholas. *L'Ecorce et le noyau*. Paris: Aubier-Flammarion, 1978.

Angenot, Marc. *Ce que l'on dit des Juifs en 1889: Antisémitisme et discours social*. Paris: Presses Universitaires de Vincennes, 1989.

Arendt, Hanna. "Philosophie et politique." *Les Cahiers du GRIF* 33. (1986): 85–97.

Atlan, Henri. *A tort ou à raison*. Paris: Seuil, 1986.

Bardèche, Maurice. *Marcel Proust, romancier*. 2 vols. Paris: Les Sept Couleurs, 1971.

Baudry, Jean-Louis. *Proust, Freud, et l'autre*. Paris: Minuit, 1984.

Beaujour, Michel. *Miroirs d'encre*. Paris: Seuil, 1980.

Beckett, Samuel. *Proust*. New York: Grove Press, 1931.

Bellak, Leopold. "Free Association: Conceptual and Clinical Aspects." *International Journal of Psychoanalysis* 42 (1961).

Bellemin-Noël, Jean. " 'Psychanalyser' le rêve de Swann?" *Poétique* 8 (1971): 447–70.

Benda, Julian. *La Jeunesse d'un clerc*. Paris: Gallimard, 1936.

Benjamin, Walter. *Correspondance*. Paris: Aubier, 1979.

——— . *Illuminations*. New York: Schocken books, 1969

Bersani, Leo. " 'The Culture of Redemption': Marcel Proust and Melanie Klein," *Critical Inquiry* 12 (Winter 1986): 399–421.

——— . "Déguisements du moi en art fragmentaire." In *Recherche de Proust*. Paris: Recherche de Proust, 1980.

——— . *Marcel Proust: The Fictions of Life and Art*. Oxford: Oxford University Press, 1965.

Blanchot, Maurice, "Les Intellectuels en question," *Le Débat* 29 (March 1984): 2–28.

——— . *Le Livre à venir*. Paris: Gallimard, 1959.

Bloom, Harold. "Introduction to Proust." In *Remembrance of Things Past*. New York: Chelsea House, 1987.

——— . *Wallace Stevens: The Poems of Our Climate*. Ithaca, N.Y.: Cornell University Press, 1977.

Booth, Wayne. *The Company We Keep*. Berkeley: University of California Press, 1988.

Bortolotto, Luigina Rossi, and Janine Bailly-Herzberg. *Monet 1870–1889*. Paris: Flammarion, 1981.

Bowie, Malcolm. *Freud, Proust, and Lacan: Theory as Fiction.* Cambridge: Cambridge University Press, 1987.

Boyer, Philippe. *Le Petit pan de mur jaune.* Paris: Seuil, 1987.

Brodsky, Claudia. "Remembering Swann: Memory and Representation in Proust." *MLN* 102/5 (December 1987).

Brombert, Victor. *The Intellectual Hero: Studies in the French Novel, 1880–1955.* Chicago: University of Chicago Press, 1960.

Brun, Bernard, "Brouillons et brouillages: Proust et l'antisémitisme," *Littérature* 70 (May 1988): 110–28.

———. "L'Edition d'un brouillon et son interprétation: Le Problème du Contre Sainte-Beuve." In *Essais de critique génétique.* Paris: Flammarion, 1979.

Brunet, Etienne. *Le Vocabulaire de Proust.* 3 vols. Geneva: Slatkine, 1983.

Buisine, Alain. *Proust et ses lettres.* Lille: Presses Universitaires de Lille, 1986.

Canavaggia, Jeanne. *Proust et la politique.* Paris: Nizet, 1986.

Caws, Mary Ann. "Gestures toward the Self: Representing the Body in Modernism—Cloaking, Re-Membering, and the Elliptical Effect." In *Modernism: Challenges and Perspectives,* ed. Monique Chefdor, Ricardo Quinones, and Albert Wachtel. Urbana: University of Illinois Press, 1986.

Chantal, René de. *Marcel Proust: Critique littéraire.* Montreal: Presses Universitaires de Montréal, 1967.

Collier, Peter. *Proust and Venice.* Cambridge: Cambridge University Press, 1989.

Compagnon, Antoine. Preface to Marcel Proust, *Du côté de chez Swann.* Paris: Folio, 1988.

———. *Proust entre deux siècles.* Paris: Seuil, 1989.

———. *La Troisième république des lettres.* Paris: Seuil, 1983.

Crémieux, Benjamin. *Du côté de Marcel Proust.* Paris: Lemarget, 1929.

Culler, Jonathan. *The Pursuit of Signs.* Ithaca, N.Y.: Cornell University Press, 1981.

Debray-Genette, Raymonde. *Métamorphoses du récit.* Paris: Seuil, 1987.

Deleuze, Gilles. *Proust and Signs.* Translated by Richard Howard. New York: Braziller, 1972.

De Man, Paul. *Allegories of Reading: Figural Language in Rousseau, Nietzsche, Rilke, and Proust.* New Haven, Conn.: Yale University Press, 1979.

Derrida, Jacques. *The Ear of the Other: Texts and Discussions with Jacques Derrida.* Edited by Christie McDonald. Lincoln: University of Nebraska Press, 1988.

––––––. *Les Fins de l'homme: A partir du travail de Jacques Derrida.* Paris: Galilée, 1981.

Descombes, Vincent. *Proust: Philosophie du roman.* Paris: Minuit, 1987.

Doubrovksy, Serge. *La place de la madeleine.* Paris: Mercure de France, 1974. Translated by Carol Mastrangelo Bové, with Paul A. Bové, as *Writing and Fantasy in Proust: La Place de la madeleine.* Lincoln: University of Nebraska Press, 1986.

Einstein, Albert. "On the General Theory of Gravitation: An Account of the Newly Published Extension of the General Theory of Relativity against Its Historical and Philosophical Background." *Scientific American* 182:4 (1950).

Ellison, David. *The Readings of Proust.* Baltimore, Md.: Johns Hopkins University Press, 1984.

Ellmann, Richard. *Oscar Wilde.* New York: Knopf, 1988.

Essais de critique génétique. Paris: Flammarion, 1979.

Favrichon, Anna. *Toilettes et silhouettes féminines.* Lyon: Presses Universitaires de Lyon, 1987.

Festa-McCormick, Diana. *Proustian Optics of Clothes: Mirrors, Masks, Mores.* Stanford, Calif.: Stanford French and Italian Studies, 1984.

Feuillerat, Albert. *Comment Marcel Proust a composé son roman.* New Haven, Conn.: Yale University Press, 1934.

Fichte, Johann Gottlieb. *Addresses to the German Nation.* Edited by G. Kelly. New York: Harper & Row, 1972.

Fraisse, Luc. *Le Processus de la création chez Marcel Proust: Le fragment expérimental.* Paris: José Corti, 1988.

Freud, Sigmund. "Psychotherapy of Hysteria." In *The Standard Edition of the Complete Works.* London: Hogarth Press, 1955.

––––––. "Screen Memories." In *The Complete Psychological Works of Sigmund Freud,* vol. 3. Translated by James Strachey, Anna Freud,

Alix Strachey, and Alan Tyson. London: Hogarth Press and the Institute of Psychoanalysis, 1962.

———. *Totem and Taboo*. London: Routledge & Kegan Paul, 1960.

Gallop, Jane. *Reading Lacan*. Ithaca, N.Y.: Cornell University Press, 1985.

Genette, Gérard. *Figures*. Paris: Seuil, 1966.

———. *Figures 2*. Paris: Seuil, 1969.

———. *Figures 3*. Paris: Seuil, 1972.

———. *Figures of Literary Discourse*. Translated by Alan Sheridan. New York: Columbia University Press, 1982.

———. *Seuils*. Paris: Seuils, 1987.

Grimaud, Michel. "La Rhétorique du rêve: Swann et la psychanalyse." *Poétique* 33 (1978): 90–106.

Hardy, Thomas. *A Pair of Blue Eyes*. Edited by Alan Manford. Oxford: Oxford University Press, 1985.

———. *The Well-Beloved*. London: Macmillan, 1975.

Hassine, Juliette. *Essai sur Proust et Baudelaire*. Paris: Nizet, 1979.

Henry, Anne. *Proust romancier: Le Tombeau égyptien*. Paris: Flammarion, 1983.

———. *Théories pour une esthétique*. Paris: Klincksieck, 1981.

Hollander, Anne. *Seeing through Clothes*. New York: Avon Books, 1975.

House, John. *Monet: Nature into Art*. New Haven, Conn: Yale University Press, 1986.

Hughes, Edward J. *Marcel Proust: A Study in the Quality of Awareness*. Cambridge: Cambridge University Press, 1983.

Jakobson, Roman. *Fundamentals of Language*. The Hague: Mouton, 1956.

Jameson, Fredric. *The Political Unconscious*. Ithaca, N.Y.: Cornell University Press, 1981.

Kristeva, Julia. *Soleil noir: Dépression et mélancolie*. Paris: Gallimard, 1987.

Lacan, Jacques. *Ecrits: A Selection*. Translated by Alan Sheridan. New York: Norton, 1977.

———. *Le Séminaire II: Le Moi dan la théorie de Freud et dans la technique de la psychanalyse*. Paris: Seuil, 1978.

Lagache, Daniel. *La Jalousie amoureuse*. Paris: Presses Universitaires de France, 1981.

Lejeune, Philippe. "Les Carafes de la Vivonne." *Poétique 31* (1977): 285–305.

Lemoine-Luccioni, Eugénie. *Essai psychanalytique sur le vêtement*. Paris: Seuil, 1983.

Leroy, Géraldi, ed. *Les Ecrivains et l'affaire Dreyfus*. Paris: Presses Universitaires de France, 1983.

Le Tourneux, Jean. "Pourquoi Einstein créa-t-il une théorie dont personne n'auait besoin?" *Etudes Françaises* 26 (Winter 1991):91–101.

Locke, John. *An Essay on Human Understanding*. 2 vols. London: J. M. Dent, 1947.

Ludwig, G., and P. Molmenti. *Vittore Carpaccio: La Vie et l'oeuvre du peintre, ouvrage traduit par H. L. de Perera illustré de 26 planches en photographie et de 229 gravures en noir tirées hors texte*. Paris: Librairie Hachette, 1910.

Lydon, Mary. "Pli selon pli: Proust and Fortuny." *Romanic Review* 82, no. 4 (November 1990): 438–54.

McDonald, Christie, and Ginette Michaud, eds. *Ça me fait penser*. *Etudes Françaises* 22 (Spring 1986).

Macé, Gérard. *Le Manteau de Fortuny*. Paris: Gallimard, 1987.

Macksey, Richard. Introduction to Marcel Proust, *On Reading Ruskin*. New Haven, Conn.: Yale University Press, 1987.

Mahony, Patrick. *Freud as a Writer*. New York: International Universities Press, 1983.

———. *Psychoanalysis and Discourse*. New York: Tavistock, 1987.

May, Georges. *Les Mille et Une Nuits d'Antoine Galland*. Paris: Presses Universitaires de France, 1986.

Mehlman, Jeffrey. *A Structural Study of Autobiography: Proust, Sartre, Leiris, Lévi-Strauss*. Ithaca, N.Y.: Cornell University Press, 1974.

Michaud, Ginette. "Monsieur Songe sans y penser dit que . . . " In Christie McDonald and Ginette Michaud, eds., *Ça me fait penser*. *Etudes Françaises* 22 (Spring 1986): 95–131.

Miller, J. Hillis. *The Ethics of Reading: Kant, de Man, Eliot, Trollope, James, and Benjamin*. New York: Columbia University Press, 1987.

Milly, Jean. "Autobiographie et littérature chez Proust." *Saggi et studi,* August 1987, pp. 3–11.

———. Introduction to Marcel Proust, *La Prisonnière.* Paris: Flammarion, 1986.

Muller, Marcel. "Proust et Flaubert: Une Dimension intertextuelle de *A la recherche du temps perdu.*" In John D. Erickson and Irène Pagès, eds., *Proust et le texte producteur.* Guelph, Ont.: University of Guelph, 1980.

Nattiez, Jean-Jacques. *Proust as Musician.* Cambridge: Cambridge University Press, 1989.

Paganini, Maria. *A la peche au poisson-loup: Chorégraphie de l'écriture proustienne.* Unpublished manuscript (translation forthcoming from University of Minnesota Press).

Piguet, Pierre. *Monet et Venise.* Paris: Herscher, 1986.

Poulet, Georges. *L'Espace proustien.* Paris: Gallimard, 1963.

———. *Proustian Space.* Translated by Elliott Coleman. Baltimore, Md.: Johns Hopkins University Press, 1977.

"Proust: Les recherches du temps perdu." *Magazine Littéraire* 246 (October 1987).

Pugh, Anthony R. *The Birth of "A la recherche du temps perdu."* Lexington: French Forum, 1987.

Quémar, Claudine. "Sur deux versions anciennes des 'côtés' de Combray." *Cahiers Marcel Proust* 7 (1975).

Raimond, Michel. *Proust romancier.* Paris: Société d'Edition d'Enseignement Supérieur, 1984.

Rapaport, David. *The History of the Concept of Association.* New York: International Universities Press, 1974.

Ribot, Th. *Essai sur l'imagination créatrice.* Paris: Librairie Félix Alcan, 1926.

Richard, Jean-Pierre. *Proust et le monde sensible.* Paris: Seuil, 1974.

———. "Proust et l'objet herméneutique." *Poétique* 13 (1973):1–28.

Ricoeur, Paul. *Temps et récit 2: La Configuration dans le récit de fiction.* Paris: Seuil, 1984.

"Le Rôle des intellectuels de l'affaire Dreyfus à nos jours." *Magazine littéraire* 248 (December 1987).

Rorty, Richard. *Contingency, Irony, and Solidarity*. Cambridge: Cambridge University Press, 1989.

Rosasco, Joan. "Le Texte et sa doublure." In John D. Erickson and Irène Pagès, eds. *Proust et le texte producteur*. Guelph, Ont.: University of Guelph, 1980.

Rosset, Clément. *L'Objet singulier* (Paris: Minuit, 1979).

Roustang, François. *Elle ne le lâche pas*. Paris: Minuit, 1980.

Ruskin, John. *The Works of John Ruskin*. 39 vols. Edited by E. T. Cook and Alexander Wedderburn. London: George Allen, 1903–12.

Saussure, Ferninand de. *Cours de linguistique générale*. Paris: Payot, 1980.

Schlanger, Judith. *Les Métamorphoses de l'organisme*. Paris: Vrin, 1971.

Schopenhauer, Arthur. *The World as Will and Representation*. 2 vols. Translated by E. F. Payne. New York: Dover, 1958.

Schor, Naomi. *Reading in Detail: Aesthetics and the Feminine*. New York: Methuen, 1987.

Schorske, Carl. *Fin-de-siècle Vienna*. New York: Vintage Books, 1981.

Serres, Michel. *Esthétique sur Carpaccio*. Paris: Hermann, 1975.

Smith, Paul. *Discerning the Subject*. Minneapolis: University of Minnesota Press, 1988.

Splitter, Randolph. *Proust's 'Recherche': A Psychoanalytic Interpretation*. London: Routledge & Kegan Paul, 1981.

Stambolian, Georges. *Marcel Proust and the Creative Encounter*. Chicago: University of Chicago Press, 1972.

Sternhell, Zeev. *La Droite révolutionnaire: Les Origines françaises du fascisme, 1885–1914* (Paris: Seuil, 1978).

Suleiman, Susan. *Authoritarian Fictions: The Ideological Novel as a Literary Genre*. New York: Columbia University Press, 1983.

———. "The Literary Significance of the Dreyfus Affair." In Norman Kleebatt, ed., *The Dreyfus Affair: Art, Truth, and Justice*. Berkeley: University of California Press, 1987.

Szondi, Peter. *On Textual Understanding and Other Essays*. Translated by Harvey Mendelsohn. Minneapolis: University of Minnesota Press, 1978.

Tadié, Jean-Yves. *Proust*. Paris: Dossiers Belfond, 1983.

Vettard, Camille. "Proust et le temps." *La Nouvelle Revue française* (special issue: "Hommage à Marcel Proust") 20, no. 112 (January 1, 1923): 204. Reprint. Paris: Gallimard, 1990.

Warren, Howard. *A History of the Association Psychology.* New York: Scribner, 1920.

Weber, Samuel. "Le Madrépore." *Poétique 13:*(1973): 28–54.

Wihl, Gary. *Ruskin and the Rhetoric of Infallibility.* New Haven, Conn.: Yale University Press, 1985.

Winton, Alison. *Proust's Additions.* 2 vols. Cambridge: Cambridge University Press, 1977.

Yoshida, Jo. "Proust contre Ruskin: La Genèse de deux voyages dans la 'Recherche' d'après des brouillons inédits." Doctoral Thesis, Université de Paris-Sorbonne, 1978.

Yoshikawa, Kazuyoshi. "Remarques sur les transformations subies par la Recherche autour des années 1913–1914 d'après des cahiers inédits." *Bulletin d'Informations Proustiennes* 7 (Spring 1978).

Zima, Pierre V. *L'Ambivalence romanesque: Proust, Kafka, Musil.* Paris: Sycomore, 1980.